EPITOME OF LACTANTIUS

FIRMIANI LACTANTII EPITOME INSTITUTIONUM DIVINARUM

LACTANTIUS' EPITOME OF THE DIVINE INSTITUTES

Edited and translated with a Commentary

BY

E. H. Blakeney

WIPF & STOCK · Eugene, Oregon

Wipf and Stock Publishers
199 W 8th Ave, Suite 3
Eugene, OR 97401

Firmiani Lactantii Epitome Institutionum Divinarum
Lactantius' Epitome of the Divine Institutes
By Lactantius, Firmiani and Blakeney, E. H.
Copyright©1950 SPCK
ISBN 13: 978-1-60899-731-2
Publication date 5/13/2010
Previously published by SPCK, 1950

This Edition reprinted by Wipf and Stock Publishers
by arrangement with SPCK, London.

CONTENTS

	Page
PREFACE	vii
INTRODUCTORY NOTES	ix
REVISED TEXT OF THE *Epitome*	1
TRANSLATION OF THE *Epitome*	59
COMMENTARY	127
ADDENDA	171
SELECT INDEX TO THE COMMENTARY	173
INDEX TO BIBLICAL REFERENCES IN THE COMMENTARY	175

PREFACE

I have long thought that the *Epitome* of Lactantius might usefully serve as a text-book in theological colleges, and in the upper forms of public schools, and might also be read by Ordination candidates. The Latinity is easy, and moreover very good. But hitherto no annotated modern edition of this interesting treatise has been available. The first complete edition of the *Epitome* is that of Pfaff (Paris, 1722), but I have not seen this book.

The text here offered is in the main that of Routh (1845), but some needful changes have been introduced. A number of these changes were first put forward by John Davies (sometime President of Queens' College, Cambridge) in the year 1718; many were taken over by Brandt, in his textual (1890) edition of the Works of Lactantius (published in the Vienna corpus); this edition I have consulted in making a final revision of the text adopted in this present volume. Those interested in the minutiae of criticism are recommended to examine Brandt's edition, which is a model of painstaking accuracy. It is no part of my scheme to deal with textual criticism, except occasionally in the annotations. I have, of course, made use of Bünemann's edition (1739), but have had less profit from it than I hoped for. My English version of the text owes a good deal to that in the Ante-Nicene Library, which I was careful to use in correcting my own rough draft. The passages in the *Institutes* corresponding to the sections in the *Epitome* have been affixed to the notes to each chapter. As for the commentary, it will, I hope, be sufficient to help the student to a proper understanding of the text itself. The English rendering given is literal for the most part, though not slavishly so. In attempting this translation I have often been puzzled how best to deal with the words *justitia* (with its corresponding adjective) and *mundus*. Sometimes I have rendered *justitia* by 'justice', sometimes by 'righteousness'; *mundus* at times by 'world', at others by 'universe'; this, as the context requires, or seems to require. I may therefore be accused of some inconsistency, but console myself with the reflection that the translators of our authorized version of the Bible do not tie themselves 'to uniformitie of phrasing or to an identity of words, as some peradventure would wish'.

There will doubtless be found some errors in translation and notes; I shall be grateful if these may be pointed out in due course, despite the sad fact that such corrections will come too late to be utilized in this volume. I would close this preface in the fine words of the Emperor Marcus Aurelius: 'if any man can show me that I am incorrect in my views, gladly would I change; for I search after truth, by which man was never yet harmed.'

E. H. B.

Postscript.—Since writing the above, I have received, when correcting proofs, help from an eminent scholar, the Rev. Dr. Srawley. The care, patience, and thoroughness he has taken in enabling me to get rid of errors will never be forgotten. I am indeed grateful to him, and also to the press reader for his help.

INTRODUCTORY NOTES

The epoch during which Lactantius[1] lived and taught is for ever memorable in the annals of civilization. The birth of this eloquent scholar, somewhere about the year A.D. 250, coincided with the Decian persecutions; he witnessed the last and fiercest of persecutions in the reign of Diocletian; and he lived to see published the famous Edict of the Emperor Constantine, which secured toleration for the Christians after more than two centuries of bitter conflict between the Church and the forces of Paganism arrayed against it. The once persecuted community, now established in the Empire as a 'religio licita', was destined, in the course of history, itself to adopt a persecuting policy—never contemplated at the time of liberation—towards the Paganism that had harassed it for so long a period:

'Thus the whirligig of Time brings in his revenges.'

Firmianus Lactantius, a pupil of Arnobius, was probably a native of Africa, and doubtless began life as a heathen. His early studies were mainly of a literary character; subsequently—we do not know when—he embraced Christianity. Invited by Diocletian to take up work in Asia Minor, he became a teacher of rhetoric; later, he sojourned in Gaul, and subsequently was appointed by the Emperor Constantine as teacher of his son Crispus. A portion of his early work as a writer still survives, but much has been lost. Among his surviving books we have a short treatise *de opificio Dei*, where he argues for the existence of God by pointing out how the human frame is, by reason of its exquisite adjustments, clear evidence of such a Being, at once all wise and beneficent: in fact it may be regarded as, in some sort, an early example of what is known as the 'teleological argument'. He was also the author of a short treatise *de ira Dei* (spoken of by Jerome as 'pulcherrimum') in which he contends that 'wrath' cannot be denied even to God Himself—this in contrast with the views of certain Pagan expositors.[2]

[1] The Latin Apologists from Tertullian to Augustine form a striking series; they are all Africans, all rhetoricians or lawyers, all converts at a mature age (Gwatkin, *Early Church History*, vol. i, p. 176). As far as I know, the *editio princeps* of Lactantius was printed at Rome in 1465.
[2] On the problems connected with the *wrath* (ὀργή) of God, consult Prof. Orr's art. in Hastings, *Dict. of Bible*, vol. i, s.v. ANGER.

His chief title to fame is his well-known treatise, in seven books, entitled the *Divinae Institutiones*.[1] As the *Epitome* is a summary, by the author himself, of this work, a brief account of its main contents may be usefully given here. In the first book he criticizes, with severity, the current polytheism, while in book two he accounts for its origin; in this he follows the example of most Christian Apologists. In the third book he deals with heathen philosophy, contrasting the truths of the Gospel with the errors and misleading inferences of the philosophers: here he is seen at his best. His learning was extensive, and his qualifications for this branch of criticism give him an undoubted right to undertake a rather formidable task, while his censure is not sullied by that violence which we find too often in Tertullian. In the fourth book he expounds his theory of true knowledge, showing how Christian doctrine finds its basis and justification in the person of Jesus the Messiah. Yet we note that the argument, in his hands, is rather philosophical than religious. The fifth book summarizes his theory of virtue, a subject continued in book six, in which he deals with the Stoic and Peripatetic theories of virtue. In this section of his work he expounds the doctrine of *The Two Ways*.[2] In the final book he discusses the doctrine of the blessed life, and the Summum Bonum, concluding with a picture of man's ultimate destiny. Theologians, we are assured, find shortcomings in his orthodoxy, and it may be true, as some have stated, that he contributed little of positive importance to the elucidation of Christian dogmatics; yet his deep moral earnestness, his eloquence—trained as it had been in the best literary tradition—his refinement, and his love for Christian teaching, as he understood it, are worthy of note and endear him to all those who prize sincerity of thought and purity of style.[3]

True, he lived in an uncritical age; he could actually cite the forged Sibylline oracles as genuinely early 'testimonia'; and he concluded his review by a description of the soon-coming end of the world, adopting an exaggerated form of chiliasm, which to

[1] Cf. *Cambridge Ancient History*, vol. xii. pp. 609, 650f. It may be worth a remark, in passing, how often the Reformers in England refer to the Institutes, in their theological works; as reference to the Index of the Parker Society's great collection will show.

[2] Cf. the opening passages in the *Didaché* (?c. A.D. 100), a moral treatise—in part—setting forth the paths of righteousness and unrighteousness respectively, and founded on an ancient work 'The Two Ways'.

[3] Lactantius was one of the Latin authors chosen by Colet for use in St. Paul's School (which he founded in 1509).

modern ears sounds fantastic.[1] These things will be found in the seventh book of the *Institutiones*, but as Lactantius' discussions there are too long and elaborate for ordinary readers, he decided to abridge his work, and this abridgement we possess in the *Epitome*. Jerome speaks of this book as 'acephalous', a book without a head, and so it appears in all but one of the MSS.; but, as Prof. H. J. Rose[2] indicates, Jerome's copy must be an ancestor of our inferior copies.

The *Institutiones*[3] must have been written, or at least published, during the reign of Constantine, for in that treatise will be found an address to the Emperor. Possibly this was an after-thought, inserted after the bulk of the volume had been composed. Notwithstanding the excellence of his Latinity (he was spoken of as the Christian Cicero) he exercised little influence on contemporary thought. Jerome, in one of his letters (the 58th) remarks that Lactantius 'has a flow of eloquence, worthy of Cicero—would he had been as ready to teach our doctrines as he was to pull down those of others!' According to that rather splenetic Father (letter 84) 'he denied the subsistence of the Holy Spirit'. One result of his apparent indifference to certain outstanding 'dogmata' of the Faith was the condemnation of his books by a fifth-century Church Council. Even his vigorous onslaught on philosophy did not secure him from the opposition of the rigorists. Whatever his shortcomings—and we do ill to lay too much stress on them—he had what Tertullian once designated the 'anima naturaliter Christiana'. Here is what he himself avers: 'Man cannot divest himself of the idea of God; his spontaneous turning to Him in every need, his involuntary explanation, prove it; the truth, on compulsion of nature, bursts from his bosom in its own despite.' We may count him the last of the Latin Apologists, and it would be well to read him in conjunction with the relevant matter in the works of such predecessors as Justin Martyr, Tertullian (in his *Apologeticus*), Minucius Felix, Arnobius, as well as in the Epistle to Diognetus, Aristides, and others.[4]

[1] Cf. Bousset, *The Antichrist Legend*, pp. 81, 124 [E.T.].
[2] In his *Handbook of Latin Literature*.
[3] Consult Sihler's treatise, *From Augustus to Augustine*, pp. 174f.
[4] For Apologists, see Gwatkin, *Early Church History*, vol. i; Bigg's *Origins of Christianity*, chap. 24; Cruttwell, *Literary History of Early Christianity*, book iii (valuable); Cadoux, *Early Church and the World*; Harnack, *History of Dogma*, vol. ii [E.T.]. I might mention here that Lactantius is probably referred to in Dante, *Paradiso*, cant. x. 118-20, though I can find no reference to him in the *Policraticus* of John of Salisbury. Augustine was familiar with his writings.

His criticism of current Paganism is in many respects illustrated by certain sections of Augustine's *de civitate Dei*: his judgement here is generally sound. But, as with most of his contemporaries, his attitude towards the various problems that exercised the mind of antiquity is rudimentary. For example: he regarded the notion of a round earth, with its antipodes, as folly. In this opinion he did not stand alone: Augustine was equally incredulous —which need not surprise us, for even Bacon, writing as late as 1612, could not bring himself to accept the Copernican discovery, which was formulated nearly a century before Bacon's day. Yet these writers should have known better, for Heraclides (a pupil of Plato) had already shown the falsity of the geocentric conception of the universe, as Aristarchus of Samos had also done in the third century B.C.[1] That Lactantius shared the opinion that daemonic agencies were everywhere abroad in the world is evident, and that, by their lying tricks, they aim at destroying mankind; these daemons are the inventors of divination, necromancy, astrology, and oracles.[2] The Early Christians regarded pagan divinities as daemons; they are the gods of the Gentiles.[3]

By way of summing up, we may add a few somewhat desultory notes on the position of Lactantius as teacher. In constructive theology he has no great significance, even in the *Institutes*: still less in the *Epitome*, which it may be assumed contained the main points he desires to emphasize. One strange view he held, that God the Father possessed a figure.[4] He was accused of denying the personality of the Holy Ghost, and indeed he shows no true consciousness of a co-equal Trinity. He represents, says Dr. Swete, a layman's point of view, which had barely gone beyond a recognition of Christ as divine. His tendency was towards 'subordinationism', which has never wholly vanished from the Church. Enough for him to concentrate on the simplest Christological formulas. In point of fact, Christianity, as conceived by him, was of a moral rather than of a mystical or metaphysical cast.

[1] See the Introd. to T. L. Heath's volume, *Greek Astronomy* (1932).
[2] Cf. what Cassels says in his *Supernatural Religion* on Patristic theories of these contaminated beings.
[3] Cf. Min. Felix xxvi. It may be observed here that the Alexandrian writers took pains to rationalize paganism. See Hegel's *Philosophy of History*, pt. iii. chap. 2. On the doctrine of daemons in its relation to heathen worship Augustine speaks in the 8th book of the *de civitate Dei*; cf. *de cat. rud.* 19, with Christopher's notes.
[4] So too Tertullian. Cf. Bigg, *The Origins of Christianity*, chap. xxxi.

Bishop Bull, in his celebrated *Defensio Fidei Nicenae* (1685) described him as 'rudis disciplinae Christianae, et in rhetorica melius quam in theologia versatus'. For example: the Atonement is barely alluded to. Lactantius was naturally inclined to reserve in expressing 'dogmata', which makes us all the more surprised by his attitude towards the theory of an endless Hell and of eternal torment for temporal sin [1]; his comments, almost worthy of the fierce Tertullian, may be found in the seventh book of the *Institutes*, where we read that the human body will be specially immortalized to resist consumption by eternal fire—an appalling doctrine, repeated unhappily by later theologists. In general, Lactantius was half-hearted in much of his theology—as Harnack points out in his *History of Dogma*—and this was forced upon him by the historical situation in which he ultimately found himself. He would probably have found himself more at home in the Epistle of St. James than in the Pauline Letters.

One may remark a curious feature in his teaching, namely the emphasis laid on the necessity of evil in the interest of morality itself, since, apart from evil, virtue would not exist.[2] Religion and morality for him lie in the realm of spirit, and can be won by man's own effort: 'non necessitas esse peccare, sed propositi ac voluntatis', a Pelagian notion, if pressed home. Another point: unlike most of the Apologists he does not, as a rule, make use of the O.T. prophets (but see chap. 46); he appears to rely on the Sibyl. As for the part assigned by him to angelic agencies, in the government of the world, this has little warrant from Scripture. His attitude towards the figures of legend and folk lore is primitive; thus he accepts the story of the Fall in Genesis as literal history. Finally, the divine Providence (Πρόνοια) is central in his belief; it was not so with Arnobius. In the main, he shows but slight interest in the historical side of Christianity, still less in the speculative.

Lactantius died, in poor circumstances we are told, somewhere about the year 325, the same year in which the Nicene creed was

[1] Cf. 1 Enoch, lxii. 12.
[2] The notion that sin is something original and unavoidable is combated in 1 Enoch, xcviii, but Lactantius' view goes beyond even this. Compare perhaps the words of Boëthius, *de cons. phil.* iv. pr. 6, § 38; Rashdall, *Theory of Good and Evil*, vol. 2, iii. 1, § 9. The Stoical position seems to have been that evil is good under disguise, and so ultimately conducive to the best. Cf. Hatch, *Hibbert Lectures*, pp. 217, 218, and see a remark by Plutarch, *de Isid.* xlv. Augustine held that Evil was negative, a notion adopted from Neoplatonism: τὸ κακὸν ἔλλειψιν τοῦ ἀγαθοῦ θεῖόν.

first set forth. He left behind him a reputation for austerity, but he had no lack of friends who could appreciate his learning and the purity of his life. Like all innovators, he was subject to adverse criticism, as we have already noted. 'If', said Dupin, 'he appears to have held that the Word was generated in time, it is easy to give a Catholic sense to this; and we may justly do so, as he plainly establishes the divinity of that Word.' Yes, we must reckon him, after all deductions are made, as a genuinely Christian teacher. He was, as his various treatises indicate, something of a philosopher, but the philosophy that appealed to him was of the practical sort: the flights of an advanced metaphysic left him uninterested. He must have felt, as did Bishop Hall, the Christian Stoic, that true light and peace of mind were to be won not at Athens but at Jerusalem. Of his literary merits we have already spoken. We remark his frequent citations from classic writers. One is glad to feel that, unlike the great Augustine in his later days, he was opposed to any attempt to force belief on the reluctant: he preferred to rely on persuasion rather than force. Religion, he wrote, cannot be forced; 'nihil est tam voluntarium quam religio'. The good old rule was, βία ἐχθρὸν Θεῷ.[1] All moral regeneration, in his view, must be based on a Christian ethic; with polytheism such regeneration was all but impossible; there was no real spiritual content in the deadness of the Pagan world. Let us find satisfaction in the knowledge that in Lactantius there was a pleasing survival of the old Roman *gravitas*, rare enough among his contemporaries.

> Kindly and wise, he followed in the wake
> Of those high souls who, for the Gospel's sake,
> Held to the law of righteousness, and trod
> In faith and hope the appointed paths of God.

[1] Cf. the Q'rân (*Surah* ii): 'Let there be no compulsion in religion' (a pity, indeed, that Muhammad proved, at the close of his life, false to this excellent doctrine). Cf. too Origen, *de prin.* I, ii. 10. Augustine appealed to Luke 14. 23 to justify compulsion, but without any justification: the word in the text ἀνάγκασον simply means 'urge', without any idea of force implied.

THE EPITOME

PROLOGUE

FIRMIANI LACTANTII
EPITOME
INSTITUTIONUM DIVINARUM

AD

PENTADIUM FRATREM

Quanquam Divinarum Institutionum libri, quos jam pridem ad illustrandam veritatem religionemque conscripsimus, ita legentium mentes instruant, ita informent, ut nec prolixitas pariat fastidium, nec oneret ubertas, tamen horum tibi Epitomen fieri, PENTADI frater, desideras; credo, ut ad te aliquid scribam, tuumque nomen in nostro qualicunque opere celebretur. Faciam quod postulas, etsi difficile videtur ea, quae septem maximis voluminibus explicata sunt, in unum conferre. Fiet enim mutilum, et minus plenum, quum tanta rerum multitudo in angustum coarctanda sit, et brevitate ipsa minus clarum, maxime quum et argumenta plurima et exempla, in quibus lumen est probationum, necesse sit praeteriri, quoniam tanta eorum copia est, ut vel sola librum conficere possint. Quibus sublatis, quid poterit utile satis plenum, quid apertum videri? Sed enitar, quantum res sinit, et diffusa substringere et prolixa breviare; sic tamen, ut neque res ad copiam, neque claritas ad intelligentiam deesse videatur in hoc opere, quo in lucem veritas protrahenda est.

CHAPTER I

Prima incidit quaestio, sitne aliqua providentia, quae aut fecerit aut regat mundum. Esse, nemini dubium est, siquidem omnium fere philosophorum, praeter scholam Epicuri, una vox, una sententia est, nec fieri sine artifice Deo potuisse mundum, nec sine rectore constare. Itaque non solum a doctissimis viris, sed et omnium mortalium testimoniis ac sensibus coarguitur Epicurus. Quis enim de providentia dubitet, quum videat coelos terramque sic disposita, sic temperata esse universa, ut non modo ad pulchritudinem ornatumque mirabilem, sed ad usum quoque hominum, ceterorumque viventium commoditatem aptissime convenirent? Non potest igitur quod ratione constat, sine ratione coepisse.

CHAPTER 2

Quoniam certum est esse providentiam, sequitur alia quaestio, utrumne Deus unus an plures, quae quidem multum habet ambiguitatis. Dissentiunt enim non modo singuli inter se, verum etiam populi atque gentes. Sed qui rationem sequetur, intelliget nec Dominum esse posse nisi unum, nec Patrem nisi unum. Nam si Deus, qui omnia condidit, et idem Dominus, et idem Pater est, unus sit necesse est, ut idem sit caput idemque fons rerum. Nec potest aliter summa consistere, nisi ad unum cuncta referantur, nisi unus teneat gubernaculum, nisi unus frena moderetur, regatque universa membra, tanquam mens una. Si multi sint in examine apum reges, peribunt aut dissipabuntur, dum

Regibus incessit magno discordia motu:

si plures in armento duces, tam diu praeliabuntur, donec unus obtineat: si multi in exercitu imperatores, nec pareri poterit a milite, quum diversa jubeantur, nec ab iis ipsis unitas obtineri, quum sibi quisque pro viribus consulat. Sic in hac mundi republica nisi unus fuisset moderator, qui et conditor, aut soluta fuisset haec moles, aut ne condi quidem potuisset. Praeterea in multis non potest esse totum, quum singuli sua officia, suas obtineant potestates. Nullus igitur eorum poterit omnipotens nuncupari, quod est verum cognomentum Dei, quoniam id solum poterit, quod in ipso est; quod autem in aliis, non audebit attingere. Non Vulcanus sibi aquam vindicabit, aut Neptunus ignem, non Ceres artium peritiam, nec Minerva fruges, non arma Mercurius, nec Mars lyram, non Jupiter medicinam, nec Asclepius fulmen: facilius illud ab alio jactum suscipiet, quam ipse torquebit. Si ergo singuli non possunt omnia, minus habent virium, minus potestatis; is autem Deus habendus est, qui potest totum, quam qui de toto minimum.

CHAPTER 3

Unus igitur Deus est, perfectus, aeternus, incorruptibilis, impassibilis, nulli rei potestative subjectus, ipse omnia possidens, omnia regens, quem nec' aestimare sensu valeat humana mens, nec eloqui lingua mortalis. Sublimior enim ac major est quam ut possit aut cogitatione hominis aut sermone comprehendi. Denique, ut taceam de prophetis unius Dei praedicatoribus, poetae quoque et philosophi testimonium singulari Deo perhibent. Orpheus principalem Deum dicit, qui coelum solemque cum ceteris astris, qui terram, qui maria condiderit. Item noster Maro summum Deum modo spiritum, modo mentem nuncupat, eamque velut membris infusam, totius mundi corpus agitare; item Deum per profunda coeli, per tractus maris terrarumque discurrere, atque ab eo universas animantes trahere vitam. Ne Ovidius quidem ignoravit a Deo instructum esse mundum, quem interdum opificem rerum, interdum mundi fabricatorem vocat.

CHAPTER 4

Sed veniamus ad philosophos, quorum certior habetur auctoritas quam poetarum. Plato monarchiam adserit, unum Deum dicens, a quo sit mundus instructus, et mirabili ratione perfectus. Aristoteles auditor ejus unam esse mentem, quae mundo praesideat, confitetur. Antisthenes unum esse dicit naturalem Deum, totius summae gubernatorem. Longum est recensere quae de summo Deo vel Thales vel Pythagoras et Anaximenes antea, vel postmodum Stoici, Cleanthes et Chrysippus et Zenon, vel nostrorum Seneca, Stoicos secutus, et ipse Tullius praedicaverint, quum hi omnes, et quid sit Deus, definire tentaverint, et ab eo solo regi mundum adfirmaverint, nec ulli subjectum esse naturae, quum ab ipso sit omnis natura generata. Hermes, qui ob virtutem multarumque artium scientiam Trismegistus meruit nominari, qui et doctrinae vetustate philosophos antecessit, quique apud Aegyptios ut deus colitur, majestatem Dei singularis infinitis adserens laudibus, Dominum et Patrem nuncupat, eumque esse sine nomine, quod proprio vocabulo non indigeat, quia solus sit, nec habere ullos parentes, quia ex se et per se ipse sit. Hujus ad filium scribentis exordium tale est: 'Deum quidem intelligere difficile est, eloqui vero impossibile, etiam cui intelligere possibile est; perfectum enim ab imperfecto, invisibile a visibili non potest comprehendi.'

CHAPTER 5

Superest de vatibus dicere. Varro decem Sibyllas fuisse tradit, primam de Persis, secundam Libyssam, tertiam Delphida, quartam Cimmeriam, quintam Erythraeam, sextam Samiam, septimam Cumanam, octavam Hellespontiam, nonam Phrygiam, decimam Tiburtem, cui sit nomen Albuneae. Ex his omnibus Cumanae solius tres esse libros, qui Romanorum fata contineant, et habeantur arcani, ceterarum autem fere omnium singulos exstare haberique vulgo, sed eos Sibyllinos velut uno nomine inscribi. Nisi quod Erythraea, quae Troici belli temporibus fuisse perhibetur, nomen suum verum posuit in libro, aliarum confusi sunt. Hae omnes, de quibus dixi, Sibyllae, praeter Cumaeam, quam legi nisi a Quindecimviris non licet, unum Deum esse testantur, principem, conditorem, parentem, non ab ullo generatum, sed a seipso satum, qui et fuerit a saeculis, et sit futurus in saecula, et idcirco solus coli debeat, solus timeri, solus a cunctis viventibus honorari. Quarum testimonia, quia breviare non poteram, praetermisi; quae si desideras, ad ipsos tibi libros recurrendum est. Nunc reliqua persequamur.

CHAPTER 6

Haec igitur tot ac tanta testimonia liquido perdocent, unum esse regimen in mundo, unam potestatem, cujus nec origo excogitari, nec vis enarrari potest. Stulti ergo, qui de concubitu natos putant deos esse, quum ipsi sexus et corporum copulatio idcirco mortalibus a Deo data sint, ut per sobolis successionem genus omne servetur. Immortalibus vero quid opus est aut sexu aut successione, quos nec voluptas nec interitus attingit? Illi ergo, qui dii putantur, quoniam et genitos esse tanquam homines et procreasse constat, mortales utique fuerunt; sed dii crediti sunt, quod, quum essent reges magni ac potentes, ob ea beneficia, quae in homines contulerant, divinos post obitum honores consequi meruerunt, positisque templis atque simulacris, memoria eorum tanquam immortalium retenta est atque celebrata.

CHAPTER 7

Sed quum sit omnibus fere gentibus persuasum deos esse, res tamen eorum gestae, quas tam poetae quam historici tradiderunt, homines eos fuisse declarant. Hercules per quae tempora fuerit, quis ignorat, quum idem et inter Argonautas navigaverit, et, expugnata Troja, Laomedontem Priami patrem ob perjurium interfecerit? Ab eo tempore paulo amplius quam mille et quingenti computantur anni. Hic ne natus quidem honeste traditur, sed Alcmenae adulterio genitus, et ipse vitiis genitoris addictus, nec feminis unquam nec maribus abstinuit, orbemque totum non tam gloriae quam libidinis causa, nec tantum ad necandas belluas quantum ad serendos liberos, peragravit. Quumque esset invictus, ab una tamen Omphale triumphatus est, cui clava et spolio leonis tradito, indutus ipse feminea veste atque ad pedes mulieris abjectus, pensa quae faceret*accepit. Idem postea instinctu furoris elatus, parvos liberos et uxorem Megaram trucidavit. Postremo sumpta Deianirae conjugis veste, quum difflueret ulceribus, doloris impatiens, rogum sibi in Oetaeo monte construxit, eoque se vivum cremavit. Sic efficitur ut, etiamsi ob virtutem deus credi potuisset, ob haec tamen homo fuisse cernatur.

CHAPTER 8

Aesculapium Tarquitius tradit ex incertis parentibus natum, et ob id expositum, atque a venatoribus collectum, caninis uberibus educatum, Chironi in disciplinam datum. Hic Epidauri moratus est, Cynosuris, ut Cicero ait, sepultus, quum esset ictu fulminis interemptus. Apollo autem pater ejus non dedignatus est alienum gregem pascere, ut acciperet uxorem, et dilectum puerum quum peremisset imprudens, gemitus suos inscripsit in flore. Marti, viro fortissimo, adulterii crimen non defuit, siquidem catenis cum adultera vinctus spectaculo fuit. Castor et Pollux alienas sponsas non impune rapuerunt, quos Homerus non poetica sed simplici fide mortuos sepultosque testatur. Mercurius, qui de stupro Veneris genuit Androgynum, deus esse meruit, quia lyram reperit et palaestram. Liber Pater, debellata India, victor, quum Cretam forte venisset, Ariadnen conspexit in litore, quam Theseus et violaverat et reliquerat. Tum amore inflammatus eam sibi in conjugium sociavit, et coronam ejus, ut poetae ferunt, inter astra signavit. Mater magna ipsa post fugam et obitum viri quum in Phrygia moraretur, vidua et anus formosum adolescentem in deliciis habuit, et quia fidem non praestiterat, ademptis genitalibus, effeminavit. Ideo etiam nunc Gallis sacerdotibus gaudet.

CHAPTER 9

Ceres unde Proserpinam nisi de stupro genuit? unde Latona geminos nisi ex crimine? Venus deorum et hominum libidinibus exposita, quum regnaret in Cypro, artem meretriciam reperit, ac mulieribus imperavit, ut quaestum facerent, ne sola esset infamis. Ipsae illae virgines Minerva et Diana num castae? Unde igitur prosilivit Erichthonius? num in terram Vulcanus semen effudit, et inde homo tanquam fungus enatus est? Aut illa cur Hippolytum, vel ad secretas sedes, vel ad mulierem relegavit, ubi solus inter ignota nemora aetatem exigeret, et, jam mutato nomine, Virbius vocaretur? Quid haec significant, nisi incestum, quod poetae non audent confiteri?

CHAPTER 10

Horum autem omnium rex et pater Jupiter, quem tenere in coelo summam credunt potestatem, quid habuit pietatis qui Saturnum patrem regno expulit, et armis fugientem persecutus est? quid continentiae, qui omnia libidinum genera exercuit? Nam idem Alcmenam Ledamque summis viris nuptas adulterio fecit infames; idem pulchritudine pueri captus, venantem ac virilia meditantem, ad femineos usus violenter abripuit. Quid virginum stupra commemorem, quarum multitudo quanta fuerit, filiorum numerus ostendit? In una tamen Thetide abstinentior fuit; erat enim praedictum, quod is, quem paritura esset, major patre suo futurus esset. Pugnavit ergo cum amore, ne quis se major nasceretur. Sciebat ergo, se non esse perfectae virtutis magnitudinis, potestatis, qui, quod ipse patri fecerat, timuit. Cur igitur optimus maximus nominatur? quum se et peccatis contaminaverit, quod est injusti ac mali, et majorem timuerit, quod est imbecilli ac minoris.

CHAPTER 11

Sed dicet aliquis ficta haec esse a poetis. Non est hoc poeticum sic fingere, ut totum mentiare, sed ut ea, quae gesta sunt, figura et quasi velamine aliquo versicolore praetexas. Hunc habet poetica licentia modum, non ut totum fingat, quod est mendacis et inepti, sed ut aliquid cum ratione commutet. In imbrem se aureum vertisse dixerunt, ut Danaen falleret. Quis est imber aureus? Utique aurei nummi, quorum magnam copiam offerens, et in sinum infundens, fragilitatem virginalis animi hac mercede corrupit. Sic et imbrem ferreum dicunt, quum volunt multitudinem significare telorum. Catamitum in aquila rapuit. Quae est aquila? Legio scilicet, quoniam figura hujus animalis insigne legionis est. Europam transvexit in tauro. Quis est taurus? Utique navis, quae tutelam habuit tauri in specie figuratam. Sic Inachi filia non utique bos facta transnavit, sed ejusmodi navigio iram Junonis effugit, quod habebat bovis formam. Denique quum in Aegyptum delata esset, Isis est facta, cujus navigium certo quodam die in memoriam fugae celebratur.

CHAPTER 12

Vides ergo, non omnia poetas confinxisse, et quaedam praefigurasse, ut, quum vera dicerent, aliquid tamen velaminis adderent iis quos deos esse dicebant, sicut etiam de regnis; quum enim dicunt Jovem coeli regnum sorte tenuisse, aut Olympum montem significant, in quo Saturnum, et Jovem postmodum, habitasse veteres historiae produnt, aut partem Orientis, quae sit quasi superior, quod inde lux nascitur; Occidentis autem velut inferior, et ideo Plutonem inferos esse sortitum; mare vero cessisse Neptuno, quod oram maritimam cum omnibus insulis obtinuerit. Multa sic poetae colorant, quod qui nesciunt, tanquam mendaces eos arguunt; verbo dumtaxat, nam re quidem credunt, quoniam deorum simulacra sic fingunt, ut, quum mares ac feminas faciant, et alios conjuges, alios parentes, alios liberos fateantur, poetis utique assentiant; haec enim sine coitu et generatione esse non possunt.

CHAPTER 13

Sed omittamus sane poetas. Ad historiam veniamus, quae simul et rerum fide et temporum nititur vetustate. Euhemerus fuit Messenius, antiquissimus scriptor, qui de sacris inscriptionibus veterum templorum et originem Jovis, et res gestas omnemque progeniem collegit; item ceterorum Deorum parentes, patrias, actus, imperia, obitus, sepulchra etiam persecutus est. Quam historiam vertit Ennius in Latinam linguam, cujus haec verba sunt: 'Haec ut scripta sunt, Jovis fratrumque ejus stirps atque cognatio;

in hunc modum nobis ex sacra scriptione traditum est.' Idem igitur Euhemerus Jovem tradit, quum quinquies orbem circumivisset, et amicis suis atque cognatis distribuisset imperia, legesque hominibus [dedisset], multaque alia bona fecisset, immortali gloria memoriaque affectum sempiterna, in Creta vitam commutasse, atque ad deos abiisse, et sepulchrum ejus esse in Creta, in oppido Gnosso, et in eo scriptum antiquis litteris Graecis *ZAN KPONOY*, quod est Jupiter Saturni. Constat ergo, ex iis quae retuli, hominem fuisse, in terraque regnasse.

CHAPTER 14

Transeamus ad superiora, ut originem totius erroris deprehendamus. Saturnus Caelo et Terra traditur natus. Hoc utique incredibile est. Sed cur ita tradatur, ratio certa est, quam qui ignorat tanquam fabulam respuit. Saturni patrem Uranum fuisse vocitatum, et Hermes auctor est, et sacra historia docet. Trismegistus paucos admodum fuisse quum diceret perfectae doctrinae viros, in iis cognatos suos enumeravit, Uranum, Saturnum, Mercurium. Euhemerus eundem Uranum primum in terra regnasse commemorat his verbis: 'Initio primus in terris imperium summum Caelus habuit, is id regnum una cum fratribus suis sibi institut atque para[vit].' *Hic plura deficiunt. Sequitur*: [ut eis per] hominum stultam benevolentiam et errorem divinitas attributa sit.

CHAPTER 20

Dixi de religionibus quae sunt communes omnium gentium. Dicam nunc de diis quos Romani proprios habent. Faustuli conjugem Romuli Remique nutricem, cujus honori Larentinalia sunt dicata, vulgati fuisse corporis quis ignorat? Et idcirco Lupa nuncupata est, et in ferae speciem figurata. Faula quoque et Flora meretrices erant, quarum altera Herculis fuit scortum, sicut Verrius tradit, altera, quum magnas opes corpore quaesivisset, populum scripsit haeredem, et ideo in honorem ejus ludi Floralia celebrantur. Tatius muliebre simulacrum in cloaca maxima repertum consecravit, et deam Cloacinam nuncupavit. Obsessi a Gallis Romani ex mulierum capillis tormenta fecerunt, et ob id Veneri Calvae aram templumque posuerunt; item Pistori Jovi, quod eos monuerat in quiete, ut ex omni fruge panem facerent, et supra hostes jacerent, quo facto desperantes Galli posse inopia Romanos subigi, ab obsidione discesserant. Pavorem ac Pallorem Tullus Hostilius deos fecit. Colitur et Mens, quam, credo, si habuissent, nunquam colendam putassent. Honorem atque Virtutem Marcellus invenit.

CHAPTER 21

Sed et alios ejusmodi commenticios deos senatus instituit, Spem, Fidem, Concordiam, Pacem, Pudicitiam, Pietatem, quae omnia, quum in animis hominum esse vera deberent, intra parietes falsa posuerunt. Hos tamen, quamvis extra hominem in nulla sint omnino substantia, mallem potius coli, quam Rubiginem, quam Febrem, quae non sacranda sunt sed exsecranda, quam Fornacem cum suis Fornacalibus sacris, quam Stercutum, qui fimo pinguefacere terram primus ostendit, quam Deam Mutam, quae Lares genuit, quam Cuninam, quae cunis infantium praeest, quam Cacam, quae ad Herculem de furto boum detulit, ut occideret fratrem: quam multa alia portenta atque ludibria, de quibus piget dicere! Terminum tamen non libet praeterire, quia ne Jovi quidem Capitolino cessisse traditur, quum lapis esset informis. Hunc finium putant habere custodiam, eique publice supplicatur, ut 'Capitoli immobile saxum' Romani imperii fines et conservet et proroget,

CHAPTER 22

Has omnes ineptias primus in Latio Faunus induxit, qui et Saturno avo cruenta sacra constituit, et Picum patrem tanquam deum coli voluit, et Fatuam Faunam conjugem sororemque inter deos conlocavit, ac Bonam Deam nominavit. Deinde Romae Numa, qui agrestes illos ac rudes viros superstitionibus novis oneravit, sacerdotia instituit, deos familiis gentibusque distribuit, ut animos ferocis populi ab armorum studiis avocaret. Ideo Lucilius deridens ineptias istorum, qui vanis superstitionibus serviunt, hos versus posuit:

    Terriculas lamias Fauni quas Pompiliique
    Instituere Numae, tremit has, hic omnia ponit.
    Ut pueri infantes credunt, signa omnia ahena
    Vivere et esse homines; sic isti omnia ficta
    Vera putant, credunt signis cor inesse in ahenis;
    Pergula pictorum, veri nihil, omnia ficta.

Tullius quoque de Natura Deorum 'commentitios ac fictos deos' queritur inductos, et hinc exstitisse 'falsas opiniones, erroresque turbulentos, et superstitiones paene aniles'. Quae sententia eo debet gravior computari, quod haec disseruit et philosophus et sacerdos.

CHAPTER 23

Diximus de diis, nunc de ritibus sacrorum culturisque dicemus. Jovi Cyprio, sicut Teucrus instituerat, humana hostia mactari solebat. Sic et Tauri Dianae hospites immolabant, Latiaris quoque Jupiter humano sanguine propitiatus est. Etiam ante [a] Saturno sexagenarii homines ex responso Apollinis de ponte in Tiberim dejiciebantur. Et eidem Saturno Carthaginienses non modo infantes prosecrabant, sed victi a Siculis, ut piaculum solverent, ducentos nobilium filios immolarunt. Nec illa his humaniora sunt, quae fiunt etiam nunc Matri Magnae atque Bellonae, in quibus antistites non alieno sanguine sed suo litant, cum amputatis genitalibus a viris migrant, nec ad feminas transeunt, aut sectis humeris detestabiles aras proprio cruore respergunt. Sed haec crudelia. Veniamus ad mitia. Isidis sacra nihil aliud ostendunt, nisi quemadmodum filium parvum, qui dicitur Osiris, perdiderit et invenerit. Nam primo sacerdotes ac ministri, derasis omnibus membris, tunsisque pectoribus, plangunt, dolent, quaerunt, affectum matris imitantes: postmodum puer per Cynocephalum invenitur. Sic luctuosa sacra laetitia terminantur. His etiam Cereris simile mysterium est, in quo, facibus accensis, per noctem Proserpina inquiritur, et, ea inventa, ritus omnis gratulatione ac taedarum jactatione finitur. Lampsaceni asellum Priapo mactant: ea enim visa est aptior victima, quae ipsi, cui mactatur, magnitudine virilis obscoeni posset aequari. Lindos est oppidum Rhodi, ubi Herculis sacra maledictis celebrantur. Hercules enim quum boves aratori abstulisset atque immolasset, ille injuriam suam convitiis ultus est, eoque ipso sacerdote postmodum constituto, sanctum est, ut iisdem maledictis et ipse et alii postea sacerdotes sacra celebrarent. Cretici autem Jovis mysterium est, quomodo infans aut subtractus sit patri, aut educatus. Capella praesto est, cujus uberibus puerum Amalthea nutrivit. Idem etiam Matris Deum sacra demonstrant: nam quia tum Corybantes galearum tinnitibus et scutorum pulsibus vagitum pueri texerant, nunc imago rei refertur in sacris; sed pro galeis cymbala, pro scutis tympana feriuntur, ne puerum vagientem Saturnus exaudiat.

CHAPTER 24

Haec sunt mysteria deorum. Nunc etiam originem religionum requiramus, ut et a quibus et per quae tempora institutae fuerint eruamus. Didymus in iis libris, qui inscribuntur *Ἐξηγήσεως Πινδαρικῆς*, Melissea fuisse tradit Cretensium regem, cujus filiae fuerint Amalthea et Melissa, quae Jovem nutrierint caprino lacte ac melle; hunc novos ritus ac pompas sacrorum introduxisse, et primum diis sacrificasse, id est Vestae, quae dicitur Tellus; unde Poeta:

—— primamque deorum
Tellurem,

et postmodum Deum Matri. Euhemerus autem in sacra historia ipsum Jovem dicit, postquam imperium ceperit, sibi multis in locis fana posuisse. Nam circuiens orbem, ut quemque in locum venerat, principes populorum amicitia sibi et hospitii jure sociabat. Cujus rei ut posset memoria servari, fanum sibi creari jubebat atque ab hospitibus suis annua festa celebrari. Sic per omnes terras cultum sui numinis seminavit. Quando autem isti fuerint, facile colligi potest. Scribit enim Thallus in historia sua, Belum regem Assyriorum, quem Babylonii colunt, quique Saturni fuerit aequalis et amicus, antiquiorem fuisse Troico bello annis CCCXXII, et sunt ab Ilio capto anni M.CCCCLXX. Unde apparet, non amplius quam M.DCCC esse annos, ex quo, novis Deorum cultibus institutis, humanum genus inciderit in errorem.

CHAPTER 25

Merito igitur poetae commutatum esse aureum saeculum memorant, quod fuerit regnante Saturno. Nulli enim tunc dii colebantur, sed unum et solum Deum noverant. Postquam se terrenis ac fragilibus subjugaverunt, colentes ligna et aera et lapides, commutatio saeculi facta est usque ad ferrum. Amissa enim Dei notitia, et uno illo vinculo humanae societatis abrupto, vastare se invicem, praedari, ac debellare coeperunt. Quod si sursum oculos suos tollerent, ac Deum intuerentur, qui eos ad adspectum coeli suique excitavit, nunquam se servos et humiles facerent terrena venerando, quorum stultitiam Lucretius graviter incusat, dicens:

> Et faciunt animos humiles formidine divum,
> Depressosque premunt ad terram,

†qua reddunt. Nec repunt†, nec intelligunt quam vanum sit ea timere, quae feceris, aut ab his aliquod sperare praesidium, quae muta et insensibilia nec vident nec audiunt supplicantem. Quid ergo majestatis aut numinis habere possunt, quae et fuerunt in hominis potestate, ne fierent, aut ut aliud fierent, et sunt etiam nunc? Nam et violari et furto subtrahi possunt, nisi illa et lex saepiat et humana custodia. Num igitur mentis suae compos videri potest, qui talibus opimas victimas caedit, dona consecrat, pretiosas vestes offert, quasi uti possunt, qui motu carent? Merito ergo Dionysius Siciliae tyrannus deos Graeciae, quum eam victor occupasset, spoliavit atque derisit, et post sacrilegia quae admiserat ad Siciliam prospera navigatione remeavit, regnumque tenuit usque ad senectutem, nec eum dii violati puniri potuerunt. Quanto satius est, spretis inanibus, ad Deum te convertere, tueri statum, quem a Deo acceperis, tueri nomen! Idcirco enim ἄνθρωπος, quia sursum spectat, nominatur: sursum autem spectat, qui Deum verum et vivum, qui est in coelo, suspicit, qui artificem, qui parentem animae suae non modo sensu ac mente, verum etiam vultu et oculis sublimibus quaerit. Qui autem se terrenis humilibusque substernit, utique illud, quod est inferius, sibi praefert. Nam, quum ipse opus Dei sit, simulacrum autem opus hominis, non potest humanum opus divino anteponi. Et sicut Deus hominis parens est, ita simulacri homo. Stultus igitur et amens, qui adorat quod ipse fabricavit; cujus artificii detestabilis et inepti auctor fuit Prometheus, patruo Jovis Iapeto natus. Nam quum primum Jupiter, summo potitus imperio, tanquam deum se constituere vellet, ac templa condere, et quaereret aliquem qui humanam figuram posset exprimere, tunc Prometheus exstitit, qui hominis effigiem de pingui luto figuraret, ita verisimiliter ut novitas ac subtilitas artis miraculo esset. Denique illum et sui temporis homines, et postea poetae, tanquam fictorem veri ac vivi hominis prodiderunt, ut nos, quoties fabrefacta signa laudamus, vivere illa et spirare dicimus. Et hic quidem auctor fuit fictilium simulacrorum. Sequentes autem

posteri et de marmore sculpserunt, et ex aere fuderunt; deinde processu temporum ex auro et ebore accessit ornatus, ut non modo similitudines oculos hominum, verum etiam fulgor ipse praestringeret. Sic illecti pulchritudine, ac verae majestatis, obliti, insensibilia sentientes, irrationabilia rationabiles, exanima viventes colenda sibi ac veneranda duxerunt.

CHAPTER 26

Nunc refellamus eos etiam, qui elementa mundi tanquam deos habent, id est, coelum, solem, atque lunam, quorum artificem non cognoscentes, ipsa opera mirantur et adorant. Qui error non imperitorum modo, verum etiam philosophorum est; siquidem Stoici universa coelestia in deorum numero habenda censent, quia certos et rationabiles motus habent, quibus succedentium sibi temporum vicissitudines constantissime servant. Non est igitur in his voluntarius motus, quia praestitutis legibus serviunt, non proprio utique sensu, sed opificio summi Conditoris, qui illa sic ordinavit, ut inerrabiles cursus et certa spatia conficerent, quibus dierum ac noctium, aestatis et hiemis, alterna variarent. Quod si effectus eorum, si meatus, si claritatem, si constantiam, si pulchritudinem admirantur, intelligere debuerunt quanto his pulchrior et praeclarior et potentior sit ipse conditor atque artifex eorum Deus. Sed illi Divinitatem humanis visibus aestimaverunt, ignorantes nec aeternum esse posse, quod veniat sub aspectum, nec, quod sit aeternum, posse oculis mortalibus comprehendi.

CHAPTER 27

Unum et ultimum restat, ut, quoniam plerumque accidit, sicuti in historiis legimus, ut majestatem suam dii ostendisse videantur per auguria, per somnia, per oracula, tum etiam poenis eorum qui sacrilegia commiserant, doceam quae ratio id effecerit; ne quis etiam nunc in eosdem laqueos incidat, quos illi veteres inciderunt. Quum Deus pro virtute majestatis suae mundum de nihilo condidisset, coelumque luminibus adornasset, terram vero et mare complesset animalibus, tum hominem, de limo ad imaginem similitudinis suae figuratum, inspiravit ad vitam, posuitque eum in paradiso, quem conseverat omni genere fructiferi ligni, et praecepit ei, ne una ex arbore, in qua posuerat scientiam boni malique, gustaret, fore interminatus ut vitam perderet, si fecisset; si vero mandatum servaret, immortalis permaneret. Tum serpens, qui erat unus ex Dei ministris, invidens homini quod esset immortalis effectus, illexit eum dolo, ut mandatum Dei legemque transcenderet. Et hoc modo scientiam quidem boni ac mali accepit, sed vitam, quam perpetuam Deus tribuerat, amisit. Ejecit ergo peccatorem de sancto loco, et in hunc orbem relegavit, ut victum quaereret per laborem, ut difficultates et aerumnas pro merito sustineret; ipsumque paradisum vallo igneo circumfudit, ne quis hominum ad diem usque judicii ad locum illum perpetuae beatitudinis conaretur irrepere. Tum secuta est hominem mors ex Dei sententia; et tamen vita ejus, licet temporalis esse coepisset, in mille annis terminum sumpsit, et id fuit humanae vitae spatium usque ad cataclysmi tempus; nam post diluvium paulatim vita hominum breviata, et ad annos centum viginti redacta est. Serpens vero ille, qui de factis, diaboli (id est, criminatoris sive delatoris) nomen accepit, non destitit semen hominis, quem a principio deceperat, persequi. Denique eum, qui primus in hoc orbe generatus est, inspirato livore, in caedem fratris armavit, ut de duobus primogenitis hominibus alterum exstingueret, alterum faceret parricidam. Nec quievit deinceps, quo minus per singulas generationes pectoribus hominum malitiae virus infunderet, corrumperet, depravaret, tantis denique sceleribus obrueret, ut justitiae jam rarum esset exemplum, sed viverent homines ritu belluarum. Quod Deus quum videret, angelos suos misit, ut vitam hominum excolerent, eosque ab omni malo tuerentur. His mandatum dedit, ut se terrenis abstinerent, ne qua labe maculati, honore angelico mulctarentur. Sed eos quoque idem ille subdolus criminator, dum inter homines commorantur, illexit ad voluptates, ut se cum mulieribus inquinarent. Tum damnati sententia Dei, et ob peccata projecti, et nomen angelorum et substantiam perdiderunt. Ita diaboli satellites facti, ut haberent solatium perditionis suae, ad perdendos homines converterunt, quos ut tuerentur advenerant.

CHAPTER 28

Hi sunt daemones, de quibus poetae saepe in carminibus suis loquuntur, quos custodes hominum appellat Hesiodus. Ita enim persuaserunt hominibus, illecebris atque fallaciis suis, ut eosdem deos esse crederent. Denique Socrates habere se a prima pueritia custodem rectoremque vitae suae daemonem praedicabat sine cujus nutu et imperio nihil agere posset. Adhaerent ergo singulis, et sub nomine Geniorum aut Penatium domos occupant. His sacraria constituuntur, his quotidie libatur ut Laribus, his honos datur tanquam malorum depulsoribus; hi a principio, ut averterent homines a Dei veri agnitione, novas religiones et cultus deorum introduxerunt; hi memorias regum mortuorum consecrari, templa constitui, simulacra fieri docuerunt, non ut honorem Dei minuerent, aut suum augerent quem peccando amiserunt, sed ut vitam hominibus eriperent, spem verae lucis auferrent, ne homines, unde illi exciderunt, ad immortalitatis coeleste praemium pervenirent. Iidem astrologiam prodiderunt, et auguratum, et aruspicinam, quae quum per se falsa sint, tamen ipsi, auctores malorum, sic ea gubernant, sic temperant, ut vera credantur. Ipsi etiam magicae artis praestigias ad circumscribendos oculos repererunt—illorum adspiratione fit, ut quod sit, non esse, et quod non sit, esse videatur; ipsi necromantias, ipsi sortes et oracula, ut mentes hominum per ambiguos exitus mentita divinatione deludant. In templis vero et sacrificiis omnibus praesentes adsunt, et, prodigiis quibusdam fallacibus editis ad miraculum praesentium sic homines circumveniunt, ut. inesse numen simulacris et imaginibus credant. Irrepunt etiam corporibus ut spiritus tenues, vitiatisque membris morbos conciunt, quos sacrificiis votisque placati postmodum relaxent; somnia immittunt, aut plena terroris, ut ipsi rogentur, aut quorum exitus respondeant veritati, ut venerationem sui augeant. Nonnunquam etiam in sacrilegos edunt aliquid ultionis, ut quisquis viderit timidior ac religiosior fiat. Sic fraudibus suis obduxerunt humano generi tenebras, ut oppressa veritate summi ac singularis Dei nomen in oblivionem veniret.

CHAPTER 29

Sed dicet quispiam, 'Cur ergo verus ille Deus patitur haec fieri? ac non potius malos vel summovet vel exstinguit? Cur vero ipse daemoniarchen a principio fecit, ut esset qui cuncta corrumperet, cuncta disperderet?' Dicam breviter, cur hunc talem esse voluerit. Quaero, utrumne virtus bonum sit, an malum? Negari non potest quin bonum. Si bonum est virtus, malum est igitur e contrario vitium. Si vitium ex eo malum est quia virtutem impugnat, et virtus ex eo bonum est quia vitium affligit, ergo non potest virtus sine vitio consistere, et, si vitium sustuleris, virtutis merita tollentur; nec enim potest ulla fieri sine hoste victoria. Ita fit, ut bonum sine malo esse non possit. Vidit hoc Chrysippus, vir acris ingenii, de Providentia disserens, eosque stultitiae redarguit, qui bonum quidem a Deo factum putant, malum autem negant. Hujus sententiam interpretatus est A. Gellius in libris Noctium Atticarum, sic dicens: 'Quibus non videtur mundus Dei et hominum causa institutus, neque res humanae providentia gubernari, gravi se argumento uti putant, quum ita dicunt: Si esset providentia, nulla essent mala. Nihil enim minus aiunt providentiae congruere, quam in eo mundo, quem propter homines fecisse dicatur, tantam vim esse aerumnarum et malorum.' Ad ea Chrysippus quum in libro περὶ προνοίας quarto dissereret, *Nihil prorsus*, inquit, *istis insulsius, qui opinantur bona esse potuisse, si non essent ibidem mala. Nam quum bona malis contraria sint, utraque necesse est opposita esse inter se, et quasi mutuo adversoque fulta nisu consistere. Nullum adeo contrarium est sine contrario altero. Quo enim pacto justitiae sensus esse posset, nisi essent injuriae? aut quid aliud justitia est, quam injustitiae privatio? Quid item fortitudo non intelligi potest, nisi ex ignaviae adpositione; quid continentia, nisi ex intemperantiae. Quo item modo prudentia esset, nisi foret contraria imprudentia? Proinde*, inquit, *homines stulti cur non hoc etiam desiderant, ut veritas sit, et non sit mendacium? Namque itidem sunt bona et mala, felicitas et importunitas, voluptas et dolor. Alterum enim ex altero, sicut Plato ait, verticibus inter se contrariis deligatum: si tuleris unum, abstuleris utrumque.* Vides ergo id, quod saepe dixi, bonum et malum ita sibi esse connexa, ut alterum sine altero constare non possit. Summa igitur prudentia Deus materiam virtutis in malis posuit, quae idcirco fecit ut nobis constitueret agonem, in quo victores immortalitatis praemio coronaret.

CHAPTER 30

Docui, ut opinor, cultus deorum non modo impios, sed etiam vanos esse; vel quod homines fuerint, quorum memoria post obitum consecrata sit; vel quod simulacra ipsa insensibilia et surda sint, quia sunt ficta de terra, nec oportere hominem, qui debeat spectare coelestia, terrenis se subjugare; vel quod spiritus, qui eas religiones sibi vindicant, incesti et impuri sint, et ideo Dei sententia condemnati ceciderint in terram; nec fas esse in eorum ditionem venire, quibus potentior sis, si Deum verum sequi velis. SUPEREST ut, quoniam de falsa religione diximus, etiam de falsa sapientia disseramus, quam philosophi profitentur, homines summa quidem doctrina et eloquentia praediti, sed longe a veritate summoti, quia nec Deum nec sapientiam Dei cognoverunt. Qui licet sint arguti ac diserti, tamen, quia humana est eorum sapientia, etiam cum his congredi non verebor, ut appareat a veritate mendacium, a coelestibus terrena facile posse superari. Quid sit philosophia hoc modo definiunt: 'Philosophia est amor vel studium sapientiae.' Non est ergo ipsa sapientia, quia necesse est aliud esse, quod amat, aliud, quod amatur. Si studium est sapientiae, ne sic quidem philosophia sapientia est; sapientia enim res est ipsa quae quaeritur; studium vero, quod quaerit. Ipsa igitur definitio, vel nominis significatio, declarat philosophiam non esse ipsam sapientiam. Dicam, ne studium quidem esse sapientiae, quo sapientia non comprehenditur. Quis enim studere dicatur ei rei, quam nullo modo possit attingere? Qui medicinae, aut grammaticae, aut oratoriae studet, studiosus ejus artis, quam discit, dici potest; ubi didicit, jam medicus, jam grammaticus, jam orator dicitur. Sic oportuit et studiosos sapientiae, postquam didicissent, sapientes nominari. Quum autem studiosi sapientiae, quamdiu vivant, vocentur, apparet illud studium non esse, quo ad ipsam rem, quae studio petitur, non potest perveniri; nisi forte qui ad finem usque vitae, ut sapiant, student, apud inferos sapientes erunt. Omni autem studio subjacet finis. Non est igitur id studium rectum quod non habet finem.

CHAPTER 31

Praeterea duo sunt, quae cadere in philosophiam videntur, scientia et opinatio, quae si auferantur, tota philosophia corruit. Atqui utrumque philosophiae ipsi philosophorum principes ademerunt. Scientiam Socrates, opinationem sustulit Zeno. Videamus an recte, Sapientia est, ut Cicero definivit, 'divinarum et humanarum rerum scientia': quae definitio si vera est, non cadit in hominem sapientia. Quis enim mortalium hoc sibi possit assumere, ut divina et humana scire se profiteatur?

Humana omitto, quae quamquam cum divinis connexa sunt, tamen quia sunt hominis, concedamus ut homo illa scire possit. Divina certe per se scire non potest, quia homo est; qui autem scit illa, divinus sit necesse est, ac propterea Deus. Homo autem nec divinus, nec Deus est. Non potest igitur per se scire homo divina. Nemo ergo sapiens, nisi Deus, aut certe is homo quem Deus docuit. Illi autem, quia nec dii sunt, nec a Deo docti, sapientes ergo, id est, divinarum et humanarum rerum scientes, esse non possunt. Recte igitur a Socrate atque Academicis scientia sublata est. Opinatio quoque non congruit sapienti. Id enim quisque opinatur quod ignorat. Opinari autem scire te, quod ignores, temeritas ac stultitia est. Recte igitur opinatio a Zenone sublata est. Si ergo scientia in homine nulla est, et opinatio esse non debet, philosophia radicitus amputatur.

CHAPTER 32

Huc accedit, quod non est uniformis, sed divisa in sectas, et in multas discrepantesque sententias dissipata, statum non habet. Quum enim singulae alias omnes impugnent et affligant, nec sit aliqua ex iis, quae non, judicio ceterarum, stultitiae condemnetur, utique discordantibus membris corpus omne philosophiae ad interitum deducitur. Hinc Academia postmodum nata est. Nam quum viderent ejus sectae principes omnem philosophiam, philosophis se invicem oppugnantibus, esse subversam, susceperunt adversus omnes bellum, ut omnia omnium dissolverent, nihil ipsi asserentes, nisi unum, nihil sciri posse. Ita, sublata scientia, philosophiam veterem subruerunt. Sed ne ipsi quidem philosophorum nomen retinuerunt, qui ignorantiam fatebantur; quia nescire omnia non modo philosophi, sed ne hominis quidem, sit. Ita [fit ut] philosophi, quia nihil munimenti habent, mutuis se vulneribus exstinguant, et ipsa tota philosophia suis se armis consumat ac finiat. At enim sola physice labat. Quid illa moralis? Num aliqua firmitate subnixa est? Videamus, an philosophi in hac saltem parte consentiant, quae ad vitae statum pertinet.

CHAPTER 33

Quod sit in vita SUMMUM BONUM quaeri necesse est, ut ad illud vita omnis et actiones nostrae dirigantur. Quum de hominis summo bono quaeritur, tale constitui debet, primum, ut id ad hominem solum pertineat, deinde, ut animi sit proprium, postremo, ut virtute quaeratur. Videamus ergo, an summum bonum, quod philosophi determinant, tale sit, ut nec mutum animal nec corpus attingat, nec possit sine virtute conquiri. Aristippus, Cyrenaicae sectae conditor, qui summum bonum esse censuit corporis voluptatem, de numero philosophorum deque coetu hominum propellendus est, quia se pecudi comparavit. Hieronymi summum bonum est nihil dolere, Diodori, dolere desinere. Sed ceterae animantes dolorem fugiunt, et, quum non dolent, aut dolere desinunt, gaudent. Quid igitur homini dabitur eximium, si bonum ejus summum commune cum belluis judicatur? Zeno summum bonum putavit, cum natura congruenter vivere. At haec definitio generalis est. Omnes enim animantes cum natura congruenter vivunt, et est sua cuique natura. Epicurus animi asseruit voluptatem. Quid est voluptas animi, nisi gaudium, quo plerumque luxuriat animus, ac relaxatur vel ad lusum vel ad risum? Sed hoc bonum etiam muta contingit, quae, quum pabulis saturata sunt, in gaudium et lasciviam resolvuntur. Dinomachus et Callipho honestam voluptatem probaverunt, sed aut idem dixerunt quod Epicurus, ut corporis sit voluptas inhonesta, aut si corporis voluptates, alias turpes, alias honestas putaverunt, jam non est summum bonum quod corpori adscribitur. Peripatetici ex bonis animi et corporis et fortunae summum bonum conflant. Animi bona probari possunt: Sed si auxilio indigent ad complendam beatitudinem, utique imbecilla sunt. Corporis vero atque fortunae non sunt in hominis potestatem, nec jam summum bonum est, quod aut corpori aut extra positis assignatur; quia et pecudes attingit hoc duplex bonum, quibus opus est, ut et bene valeant, et victu non indigeant. Stoici aliquanto melius sensisse creduntur, qui summum bonum virtutem esse dixerunt. Sed virtus non potest esse summum bonum, quoniam, si malorum laborumque tolerantia est, beata per se non est, sed efficere aut procreare summum bonum debet; quia pervenire ad illud sine difficultate ac labore maximo non potest. At vero Aristoteles longe a ratione aberravit, qui honestatem virtuti copulavit; quasi aliquando virtus aut ab honestate secerni, aut turpitudini posset adjungi. Herillus Pyrrhonius scientiam fecit summum bonum. Haec quidem et hominis et animi solius est, sed potest sine virtute contingere. Nec enim beatus putandus est, qui vel auditu aliquid didicerit, vel parva lectione cognoverit; nec est summi boni definitio, quia potest esse aut rerum malarum aut certe inutilium scientia. Et si sit bonarum et utilium, quam labore sis assecutus, summum tamen bonum non est, quia non propter se expetitur scientia, sed propter aliud. Nam idcirco artes discuntur, ut sint nobis aut victui, aut gloriae, aut etiam voluptati, quae utique summa bona esse non possunt. Ergo ne in ethica quidem philosophi regulam tenent; quandoquidem in ipso cardine, id est, in ea disputatione qua vita formatur, inter se pugnant; nec enim possunt paria esse aut similia praecepta, quum alii forment ad voluptatem, alii ad honestatem, alii vero ad naturam, alii ad scientiam, alii ad quaerendas, alii ad fugiendas opes, alii ad nihil dolendum, alii ad patientiam malorum; in quibus omnibus, sicut superius ostendi, a ratione declinant, quia Deum nesciunt.

CHAPTER 34

Videamus nunc, quod sit propositum sapienti summum bonum. Ad justitiam nasci homines non modo literae sacrae docent, verum etiam idem ipsi philosophi nonnunquam fatentur. Cicero sic ait: 'Sed omnium quae in doctorum hominum disputatione versantur, nihil est profecto praestabilius, quam plane intelligi nos ad justitiam esse natos.' Est hoc verissimum. Nec enim ad scelus nascimur, quum simus animal sociale atque commune. Ferae ad saevitiam gignuntur; aliter enim nequeunt quam praeda et sanguine victitare. Eaedem tamen, etsi ultima fames urgeat, nihilominus generis sui animalibus parcunt. Idem faciunt et aves, quas aliorum visceribus pasci necesse est. Quanto magis hominem, qui cum homine et commercio linguae et communione sensus copulatus est, parcere homini oportet, eumque diligere! Haec est enim justitia. Sed quoniam soli homini sapientia data est, ut Deum intelligat, et haec sola hominis mutorumque distantia est, duobus officiis obstricta est ipsa justitia. Unum Deo debet ut patri, alterum homini velut fratri. Ab eodem enim Deo geniti sumus. Merito ergo ac recte dictum est, sapientiam esse divinarum et humanarum rerum scientiam. Oportet enim scire nos quid Deo, quid homini debeamus—Deo scilicet religionem, homini caritatem. Sed illud superius sapientiae, hoc posterius virtutis est; et utrumque justitia comprehendit. Si ergo constat ad justitiam nasci hominem, necesse est justum malis esse subjectum, ut virtutem, qua est praeditus, in usu habeat; virtus enim malorum sustinentia est. Voluptates fugiet ut malum; opes contemnet, quia fragiles sunt; si habuerit, dilargietur, ut miseros servet; honores non appetet, quia sunt breves et caduci; injuriam nulli faciet; si fuerit passus, non retribuet, et diripientem sua non persequetur, nefas enim judicabit hominem laedere; et si quis exstiterit qui cogat desciscere a Deo, nec cruciatus nec mortem recusabit. Ita fiet, ut eum necesse sit et inopem, et humilem, et in contumeliis, aut etiam cruciatibus vivere.

CHAPTER 35

Quis igitur erit fructus justitiae atque virtutis, si nihil habebit in vita nisi malum? Quod si virtus, quae bona omnia terrena contemnit, mala universa patientissime perfert, ipsamque mortem pro officio suscipit, sine praemio esse non potest; quid superest nisi ut merces ejus immortalitas sola sit? Nam si cadit in hominem beata vita, ut philosophi volunt, in eo solo non dissidentes, cadit ergo et immortalitas. Id enim solum beatum est quod incorruptum, id solum incorruptum quod aeternum. Immortalitas ergo est summum bonum, quia et hominis, et animi, et virtutis est tantum. Ad hanc dirigimur, ad hanc capiendam nati sumus. Idcirco nobis Deus virtutem justitiamque proponit, ut aeternum illud praemium nostris laboribus assequamur. De ipsa vero immortalitate suo loco disseremus. Restat λογική philosophia, quae ad beatam vitam nihil confert: sapientia enim non in sermonis ornatu, sed in corde atque sensu [est]. Quod si et physica supervacua est, et haec logica; in ethica vero, quae sola necessaria est, philosophi erraverunt, qui summum bonum nullo modo invenire potuerunt; inanis igitur et inutilis omnis philosophia reperitur, quae nec rationem hominis comprehendere, nec officium potuit munusque complere.

CHAPTER 36

Quoniam de philosophia dixi breviter, nunc etiam de philosophis pauca dicam. Epicuri doctrina haec est inprimis, nullam esse providentiam; et idem deos esse non abnuit. Utrumque contra rationem. Sed si sunt dii, est igitur providentia. Aliter enim Deus intelligi non potest, cujus est proprium providere.

'Nihil', inquit, 'curat.' Ergo non modo humana, sed ne coelestia quidem curat. Quomodo igitur, aut unde esse illum affirmas? exclusa enim providentia curaque divina, consequens erat ut non esse omnino Deum diceres. Nunc eum verbo reliquisti, re sustulisti. Unde ergo rerum natura est, si Deus nihil curat? 'Semina', inquit, 'sunt minuta, quae nec videri, nec tangi possunt, quorum coitu fortuito et orta sunt omnia, et semper oriuntur.' Si nec videntur, nec ulla corporis parte sentiuntur, unde esse illa scire potuisti? Deinde si sunt, qua mente conveniunt ut aliquid efficiant? Si sunt laevia, cohaerere non possunt: si hamata et angulata, ergo secabilia sunt. Hami enim et anguli exstant et possunt amputari. Sed haec delira et inutilia. Quid quod idem animas exstinguibiles facit? Quem refellunt non modo philosophi omnes et publica persuasio, verum etiam responsa vatum, carmina Sibyllarum, ipsae denique divinae voces Prophetarum; ut mirum sit exstitisse unum Epicurum, qui cum pecoribus ac belluis sortem hominis aequaret, Quid Pythagoras, qui primus est philosophus nominatus, qui animas quidem immortales esse asserit, in alia tamen corpora vel pecudum, vel avium, vel bestiarum commeare? Non satius fuerat eas cum suis corporibus exstingui, quam sic ad aliena damnari? satius omnino non esse, quam post hominis formam, vel suem vel canem vivere? Et homo ineptus, ut fidem dicto adderet, seipsum Trojano bello Euphorbum fuisse dixit, quo occiso, in alias figuras animalium transiisse, postremo Pythagoram factum. O felicem, cui soli tanta memoria concessa est! vel potius infelicem, cui translato in pecudem non licuit nescire quid fuerit! Atque utinam solus delirasset. Invenit etiam qui crederent, et quidem non indoctos homines, ad quos stultitiae transiret haereditas.

CHAPTER 37

Post hunc Socrates philosophiae tenuit principatum, sapientissimus etiam oraculo dictus, quia se fatebatur unum scire, quod nihil sciret. Cujus oraculi auctoritate abstinere se physicos oportebat, ne aut quaererent ea quae scire non poterant, aut scire se putarent quae ignorabant. Videamus tamen an sapientissimus Socrates, sicut Pythius praedicavit. Usurpabat hoc saepe proverbium, 'Quod supra nos, nihil ad nos pertinere.' Jam excessit scientiae suae terminos; nam, qui unum se scire dicebat [quod nihil sciret], aliud invenit, quod tanquam sciens diceret; sed id frustra. Nam et Deus, qui utique supra nos est, quaerendus est, et religio suscipienda, quae sola nos discernit a belluis; quam quidem Socrates non modo repudiavit, verum etiam derisit, per anserem canemque jurando; quasi vero per Aesculapium non posset, cui voverat gallum. En sapientis viri sacrificium! Et quia eum prosecrare ipse non potuit, amicos moriturus oravit, ut post se solverent votum, scilicet ne apud inferos velut debitor teneretur. Hic profecto et pronunciavit, quod nihil scierit, et probavit.

CHAPTER 38

Hujus auditor Plato, quem 'deum philosophorum' Tullius nominat, qui solus omnium sic philosophatus est ut ad veritatem propius accederet, tamen, quia Deum ignoravit, in multis ita lapsus est ut nemo deterius erraverit, inprimis quod in libris civilibus omnia omnibus voluit esse communia. De patrimoniis tolerabile est, licet sit injustum; nec enim aut abesse cuiquam debet, si sua industria plus habet, aut prodesse, si sua culpa minus. Sed, ut dixi, potest aliquo modo ferri. Etiamne conjuges, etiamne liberi, communes erunt? Non erit sanguinis ulla distinctio; nec genus certum, nec familiae, nec cognationes, nec affinitates; sed, sicut in gregibus pecudum confusa et indiscreta omnia, nulla erit in viris continentia, nulla in feminis pudicitia. Quis esse in utrisque amor conjugalis potest, in quibus non est certus aut proprius affectus? Quis erit in patrem pius, ignorans unde sit natus? Qui filium diliget, quem putabit alienum? Quin etiam feminis curiam reseravit; militiam, et magistratus, et imperia permisit. Quanta erit infelicitas urbis illius, in qua virorum officia mulieres occupabunt! Sed haec alias latius. Zeno Stoicorum magister, qui virtutem laudat, misericordiam—quae summa est virtus—tanquam morbum animi amputandam judicavit, quae et Deo cara est, et hominibus necessaria. Quis est enim, qui aliquo in malo constitutus nolit esse miserabilis, ac non desideret auxilia succurrentium? qui ad opem ferendam nonnisi misericordiae affectu excitantur. Hanc ille licet humanitatem, licet pietatem vocet, non rem sed nomen immutat. Hic est affectus, qui soli homini datus est, ut imbecillitatem nostram mutuis adjumentis levaremus, quem qui tollit, ad vitam nos redigit belluarum. Nam, quod dicit paria esse peccata, ex eadem immanitate est, qua misericordiam veluti morbum insectatur. Qui enim nullam facit differentiam delictorum, aut levia magnis suppliciis afficienda censet, quod est crudelis judicis; aut gravia parvis, quod est dissoluti. Utrumque reipublicae incommodum; si enim summa scelera leviter puniantur, audacia malis crescet ad facinora majora; et si levibus delictis poena gravior irrogetur, multi cives, quoniam nemo esse sine delicto potest, in periculum venient, qui correpti possent esse meliores.

CHAPTER 39

Alia vero levia; sed ex eadem vanitate nascuntur. Xenophanes orbem lunae decem et octo partibus dixit esse majorem quam haec nostra sit terra. Itaque intra sinum ejus aliam terram contineri, quae ab hominibus et omnis generis animalibus incolatur. De antipodibus quoque sine risu nec audiri nec dici potest. Asseritur tamen quasi aliquid serium, ut credamus esse homines, qui vestigiis nostris habeant adversa vestigia. Tolerabilius Anaxagoras deliravit, qui nigram nivem dixit. Quorundam non modo dicta, sed etiam facta ridenda sunt. Democritus agrum suum a patre sibi relictum deseruit, et pascua publica fieri passus est. Diogenes cum choro 'canum' suorum, qui virtutem illam summam et exactam rerum omnium contemptum profitetur, mendicare victum maluit, quam honesto labore conquirere, aut habere ullam rem familiarem. Certe vita sapientis exemplum esse vivendi ceteris debet. Si horum sapientiam omnes imitentur, quomodo stabunt civitates? Sed forsitan iidem Cynici exemplum verecundiae praebere potuerunt, qui palam cum conjugibus suis cubitaverunt. Nescio quam possent virtutem defendere, qui pudorem sustulerunt. Non melior his Aristippus, qui, credo, ut amiculae suae Laidi placeret, Cyrenaicam instituit disciplinam, qua summi boni finem in voluptate corporis collocavit, ne aut peccatis auctoritas, aut vitiis doctrina deesset. An illi fortiores magis sunt probandi, qui, ut mortem contempsisse dicerentur, voluntariam necem sibi intulerunt—Zeno, Empedocles, Chrysippus, Cleanthes, Democritus, et hos imitatus Cato; nec scierunt homicidii crimine teneri secundum jus legemque divinam eum, qui se interfecerit? Deus enim nos in hoc domicilium carnis induxit, ille nobis temporale corporis habitaculum dedit, ut incolamus, quamdiu idem voluerit. Nefas igitur habendum est, sine Dei jussu velle migrare. Non est ergo vis adhibenda naturae. Scit ille quemadmodum opus suum resolvat. Cui operi si quis manus impias adhibuerit, ac divini opificii vincula diruperit, Deum conatur effugere, cujus sententiam nec vivus quisquam nec mortuus poterit evadere. Scelerati ergo et nefarii quos superius nominavi, qui etiam docuerunt, quas causas habere debeat mors voluntaria; ut parum sit sceleris, quod homicidae in semetipsos exstiterunt, nisi ad hoc nefas, et alios erudirent.

CHAPTER 40

Innumerabilia sunt philosophorum dicta factaque, quibus eorum insipientia redargui possit. Itaque quoniam cuncta enumerare non possumus, pauca suffecerint. Satis est intelligi, philosophos neque justitiae, quam ignorabant, neque virtutis, quam mentiuntur, esse doctores. Quid enim doceant, qui suam saepe ignorantiam confitentur? Mitto Socratem, cujus est nota sententia. Anaxagoras omnia circumfusa tenebris esse pronunciat: Empedocles angustas ad inveniendam veritatem sensuum semitas esse. Democritus in profundo quodam puteo demersam veritatem jacere testatur, quam quia nusquam reperiunt, idcirco adfirmant neminem adhuc exstitisse sapientem. Quoniam igitur nulla est (ut apud Platonem Socrates dicit) humana sapientia, sequamur ergo divinam, Deoque gratias agamus, qui eam nobis et revelavit et tradidit; ac nobis gratulemur, quod veritatem ac sapientiam coelesti beneficio tenemus, quam tot ingeniis tot aetatibus requisitam philosophia non potuit invenire.

CHAPTER 41

NUNC quoniam falsam religionem, quae est in deorum cultibus, et falsam sapientiam, quae est in philosophis, refutavimus, ad veram religionem sapientiamque veniamus. Et quidem conjuncte, quia cohaerent, de utraque dicendum est. Nam Deum verum colere, id est nec aliud quidquam, quam sapientia. Ille enim summus et conditor rerum Deus, qui hominem velut simulacrum suum fecit, idcirco utique soli ex omnibus animalibus rationem dedit, ut honorem sibi tanquam patri et [timorem] tanquam Domino referret, et hac pietate atque obsequio immortalitatis praemium mereretur. Hoc est verum divinumque mysterium. Illis autem, quia vera non sunt, nulla concordia. Neque in philosophia sacra celebrantur, neque in sacris philosophia tractatur; et ideo falsa religio est, quia non habet sapientiam, ideo falsa sapientia, quia non habet religionem. Ubi autem utraque conjuncta sunt, ibi esse veritatem necesse est, ut, si quaeratur ipsa veritas quid sit, recte dici possit aut sapiens religio, aut religiosa sapientia.

CHAPTER 42

Dicam nunc, quid sit vel sapiens religio, vel sapientia religiosa. Deus in principio, antequam mundum institueret, de aeternitatis suae fonte, deque divino ac perenni Spiritu suo, Filium sibi ipse progenuit incorruptum, fideliter virtuti ac majestati patriae respondentem. Hic est virtus, hic ratio, hic sermo Dei, hic sapientia. Hoc opifice, ut Hermes ait, et consiliatore, ut Sibylla, praeclaram et mirabilem hujus mundi fabricam machinatus est. Denique ex omnibus Angelis, quos idem Deus de suis spiritibus figuravit, solus in consortium summae potestatis adscitus est, solus Deus nuncupatus. *Omnia* enim *per ipsum, et sine ipso nihil.* Denique Plato de primo ac secundo Deo, non plane ut philosophus, sed ut vates locutus est, fortasse in hoc Trismegistum secutus, cujus verba de Graecis conversa subjeci: *Dominus et factor universorum, quem Deum vocare existimavimus, secundum fecit Deum visibilem et sensibilem. Sensibilem autem dico, non quod ipse sensum accipiat, sed quod in sensum mittat et visum. Quum ergo hunc fecisset primum, et solum, et unum, optimus ei apparuit, et plenissimus omnium bonorum.* Sibylla quoque *Deum* dicit *ducem omnium a Deo factum*; et alia, *Deum Dei filium esse noscendum*; sicut ea, quae in libris posui, exempla declarant. Hunc Prophetae Divino Spiritu pleni praedicaverunt, quorum praecipue Salomon in libro Sapientiae, item pater ejus coelestium scriptor hymnorum, ambo clarissimi Reges, qui Trojani belli tempora CLXXX annis antecesserunt, hunc ex Deo natum esse testantur: hujus nomen nulli est notum, nisi ipsi et Patri, sicut docet Joannes in Revelatione. Hermes ait *non posse nomen ejus mortali ore proferri.* Ab hominibus tamen duobus vocabulis nuncupatur, Jesus, quod est Salvator, et Christus, quod est Rex. Salvator ideo, quia est sanatio et salus omnium qui per eum credunt in

Deum: Christus ideo, quia ipse de coelo in saeculi hujus consummatione venturus est, ut judicet mundum, et, resurrectione mortuorum facta, regnum sibi constituat aeternum.

CHAPTER 43

Sed ne qua forte sit apud te haesitatio, cur eum, qui ante mundum ex Deo natus sit, Jesum appellemus, qui ante annos ccc natus ex homine est, rationem tibi breviter exponam. Idem est Dei et hominis filius. Bis enim natus est; primum de Deo in'spiritu ante ortum mundi; postmodum in carne ex homine, Augusto imperante: cujus rei praeclarum et grande mysterium est, in quo et salus hominum, et religio summi Dei, et omnis veritas continetur. Nam quum primum scelerati atque impii deorum cultus per insidias daemonum irrepserunt, tum penes solos Hebraeos religio Dei mansit, qui tamen non lege aliqua, sed traditum sibi per successionem cultum patrio more tenuerunt usque ad id tempus quo de Aegypto exierunt, Moyse duce, primo omnium Prophetarum, per quem illis lex est a Deo imposita, iique Judaei sunt postmodum nominati: servierunt igitur Deo vinculis legis obstricti. Sed iidem paulatim ad profanos ritus aberrantes, alienos deos susceperunt, et derelicto patrio cultu,. insensibilibus simulacris immolaverunt.' Propterea Deus Prophetas ad eos misit, Divino Spiritu adimpletos, qui illis peccata exprobrarent, et poenitentiam indicerent; qui secuturam ultionem minarentur, ac denuntiarent futurum, si in iisdem delictis perseverassent, ut alium mitteret novae legis latorem, et, ingrato populo ab haereditate summoto, aliam sibi plebem fideliorem de exteris gentibus congregaret. Illi autem non modo perseverarunt, verum etiam eos ipsos, qui mittebantur, interfecerunt. Itaque damnavit eos ob haec facinora, nec adjecit ulterius Prophetas mittere ad populum contumacem, sed Filium suum misit, ut gentes universas ad gratiam Dei convocaret. Nec illos tamen, licet impios et ingratos, ab spe salutis exclusit, sed ad ipsos potissimum misit, ut, si forte paruissent, non amitterent quod acceperant; si autem Deum suum non suscepissent, tum, haeredibus abdicatis, gentes in adoptionem venirent. Jussit igitur eum summus Pater descendere in terram, et humanum corpus induere, ut subjectus passionibus carnis, virtutem ac patientiam non solum verbis, sed etiam factis doceret. Renatus est ergo ex virgine sine patre tanquam homo; ut quemadmodum in prima nativitate spiritali creatus, ex solo Deo sanctus spiritus factus est, sic in secunda carnali ex sola matre genitus, caro sancta fieret, ut per eum caro, quae subjecta peccato fuerat, ab interitu liberaretur.

CHAPTER 44

Haec sic futura, ut exposui, Prophetae ante praedixerant. Apud Salomonem ita scriptum est: *Infirmatus est uterus virginis et accepit foetum, et gravata est, et facta est in multa miseratione mater virgo.* Apud Esaiam sic: *Ecce virgo accipiet in uterum, et pariet filium, et vocabitis nomen ejus Emmanuel,* quod significat nobiscum Deus; fuit enim nobiscum in terra, quum induit carnem, et nihilominus Deus fuit in homine, et homo in Deo. Utrumque autem eum fuisse a Prophetis ante praedictum est. Quod Deus fuerit, Esaias ita dicit: *Adorabunt te, et in te precabuntur, quoniam in te Deus est* [*et non alius Deus praeter te. Tu enim.Deus es*], *et nos nesciebamus, Deus Israel. Confundentur et reverebuntur omnes, qui adversantur tibi, et cadent in confusionem.* Item Jeremias: *Hic Deus noster est, et non deputabitur alius absque illo, qui invenit omnem viam prudentiae, et dedit eam Jacob puero suo, et Israel dilecto sibi. Posthaec in terris visus est, et cum hominibus conversatus est.* Item, quod homo fuerit, idem Jeremias dicit: *Et homo est, et quis cognovit eum?* Esaias quoque sic tradit: *Et mittet eis Dominus hominem, qui salvabit eos, et judicans sanabit eos.* Item Moyses ipse in Numeris: *Orietur stella ex Jacob, et exsurget homo ex Israel.* Idcirco igitur quum Deus esset, suscepit carnem, ut inter Deum et hominem medius factus, hominem ad Deum magisterio suo superata morte perduceret.

CHAPTER 45

Diximus de nativitate. Nunc de virtute operibusque dicamus; quae quum magna inter homines ac mirabilia faceret, videntes illa Judaei, magica potentia fieri putabant, ignorantes ea omnia quae fiebant ab eo praedicta esse a Prophetis. Aegros et vario morborum genere languentes non medela aliqua, sed vi ac potestate verbi sui protinus roborabat, debiles resanabat, claudos ad gressum erigebat, caecis visum restituebat, mutis eloquium dabat, surdos inauribat, pollutos maculatosque purgabat, furiatis daemonum incursu mentem propriam reponebat, mortuos et jam sepultos ad vitam lucemque revocabat. Idem quinque millia hominum quinque panibus et duobus piscibus saturavit. Idem super mare ambulavit. Idem in tempestate praecepit vento ut conquiesceret, statimque tranquillitas facta est: quae omnia et in Prophetarum libris et in carminibus Sibyllinis praedicta invenimus. Ob haec miracula quum ad eum magna concurreret multitudo, et, ut erat, Dei Filium et a Deo missum crederet, repleti invidia sacerdotes ac principes Judaeorum, simul ira concitati, quod eorum peccata et injustitiam coarguebat, coierunt ut eum occiderent. Quod futurum ante annos mille paulo amplius Salomon in Sapientia pronunciaverat his verbis: *Circumveniamus justum, quoniam insuavis est nobis, et exprobrat nobis peccata legis. Promittit scientiam Dei se habere, et filium Dei se nominat. Factus est nobis in traductionem cogitationum nostrarum, gravis est nobis etiam ad videndum, quoniam dissimilis est aliis vita illius, et mutatae sunt viae illius. Tanquam nugaces aestimati sumus, ab illo. Continet se a viis nostris, quasi ab immunditiis, et praefert novissima justorum, et gloriatur patrem [Dominum] Deum. Videamus ergo si sermones illius veri sunt, et tentemus, quae eventura sunt illi. Contumelia et tormento interrogemus eum, ut sciamus reverentiam illius, et probemus patientiam illius. Morte turpissima condemnemus eum. Haec cogitaverunt et erraverunt. Excaecavit enim illos stultitia ipsorum, et nescierunt sacramenta Dei.* Harum igitur litterarum immemores, quas legebant, incitaverunt populum tanquam adversus impium, ut eum comprehensum ad judicium ducerent, mortemque ejus impiis vocibus flagitarent. Intentabant autem pro crimine id ipsum, quod se Dei Filium diceret, et quod legem solveret, curando homines in sabbato, quam ille se non solvere sed implere dicebat. Quumque Pontius Pilatus, qui tum legatus in Syria judicabat, perspiceret causam illam ad officium Romani judicis non pertinere, misit eum ad Herodem tetrarcham, permisitque Judaeis ut ipsi legis suae disceptatores essent, qui, accepta sceleris potestate, adfixerunt eum cruci; sed prius flagellis et palmis verberaverunt, spinis coronarunt, faciem conspuerunt, in cibum et potum dederunt ei fel et acetum; et inter haec nulla vox ejus audita est: tunc carnifices sortiti de tunica ejus et pallio, suspenderunt patibulo atque adfixerunt, quum postridie Pascha—id est, festum diem suum—celebraturi essent. Quod facinus prodigia secuta sunt, ut intelligerent nefas quod admiserant.

Eodem namque momento quo spiritum posuit, et terrae motus magnus, et deliquium solis fuit ut in noctem dies verteretur.

CHAPTER 46

Quae omnia Prophetae sic futura esse praedixerant. Esaias ita dicit: *Non sum contumax, neque contradico, dorsum meum posui ad flagella, et maxillas meas ad palmas, faciem autem meam non averti a foeditate sputorum.* Idem de silentio: *Sicut ovis, ad immolandum adductus sum, et sicut agnus coram tondentibus sine voce, sic non aperuit os suum.* Item David, in Psalmo xxxiv, *Congregata sunt in me flagella, et ignoraverunt; dissoluti sunt, nec compuncti sunt, tentaverunt me, et striderunt super me dentibus suis.* Idem de cibo et potu, Psalmo lxviii, *Et dederunt in escam meam fel, et in siti mea potum mihi dederunt acetum.* Item de cruce Christi: *Et foderunt manus meas et pedes meos, dinumeraverunt omnia ossa mea; ipsi autem contemplati sunt, et viderunt me; diviserunt vestimenta mea sibi, et super vestem meam sortem miserunt.* Moyses in Deuteronomio: *Et erit pendens vita tua ante oculos tuos, et timebis die et nocte, et non credes vitae tuae.* Item in Numeris: *Non quasi homo Dominus suspenditur, neque quasi filius hominis minas patitur.* Item Zacharias: *Et intuebuntur in me, quem trafixerunt.* De solis obscuratione Amos ita dicit: *In illo die, dicit Dominus, occidet sol meridie, et obtenebrabitur dies lucis; et convertam dies festos vestros in luctum, et cantica vestra in lamentationem.* Item Jeremias de civitate Hierosolyma, in qua passus est: *Et subivit sol ei, quum adhuc medius dies esset; confusa est et maledicta; reliquos eorum in gladium dabo.* Nec frustra haec dicta sunt: siquidem post breve tempus Imperator Vespasianus Judaeos debellavit, et terras eorum ferro ignique depopulatus est, obsessos fame subegit, Hierosolymam evertit, captivos triumphavit, ceteris, qui reliqui fuerunt, terris suis interdixit, nequando iis ad solum patrium reverti liceret. Quae a Deo, propter illam Christi crucem, facta sunt, ut hoc in Scripturis eorum Salomon ante testatus sit, dicens: *Et erit Israel in perditionem, et in improperium populo, et domus haec erit deserta, et omnis qui transiet per illam admirabitur, et dicet, Propter quam rem Deus fecit terrae huic, huic domui haec mala? Et dicent, quia dereliquerunt Dominum Deum suum, et persecuti sunt Regem suum dilectissimum Deo, et cruciaverunt illum in humilitate magna: propter hoc importavit illis Deus mala haec.* Quid enim non mererentur, qui Dominum, qui ad salutem ipsorum venerat, peremerunt?

CHAPTER 47

Post haec detractum patibulo corpus monumento condiderunt. Verum tertio die ante lucem, terrae motu facto, ac revoluto lapide quo sepulchrum clauserant, resurrexit. In sepulchro autem nihil nisi exuviae corporis sunt repertae. Ipsum vero resurrecturum die tertio jam olim Prophetae fuerant praelocuti. David in Psalmo xv: *Non derelinques animam meam ad inferos, nec dabis sanctum tuum videre corruptionem.* Item Osee: *Hic filius meus sapiens, propter quod nunc non resistet in contribulatione filiorum suorum, et de manu inferorum eruam eum. Ubi est judicium tuum, mors, ubi est aculeus tuus?* Idem rursus: *Vivificabit nos post biduum, die tertio.* Profectus igitur in Galilaeam post resurrectionem, discipulos suos rursus, quos metus in fugam verterat, congregavit; datisque mandatis quae observari vellet, et ordinata Evangelii praedicatione per totum orbem, inspiravit in eos Spiritum Sanctum, ac dedit eis potestatem mirabilia faciendi, ut in salutem hominum tam factis, quam verbis operarentur; ac tum demum quadragesimo die remeavit ad Patrem, sublatus in nubem. Hoc Daniel Propheta jampridem ostenderat, dicens: *Videbam in visu noctis, et ecce in nubibus coeli ut Filius Hominis veniens, et usque ad Antiquum dierum pervenit, et qui assistebant, obtulerunt eum; et datum est ei regnum, et honor, et imperium, et omnes populi, tribus, linguae servient ei, et potestas ejus aeterna, quae nunquam transibit, et regnum ejus non corrumpetur.* Item David in Psalmo cix, *Dixit Dominus domino meo: Sede ad dexteram meam, donec ponam inimicos tuos suppedaneum pedum tuorum.*

CHAPTER 48

Quum igitur ad dexteram Dei sedeat, calcaturus inimicos suos qui eum cruciaverunt, quando ad judicandum orbem venerit, apparet nullam spem reliquam esse Judaeis, nisi conversi ad poenitentiam, et a sanguine, quo se polluerunt, abluti, sperare in eum coeperint, quem negaverunt. Ideo sic dicit Hesdra: *Hoc pascha Salvator noster est in refugium nostrum. Cogitate, et ascendat in cor vestrum, quoniam habemus humiliare eum in signo, et posthaec sperabimus in eum.* Exhaeredatos autem esse Judaeos, quia Christum reprobaverunt, et nos, qui sumus ex gentibus, in eorum locum adoptatos, Scripturis adprobatur. Jeremias ita dicit: *Dereliqui domum meam, dimisi haereditatem meam in manus inimicorum ejus. Facta est haereditas mea mihi sicut leo in sylva; dedit ipsa super me vocem suam, ideo odivi eam.* Item Malachias: *Non est mihi voluntas circa vos, dicit Dominus, et sacrificium acceptum non habebo ex manibus vestris; quia a solis ortu usque ad occasum clarificabitur nomen meum apud gentes.* Esaias quoque sic: *Venio colligere omnes gentes et linguas, et venient, et videbunt claritatem meam.* Idem alio loco ex persona Patris ad Filium: *Ego Dominus Deus vocavi te in justitiam, et tenebo manum tuam, et confirmabo te, et dedi te in testamentum generis mei, in lucem gentium aperire oculos caecorum, producere ex vinculis alligatos, et de domo carceris sedentes in tenebris.*

CHAPTER 49

Si ergo Judaei a Deo rejecti sunt, sicut sacrarum Scripturarum fides indicat, gentes autem, sicut videmus, adscitae, ac de tenebris hujus vitae saecularis, deque vinculis daemonum liberatae, nulla igitur alia spes homini proposita est, nisi veram religionem veramque sapientiam, quae in Christo est, fuerit secutus; quem qui ignorat a veritate ac Deo semper alienus est. Nec sibi de summo Deo, vel Judaei, vel philosophi blandiantur. Qui Filium non agnovit, nec Patrem potuit adnoscere. Haec est sapientia, et hoc mysterium summi Dei. Per illum se Deus et agnosci et coli voluit. Ideo Prophetas ante praemisit, qui de adventu ejus praedicarent, ut, quum facta essent in eo quaecunque praedicata sunt, tunc ab hominibus et Dei Filius et Deus crederetur. Nec tamen sic habendum est, tanquam duo sint Dii. Pater enim ac Filius unum sunt; quum enim Pater Filium diligat, omniaque ei tribuat, et Filius Patri fideliter obsequatur, nec velit quidquam nisi quod Pater, non potest utique necessitudo tanta divelli, ut duo esse dicantur, in quibus et substantia, et voluntas, et fides una est. Ergo et Filius per Patrem, et Pater per Filium. Unus est honos utrique tribuendus tanquam uni Deo, et ita dividendus est per duos cultus, ut divisio ipsa compage inseparabili vinciatur. Neutrum sibi relinquet, qui aut Patrem a Filio, aut Filium a Patre secernit.

CHAPTER 50

Superest respondere etiam iis, qui putant inconveniens fuisse nec habere rationem, ut Deus mortali corpore indueretur, ut hominibus subjectus esset, ut contumelias sustineret, cruciatus etiam mortemque pateretur. Dicam quod sentio, et rem immensam paucis, ut potero, substringam. Qui aliquid docet, debet, ut opinor, facere ipse quae docet, ut cogat homines obtemperare; nam si non fecerit, praeceptis suis fidem derogabit. Exemplis igitur opus est, ut ea quae praecipiuntur habeant firmitatem; et si quis contumax exstiterit ac dixerit non posse fieri, praeceptor illum praesenti opere convincat. Non potest ergo perfecta esse doctrina, quum verbis tantum traditur; sed tum perfecta est, quum factis adimpletur. Christus itaque, quum doctor virtutis ad homines mitteretur, utique et doctrina ejus perfecta esset, et docere et facere debuerat. Sed, si corpus hominis non induisset, non posset facere quae docebat—id est, non irasci, non cupere divitias, non libidine inflammari, dolorem non timere, mortem contemnere. Haec sunt utique virtutes, sed fieri sine carne non possunt. Ergo ideo corporatus est, ut, quum vincenda esse carnis desideria doceret, ipse faceret prior, ne quis excusationem de carnis fragilitate praetenderet.

CHAPTER 51

Dicam nunc de sacramento crucis, ne quis forte dicat, Si suscipienda illi mors fuerat, non utique infamis ac turpis, sed quae haberet aliquid honestatis. Scio equidem multos, dum abhorrent nomen crucis, refugere a veritate, quum in ea et ratio magna sit et potestas. Nam quum ad hoc missus esset, ut humillimis quibusque viam panderet ad salutem, se ipse humilem fecit, ut eos liberaret. Suscepit ergo id genus mortis, quod solet humilibus irrogari, ut omnibus facultas daretur imitandi. Praeterea quum esset resurrecturus, amputari partem corporis ejus fas non erat, nec os infringi, quod accidit iis qui capite plectuntur. Crux ergo potior fuit, quae resurrectioni corpus integris ossibus reservavit. His etiam illud accedit, quod passione ac morte suscepta sublimem fieri oportebat. Adeo illum crux et re et significatione exaltavit, ut omnibus majestas ejus ac virtus cum ipsa passione notuerit. Nam quod extendit in patibulo manus, utique alas suas in Orientem Occidentemque porrexit, sub quas universae nationes ab utraque mundi parte ad requiem convenirent. Quantum autem valeat hoc signum, et quid habeat potestatis, in promptu est, quum omnis daemonum cohors hoc signo expellitur ac fugatur. Et sicut ipse ante passionem daemones verbo et imperio proturbabat, sic nunc nomine ac signo passionis ejus iidem spiritus immundi, quando in corpora hominum inrepserint, exiguntur, quum extorti et excruciati ac se daemonas confitentes verberanti se Deo cedunt. Quid ergo speraverint de suis religionibus cunctaque sua sapientia Graeci, quum videant, Deos suos, quos eosdem daemonas esse non negant, per crucem ab hominibus triumphari?

CHAPTER 52

Una igitur spes hominibus vitae est, unus portus salutis, unum refugium libertatis, si abjectis, quibus tenebantur, erroribus, aperiant oculos mentis suae Deumque cognoscant, in quo solo domicilium veritatis est; terrena et de terra ficta contemnant; philosophiam, quae apud Deum stultitia est, pro nihilo computent; et vera sapientia, id est, religione suscepta, fiant immortalitatis haeredes. At enim repugnant non tam veritati quam propriae saluti; quumque haec audiunt, velut aliquod inexpiabile nefas detestantur. Sed ne audire quidem patiuntur: violari aures suas sacrilegio putant, si audierint; nec jam maledictis abstinent, sed, quantis possunt, verborum contumeliis insectantur; ideoque si potestatem nacti fuerint, velut hostes publicos persequuntur, immo etiam plus quam hostes; quorum, quum bello victi fuerint, aut mors aut servitus poena est, nec ullus post arma deposita cruciatus, quamvis omnia pati meruerint, qui facere voluerunt, et inter mucrones locum pietas habet. Inaudita est crudelitas, quum innocentia nec victorum hostium conditionem meretur. Quae tanta hujus furoris est causa? Scilicet, quia ratione congredi non queunt, violentia premunt; incognita causa tanquam nocentissimos damnant, quia constare de ipsa innocentia noluerunt. Nec satis putant, si celeri ac simplici morte moriantur quos irrationabiliter oderunt, sed eos exquisitis cruciatibus lacerant, ut expleant odium, quod non peccatum aliquod, sed veritas parit; quae idcirco male viventibus odiosa est, quia aegre ferunt

CHAPTER 53

Sed haec facere se dicunt, ut deos suos defendant. 'Primum si dii' sunt et habent aliquid potestatis ac numinis, defensione hominis patrocinioque non indigent, sed seipsos utique defendunt. Aut quomodo ab iis homo sperare auxilium potest, si ne suas quidem injurias possunt vindicare? Stultum igitur et vanum, deorum esse vindices velle, nisi quod ex eo magis apparet diffidentia. Qui enim patrocinium Dei, quem colit, suscipit, illum esse nihili confitetur; si autem ideo colit, quia potentem arbitratur, non debet eum velle defendere, a quo ipse est defendendus. Nos igitur recte. Nam quum isti 'defensores falsorum deorum, adversus verum Deum rebelles, nomen ejus in nobis persequuntur, nec re nec verbo repugnamus, sed mites, et taciti, et patientes perferimus omnia, quaecunque adversus nos potest crudelitas machinari; habemus enim fiduciam in Deo, a quo exspectamus secuturam 'protinus ultionem. Nec est inanis ista fiducia; siquidem eorum omnium, qui hoc facinus ausi sunt, miserabiles exitus partim cognovimus, partim vidimus; nec ullus habuit impune, quod Deum laesit; sed qui sit verus Deus, qui verbo discere noluit, supplicio suo didicit. Vellem scire, quum invitos adigunt ad sacrificium, quid secum habeant rationis, aut cui praestent quod faciunt. Si diis, non est ille cultus, nec acceptabile sacrificium, quod fit ingratis, quod extorquetur per injuriam, quod eruitur per dolorem. Si autem ipsis quos cogunt, non est utique beneficium, quod quis, ne accipiat, etiam mori mavult. Si bonum est, ad quod me vocas, cur malo invitas? cur non verbis, sed verberibus, cur non ratione, sed cruciatibus corporis? Unde apparet malum esse illud, ad quod non illicis volentem, sed trahis recusantem. Quae stultitia est, consulere velle nolenti? An si aliquis prementibus malis ad mortem confugere conatur, num potes, si aut gladium extorseris, aut laqueum ruperis, aut praecipitio retraxeris, aut venenum effuderis, conservatorem te hominis gloriari, quum ille, quem servasse te putas, nec gratias agat, et te male secum arbitratur egisse, quod mortem sibi prohibueris optatam, quod ad finem, quod ad requiem malorum pervenire non siveris? Beneficium enim non ex qualitate rei debet, sed ex animo ejus qui accipit, ponderari. Cur pro beneficio imputes, quod mihi maleficium est? Vis me deos tuos colere, quod ego mihi mortiferum duco. Si bonum est, non invideo. Fruere solus bono tuo. Non est quod velis errori meo succurrere, quem judicio ac voluntate suscepi. Si malum, quid me ad consortium mali rapis? 'Utere sorte tua.' Ego malo in bono mori, quam in malo vivere.

CHAPTER 54

Haec quidem juste dici possunt. Sed quis audiet, quum homines furiosi et impotentes minui dominationem suam putent, si sit aliquid in rebus humanis liberum? Atqui religio sola est, in qua libertas domicilium collocavit; res est enim praeter ceteras voluntaria, nec imponi cuiquam necessitas potest, ut colat quod non vult. Potest aliquis forsitan simulare, non potest velle. Denique quum metu tormentorum aliqui aut cruciatibus victi ad exsecranda sacrificia consenserint, nunquam ultro faciunt quod necessitate fecerunt, sed, data rursus facultate, ac reddita libertate, referunt se ad Deum, eumque precibus et lachrimis placant, agentes non voluntatis, quam non habuerunt, sed necessitatis, quam pertulerunt, poenitentiam; et venia satisfacientibus non negatur. Quid ergo promovet, qui corpus inquinat, quando immutare non potest voluntatem? Atenim homines inanis cerebri, si quem fortem adegerint libare diis suis, incredibili alacritate insolenter exsultant, et, quasi hostem sub jugum miserint, gaudent. Si vero aliquis, nec minis nec tormentis territus, fidem vitae anteferre maluerit, in hunc ingenium suum crudelitas exserit, infanda et intolerabilia molitur; et quia sciunt gloriosam esse pro Deo mortem, et hanc nobis esse victoriam, si superatis tortoribus animam pro fide ac religione ponamus, et ipsi enituntur, ut vincant. Non afficiunt morte, sed excogitant novos inauditosque cruciatus, ut fragilitas viscerum doloribus cedat; et, si non cesserit, differunt, adhibentque vulneribus curam diligentem, ut crudis adhuc cicatricibus repetita tormenta plus doloris immittant. Et dum hanc adversus innocentes carnificinam exercent pios utique se et justos et religiosos putant—talibus enim sacris dii eorum delectantur—illos vero impios et desperatos nuncupant. Quae ista est perversitas, ut qui torquetur innocens, desperatus atque impius nominetur, carnifex autem justus piusque dicatur?

CHAPTER 55

Sed recte ac merito' puniri eos aiunt, qui publicas religiones a majoribus traditas exsecrantur. Quid si majores illi stulti fuerunt in suscipiendis religionibus vanis, sicut jam supra ostendimus, praescribetur nobis quo minus vera et meliora sectemur? Cur nobis auferimus libertatem, sed quasi addicti alienis servimus erroribus? Liceat sapere, liceat inquirere veritatem. Sed tamen, si libet majorum defendere [religiones] cur impune habent Aegyptii, qui pecudes, et omnis generis bestias pro diis colunt? Cur de diis ipsis mimi aguntur, et qui eos facetius deriserit honoratur? Cur audiuntur philosophi, qui aut nullos Deos esse aiunt, aut si sunt, nihil curare, nec humana respicere, aut nullam esse omnino, quae regat mundum providentiam, disserunt; sed soli ex omnibus impii judicantur, qui Deum, qui veritatem sequuntur? Quae quum sit eadem justitia, eadem sapientia, hanc isti vel impietatis vel stultitiae crimine infamant, nec perspiciunt quid sit quod eos fallat, quum et malo vocabulum boni et bono mali nomen imponunt. Plurimi quidem philosophorum, sed maxime Plato et Aristoteles, de justitia multa dixerunt, asserentes et extollentes eam summa laude virtutem, quod suum cuique tribuat, quod aequitatem in omnibus servet, et quum ceterae virtutes quasi tacitae sint et intus inclusae, solam esse justitiam, quae nec sibi tantum conciliata sit, nec occulta, sed foras tota promineat, et ad bene faciendum prona sit ut quamplurimis prosit. Quasi vero in judicibus solis, atque in potestate aliqua constitutis justitia esse debeat, et non in omnibus! Atquin nullus est hominum, ne infimorum quidem ac mendicorum, in quem justitia cadere non possit. Sed quia ignorabant quid esset, unde profluerit, quid operis haberet, summam illam virtutem, id est, commune omnium bonum, paucis tribuerunt, eamque nullas utilitates proprias aucupari, sed alienis tantum commodis studere dixerunt. Nec immerito exstitit Carneades, homo summo ingenio et acumine, qui refelleret istorum orationem, et justitiam, quae fundamentum stabile non habebat, everteret, non quia vituperandam esse justitiam sentiebat, sed ut illos defensores ejus ostenderet nihil certi, nihil firmi, de justitia disputare.

CHAPTER 56

Nam si justitia est veri Dei cultus (quid enim tam justum ad aequitatem, tam pium ad honorem, tam necessarium ad salutem, quam Deum agnoscere ut parentem, venerari ut Dominum, ejusque legi et praeceptis obtemperare?), nescierunt ergo justitiam philosophi, quia nec ipsum Deum agnoverunt, nec cultum ejus legemque tenuerunt, et ideo refelli potuerunt a Carneade, cujus haec fuit disputatio: 'nullum esse jus naturale; itaque omnes animantes, ipsa ducente natura, commoda sua defendere; et ideo justitiam, si alienis utilitatibus consulit, suas negligit, stultitiam esse dicendam. Quod si omnes populi, penes quos sit imperium, ipsique Romani, qui orbem totum possederint, justitiam sequi velint, ac suum cuique restituere, quod vi et armis occupaverunt, ad casas et egestatem revertentur. Quod si fecerint, justos quidem, sed tamen stultos judicari necesse est, qui, ut aliis prosint, sibi nocere contendant. Deinde, si reperiat aliquis hominem, qui aut aurum pro aurichalco, aut argentum pro plumbo vendat per errorem, atque id emere necessitas cogat, utrum dissimulabit et emet parvo, an potius indicabit? Si indicabit, justus utique dicetur, quia non fefellit; sed idem stultus, qui alteri fecerit lucrum, sibi damnum. Sed facile de damno est. Quid, si vita ejus in periculum veniet, ut eum necesse sit aut occidere aut mori, quid faciet? Potest hoc evenire, ut, naufragio facto, inveniat aliquem imbecillem tabulae inhaerentem, aut victo exercitu fugiens, reperiat aliquem vulneratum equo insidentem, utrumne aut illum tabula, aut hunc equo deturbabit, ut ipse possit evadere? Si volet justus esse, non faciet; sed idem stultus judicabitur, qui, dum alterius vitae parcit, suam prodit. Si faciet, sapiens quidem videbitur, quia sibi consulet; sed idem malus, quia nocebit.'

CHAPTER 57

Acuta ista sane; sed respondere ad ea facillime possumus. Immutatio enim nominum facit, ut sic esse videatur. Nam et justitia imaginem habet stultitiae, non tamen est stultitia; et malitia imaginem sapientiae, non tamen sapientia est. Sed sicut malitia ista in conservandis utilitatibus suis intelligens et arguta, non sapientia, sed calliditas et astutia est, ita et justitia non debet stultitia, sed innocentia nominari; quia necesse est et justum esse sapientem, et eum, qui sit stultus, injustum. Nam neque ratio neque natura ipsa permittit, ut is qui justus est, sapiens non sit; quoniam justus nihil utique facit nisi quod rectum et bonum est, pravum et malum semper fugit. Quis autem discernere bonum et malum, pravum et rectum, potest, nisi qui sapiens fuerit? Stultus autem male facit, quia bonum et malum quid sit ignorat: ideo peccat, quia non potest prava et recta discernere. Non potest ergo neque stulto justitia, neque injusto sapientia convenire. Stultus igitur non est, qui nec tabula naufragum, nec' equo saucium dejecerit, quia se abstinuit a nocendo, quod est peccatum; peccatum autem vitare sapientis est. Sed ut stultus prima facie videatur, illa res efficit, quod exstingui animam cum corpore aestimant: idcirco omne commodum ad hanc vitam referunt. Si enim post mortem nihil est, utique stulte facit, qui alterius animae parcit cum dispendio suae, aut qui alterius lucro magis quam suo consulit. Si mors animam delet, danda est opera, quo diutius commodiusque vivamus; si autem vita post mortem superest aeterna et beata, hanc utique corporalem cum omnibus terrae bonis justus et sapiens contemnet, quia sciet quale a Deo sit praemium recepturus. Teneamus igitur innocentiam, teneamus justitiam, subeamus imaginem stultitiae, ut veram sapientiam tenere possimus. Et si hominibus ineptum videtur ac stultum, torqueri et mori malle, quam libare diis et abire sine noxa, nos tamen omni virtute omnique patientia fidem Deo exhibere nitamur. Non mors terreat, non dolor frangat, quo minus vigor animi, et constantia inconcussa servetur. Stultos vocent, dummodo ipsi stultissimi sint, et caeci, et hebetes, et pecudibus aequales, qui non intelligunt esse mortiferum, relicto Deo vivo, prosternere se atque adorare terrena; qui nesciunt, et illos aeternam poenam manere, qui figmenta insensibilia fuerint venerati; et eos, qui nec tormenta nec mortem pro cultu et honore veri Dei non recusaverint, vitam perpetuam consecuturos. Haec est fides summa, haec est vera sapientia, haec perfecta justitia. Nihil ad nos attinet stulti quid homunculi sentiant. Nos judicium Dei exspectare debemus, ut eos postmodum, qui de nobis judicant, judicemus.

CHAPTER 58

Dixi de justitia, quid esset. Sequitur ut ostendam quod sit verum sacrificium Dei, qui sit justisimus ritus colendi; ne quis arbitretur, aut victimas, aut odores, aut dona pretiosa desiderari a Deo. A quo si fames, si sitis, si algor, si rerum omnium terrenarum cupiditas abest, non ergo utitur his omnibus quae templis diisque fictilibus inferuntur; sed sicut corporalibus corporalia, sic utique incorporali incorporale sacrificium necessarium est. Illis autem, quae in usum tribuit homini Deus, ipse non indiget, quum omnis terra ipsius sit sub potestate; non indiget templo, cujus domicilium mundus est; non indiget simulacro, qui est et oculis et mente incomprehensibilis; non indiget terrenis luminibus, qui solem cum ceteris astris in usum hominis potuit accendere. Quid igitur ab homine desiderat Deus, nisi cultum mentis qui est purus et sanctus? Nam illa, quae aut digitis fiunt, aut extra hominem sunt, inepta, fragilia, ingrata sunt. Hoc est sacrificium verum, non quod ex arca, sed quod ex corde profertur; non quod manu, sed quod mente libatur. Haec acceptabilis victima est, quam de seipso animus immolat. Nam quid hostiae, quid tura, quid vestes, quid argentum, quid aurum, quid pretiosi lapides conferunt, si colentis pura mens non est? Sola ergo justitia est, quam Deus expetit. In hac sacrificium, in hac Dei cultus est, de quo nunc mihi disserendum est, docendumque in quibus operibus justitiam necesse sit contineri.

CHAPTER 59

Duas esse humanae vitae vias nec philosophis ignotum fuit, nec poetis; sed eas utrique diverso modo induxerunt; philosophi alteram industriae, alteram inertiae esse voluerunt. Sed hoc minus recte, quod eas ad sola vitae hujus commoda retulerunt. Melius poetae, qui alteram justorum, alteram impiorum esse dixerunt. Sed in eo peccant, quod eas non in hac vita, sed apud inferos esse aiunt. Nos utique rectius, qui alteram vitae, alteram mortis, et hic tamen esse has vias, dicimus. Sed illa dexterior, qua justi gradiuntur, non in Elysium fert, sed in coelum; immortales enim fiunt. Sinisterior ad Tartarum; aeternis enim cruciatibus addicuntur injusti. Tenenda est igitur nobis justitiae via, quae ducit ad vitam. Primum autem justitiae officium est, Deum agnoscere ut praesentem, eumque metuere ut dominum, diligere ut patrem. Idem enim qui nos genuit, qui vitali spiritu animavit, qui alit, qui salvos facit, habet in nos, non modo ut pater, verum etiam ut dominus, licentiam verberandi, et vitae ac necis potestatem; unde illi ab homine duplex honos, id est, amor cum timore, debetur. Secundum justitiae officium est, hominem agnoscere velut fratrem. Si enim nos idem Deus fecit, et universos ad justitiam vitamque aeternam pari conditione generavit, fraterna utique necessitudine cohaeremus; quam qui non agnoscit, injustus est. Sed origo hujus mali, quo societas inter se hominum, quo necessitudinis vinculum dissolutum est, ab ignoratione veri Dei nascitur. Qui enim fontem illum benignitatis ignorat, bonus esse nullo pacto potest. Inde est, quod ex eo tempore quo dii multi consecrari ab hominibus colique coeperunt, fugata—sicut poetae ferunt—justitia, direptum est omne foedus, direpta societas generis humani. Tum sibi quisque consulens jus in viribus computare, nocere invicem, fraudibus aggredi, dolis circumscribere, commoda sua aliorum incommodis adaugere, non cognatis, non liberis, non parentibus parcere, ad necem hominum pocula temperare, obsidere cum ferro vias, maria infestare, libidini autem, quo furor duxerit, frena laxare, nihil denique sancti habere, quod non cupiditas infanda violaret. Quum haec fierent, tum leges sibi homines condiderunt pro utilitate communi, ut se invicem tutos ab injuriis facerent. Sed metus legum non scelera comprimebat, sed licentiam submovebat. Poterant enim leges delicta punire, conscientiam punire non poterant. Itaque quae ante palam fiebant, clam fieri coeperunt; circumscribi etiam jura, siquidem ipsi praesides legum, praemiis muneribusque corrupti, vel in remissionem malorum, vel perniciem justorum sententias venditabant. His accedebant dissensiones, et bella, et mutuae depraedationes, et oppressis legibus saeviendi potestas licenter assumpta.

CHAPTER 60

In hoc statu quum essent humanae res, misertus est nostri Deus, revelavit se nobis et ostendit, ut in ipso religionem, fidem, castitatem, misericordiam disceremus; ut errore vitae prioris abjecto, simul cum ipso Deo nosmetipsos, quos impietas dissociaverat, nosceremus, legemque divinam, quae humana cum coelestibus copulat, tradente ipso Domino, sumeremus: qua lege universi, quibus irretiti fuimus, errores cum vanis et impiis superstitionibus tollerentur. Quid igitur homini debeamus, eadem illa lex praescribit quae docet, quicquid homini praestiteris, Deo praestari. Sed radix justitiae, et omne fundamentum aequitatis est illud, ut non facias quod pati nolis, sed alterius animum de tuo metiaris. Si acerbum est injuriam ferre, et qui eam fecerit videtur injustus, transfer in alterius personam quod de te sentis, et in tuam quod de altero judicas, et intelliges tam te injuste facere, si alteri noceas, quam alterum, si tibi. Haec si mente volvamus, innocentiam tenebimus, in qua justitia velut primo gradu insistit. Primum est enim non nocere, proximum prodesse. Et sicut in rudibus agris, priusquam serere incipias, evulsis sentibus, et omnibus stirpium radicibus amputatis, arva purganda sunt; sic de nostris animis prius vitia detrahenda, et tunc demum virtutes inserendae, de quibus seminatae per verbum Dei fruges immortalitatis oriantur.

CHAPTER 61

Tres affectus, vel, ut ita dicam, tres Furiae sunt, quae in animis hominum tantas perturbationes cient, et interdum cogunt ita delinquere, ut nec famae nec periculi sui respectum habere permittant: ira quae vindictam cupit, avaritia quae desiderat opes, libido quae appetit voluptates. His vitiis ante omnia resistendum est, hae stirpes eruendae, ut virtutes inseri possint. Hos affectus Stoici amputandos, Peripatetici temperandos putant. Neutri eorum recte; quia neque in totum detrahi possunt, siquidem natura insiti certam habent magnamque rationem; neque diminui, quoniam si mala sunt, carendum est etiam temperatis et mediocribus; si bona, integris abutendum est. Nos vero neque detrahendos neque minuendos esse dicimus. Non enim per se mala sunt, quae Deus homini rationabiliter insevit; sed quum sint utique natura bona, quoniam ad tuendam vitam sunt attributa, male utendo fiunt mala; et sicut fortitudo, si pro patria dimices, bonum est, si contra patriam, malum, sic et affectus, si ad usus bonos habeas, virtutes erunt, si ad malos, vitia dicentur. Ira igitur ad coercitionem peccatorum, id est, ad regendam subjectorum disciplinam, data est, ut metus licentiam comprimat et compescat audaciam. Sed qui terminos ejus ignorant, irascuntur paribus aut etiam potioribus. Inde ad immania facinora prosilitur, inde ad caedes, inde ad bella consurgitur. Cupiditas quoque ad desideranda et conquirenda vitae necessaria tributa est.

Sed qui nesciunt fines ejus, insatiabiliter opes congerere nituntur. Hinc venena, hinc circumscriptiones, hinc falsa testamenta, hinc omnia fraudum genera erupere. Libidinis autem affectus ad procreandos liberos insitus et innatus est; sed qui limites ejus in animo non tenent, utuntur eo ad solam voluptatem. Inde illiciti amores, inde adulteria et stupra, inde omnes corruptelae oriuntur. Redigendi sunt ergo isti affectus intra fines suos, et in viam rectam dirigendi, in qua etiamsi sint vehementes, culpam tamen habere non possunt.

CHAPTER 62

Cohibenda est ira quum patimur injuriam, ut et malum comprimatur, quod ex certamine impendet, et ut duas maximas virtutes, innocentiam patientiamque, teneamus. Avaritia frangatur, quum habemus quod satis est. Quis enim furor est, in his coacervandis laborare, quae aut latrocinio, aut proscriptione, aut morte ad alios necesse sit pervenire? Libido extra legitimum torum non evagetur, sed creandis liberis serviat. Appetentia enim nimia voluptatis et periculum parit et infamiam generat, et (quod est maxime cavendum) mortem adquirit aeternam. Nihil est tam invisum Deo quam mens incesta et animus impurus. Nec hac sola voluptate abstinendum sibi quis putet, quae capitur ex feminei corporis copulatione, sed et ceteris voluptatibus sensuum reliquorum; quia et ipsae sunt vitiosae, et ejusdem virtutis est eas contemnere. Oculorum voluptas percipitur ex rerum pulchritudine, aurium de vocibus canoris et suavioribus, narium de odore jucundo, saporis de cibis dulcibus, quibus omnibus virtus repugnare fortiter debet, ne his illecebris irretitus animus, a coelestibus ad terrena, ab aeternis ad temporalia, a vita immortali ad poenam perpetuam deprimatur. In saporis et odoris voluptatibus hoc periculum est, quod trahere ad luxuriem possunt. Qui enim fuerit his deditus, aut non habebit ullam rem familiarem, aut, si habuerit, absumet, et aget postmodum vitam detestabilem. Qui autem rapitur auditu, (ut taceam de cantibus, qui sensus intimos ita saepe deliniunt, ut etiam statum mentis furore perturbent,) compositis certe orationibus, numerosisque carminibus, aut argutis disputationibus, ad impios cultus facile traducitur. Inde est quod scriptis coelestibus, quia videntur incompta, non facile credunt, qui aut ipsi sunt diserti, aut diserta legere malunt. Non quaerunt vera, sed dulcia: immo illis haec videntur esse verissima quae auribus blandiuntur. Ita respuunt veritatem, dum sermonis suavitate capiuntur. Voluptas vero, quae spectat ad visum, multiformis est. Nam quae percipitur ex rerum pretiosarum pulchritudine, avaritiam concitat, quae aliena esse debet a sapiente atque justo; quae autem capitur de specie mulierum, in alteram rapit voluptatem, de qua jam superius locuti sumus.

CHAPTER 63

Superest de spectaculis dicere, quae quoniam potentiora sunt ad corrumpendos animos, vitanda sapientibus et cavenda sunt; tum quod ad celebrandos deorum honores inventa memorantur. Nam munerum editiones Saturni festa sunt: Scena Liberi Patris est: Ludi vero Circenses Neptuno dicati putantur: ut jam qui spectaculis interest, relicto Dei cultu, ad profanos ritus transiisse videatur. Sed ego de re malo dicere, quam de origine. Quid tam horribile, tam tetrum, quam hominis trucidatio? Ideo severissimis legibus vita nostra munitur, ideo bella exsecrabilia sunt. Invenit tamen consuetudo, quatenus homicidium sine bello ac sine legibus faciat, et hoc sibi voluptas quod scelus vindicavit. Quod si interesse homicidio sceleris conscientia est, et eidem facinori spectator obstrictus est cui et admissor, ergo et in his gladiatorum caedibus non minus cruore perfunditur qui spectat, quam ille qui facit; nec potest esse immunis a sanguine qui voluit effundi, aut videri non interfecisse, qui interfectori et favit et praemium postulavit. Quid scena? num sanctior? in qua comoedia de stupris et amoribus, tragoedia de incestis et parricidiis fabulatur. Histrionum etiam impudici gestus, quibus infames feminas imitantur, libidines, quas saltando exprimunt, docent. Nec minus mimus corruptelarum disciplina est, in quo fiunt per imaginem quae pudenda sunt, ut fiant sine pudore quae vera sunt. Spectant haec adolescentes, quorum lubrica aetas, quae frenari ac regi debet, ad vitia et peccata his imaginibus eruditur. Circus vero innocentior existimatur; sed major hic furor est, siquidem mentes spectantium tanta efferuntur insania, ut non modo in convitia, sed etiam in rixas nec non et proelia et contentiones saepe consurgant. Fugienda igitur omnia spectacula, ut tranquillum mentis statum tenere possimus. Renuntiandum noxiis voluptatibus, ne, deleniti suavitate pestifera, in mortis [laqueos et] plagas incidamus.

CHAPTER 64

Placeat sola virtus, cujus merces immortalitas est quum vicerit voluptatem. Superatis autem affectibus et perdomitis voluptatibus, facilis in comprimendis ceteris labor est ei, qui sit Dei veritatisque sectator. Non maledicet unquam, qui speraverit a Deo benedictionem: non pejerabit, ne Deum ludibrio habeat; sed ne jurabit quidem, ne quando vel necessitate vel consuetudine in perjurium cadat: nihil subdole, nihil dissimulanter loquetur; neque abnegabit quod spoponderit, neque promittet quod facere non possit: non invidebit cuiquam, qui se suoque contentus sit; nec detrahet aut male alteri volet, in quem forsitan beneficia Dei proniora sunt: non furabitur, nec omnino quicquam concupiscet alienum; non dabit in usura pecuniam, (hoc est enim de alienis malis lucra captare,) nec tamen negabit, si qui sit quem necessitas coget mutuari. Non sit asper in filium neque in servum: meminerit quod et ipse Patrem habeat et Dominum. Ita cum his agat, quemadmodum secum agi vellet. Munera superabundantia non accipiat a tenuioribus; nec enim justum est augeri patrimonia locupletum per damna miserorum. Vetus praeceptum est, non occidere; quod non sic accipi debet, tanquam jubeamur ab homicidio tantum, quod etiam legibus publicis vindicatur, manus abstinere; sed hac jussione interposita, nec verbo licebit periculum mortis inferre, nec infantem necare aut exponere, nec seipsum voluntaria morte damnare. Item non adulterare; sed hoc praecepto non solum corrumpere alienum matrimonium prohibemur, quod etiam communi gentium jure damnatur, verum etiam prostitutis corporibus abstinere. Supra leges enim Dei lex est: ea quoque, quae pro licitis habentur, vetat, ut justitiam consummet. Ejusdem legis est, falsum testimonium non dicere, quod et ipsum latius patet. Nam si falsum testimonium mendacio nocet ei contra quem dicitur, et fallit eum apud quem dicitur, nunquam igitur mentiendum est, quia mendacium semper aut fallit aut nocet. Non est ergo vir justus, qui etiam sine noxa in otioso sermone mentitur. Huic vero nec adulari licet, perniciosa est enim ac deceptrix adulatio; sed ubique custodiet veritatem, quae licet sit ad praesens insuavis, tamen, quum fructus ejus atque utilitas apparuerit, non odium pariet, ut ait Poeta, sed gratiam.

CHAPTER 65

Dixi de iis quae vetantur: dicam nunc breviter quae jubentur. Innocentiae proxima est misericordia. Illa enim malum non facit, haec bonum operatur: illa inchoat justitiam, haec complet. Nam quum imbecillior sit hominum natura quam ceterarum animantium, quas Deus et instructas ad inferendam et munitas ad vim repellendam figuravit, affectum nobis misericordiae dedit, ut omne praesidium vitae nostrae in mutuis auxiliis poneremus. Si enim ficti ab uno Deo, et orti ab uno homine, consanguinitatis jure sociamur, omnem igitur hominem diligere debemus. Itaque non tantum inferre injuriam non oportet, sed ne illatam quidem vindicare, ut sit in nobis perfecta innocentia. Et ideo jubet nos Deus etiam pro inimicis precem facere semper. Ergo animal commune atque consors esse debemus, ut nos invicem praestandis et accipiendis auxiliis muniamus. Multis enim casibus et incommodis fragilitas nostra subjecta est. Spera et tibi accidere posse, quod alteri videas accidisse. Ita demum excitaberis ad opem ferendam, si sumpseris ejus animum, qui opem tuam in malis constitutus implorat. Si quis victu indiget, impertiamus; si quis nudus occurrit, vestiamus; si quis a potentiore injuriam sustinet, eruamus. Pateat domicilium nostrum peregrinis vel indigentibus tecto. Pupillis defensio, viduis tutela nostra non desit. Redimere ab hoste captivos magnum misericordiae opus est, aegros item et pauperes visere atque refovere. Inopes aut advenae si obierint, non patiamur insepultos jacere. Haec sunt opera, haec officia misericordiae, quae si quis obierit, verum et acceptum sacrificium Deo immolabit. Haec litabilior victima est apud Deum, qui non pecudis sanguine, sed hominis pietate placatur; quem Deus, quia justus est, suamet ipsum lege, sua et conditione prosequitur: miseretur ejus, quem viderit misericordem: inexorabilis est ei, quem precantibus cernit immitem. Ergo, ut haec omnia, quae Deo placent, facere possimus, contemnenda est pecunia, et ad coelestes transferenda thesauros, *ubi nec fur effodiat, nec rubigo consumat*, nec tyrannus eripiat, sed nobis ad aeternam opulentiam, Deo custode, servetur.

CHAPTER 66

Fides quoque magna justitiae pars est, quae maxime a nobis, qui nomen fidei gerimus, conservanda est, praecipue in religione, quia Deus prior est et potior quam homo. Et si est gloriosum pro amicis, pro parentibus, pro liberis, id est, pro homine suscipere mortem, et qui hoc fecerit, diuturnam memoriam laudemque consequitur, quanto magis pro Deo, qui potest aeternam vitam pro temporali morte praestare? Itaque quum inciderit ejusmodi necessitas, ut desciscere a Deo atque ad ritus gentium transire cogamur, nullus nos metus, nullus terror inflectat, quo minus traditam nobis fidem custodiamus. Deus sit ante oculos, sit in corde, cujus interno auxilio dolorem viscerum, et adhibita corpori tormenta superemus. Nihil tunc aliud quam vitae immortalis praemia cogitemus. Ita facile, etsi dissipandi aut urendi, artus fuerint, tolerabimus universa quae in nos tyrannicae crudelitatis amentia molietur. Postremo ipsam mortem non inviti aut timidi, sed libentes et interriti, subire nitamur, ut qui sciamus quali apud Deum gloria simus fruituri; triumphato saeculo ad promissa venientes, quibus bonis, quanta beatitudine brevia haec poenarum mala et hujus vitae damna pensemus! Quod si facultas hujus gloriae deerit, habebit fides etiam in pace mercedem. Teneatur ergo in omnibus vitae officiis: teneatur in matrimonio; non enim satis est, si aut alieno toro aut lupanari abstineas. Qui habet conjugem, nihil quaerat extrinsecus, sed contentus ea sola, casti et inviolati cubilis sacramenta custodiat. Adulter est enim Deo et incestus, qui abjecto jugo, vel in liberam, vel in servam peregrina voluptate luxuriat. Sed sicut femina castitatis vinculis obligata est, ne aliud concupiscat, ita vir eadem lege teneatur, quoniam Deus virum et uxorem unius corporis compage solidavit. Ideo praecepit, non dimitti uxorem, nisi crimine adulterii revictam: ut nunquam conjugalis foederis vinculum, nisi quod perfidia ruperit, resolvatur. Illud quoque ad consummandam pudicitiam jungitur, ut non modo peccatum absit, verum etiam cogitatio; pollui enim mentem quamvis inani cupiditate; itaque justum hominem, quod sit secus, nec facere oportere, nec velle. Purganda est igitur conscientia, quam Deus pervidet, qui falli non potest. Emaculetur omni labe pectus ut templum Dei esse possit, quod non auri nec eboris nitor sed fidei et castitatis fulgor illustret.

CHAPTER 67

Sed enim haec omnia difficilia sunt homini, nec patitur conditio fragilitatis naturae esse quemquam sine macula. Ultimum ergo remedium illud est, ut confugiamus ad poenitentiam, quae non minimum locum inter virtutes habet, quia sui correctio est; ut, quum forte aut re aut verbo lapsi fuerimus, statim resipiscamus, ac nos deliquisse fateamur, oremusque a Deo veniam, quam pro sua misericordia non negabit, nisi perseverantibus in errore. Magnum est poenitentiae auxilium, magnum solatium. Illa est vulnerum peccatorumque sanatio: illa spes, illa portus salutis; quam qui tollit, viam vitae sibi amputat: quia nemo esse tam justus potest ut nunquam sit ei poenitentia necessaria. Nos vero, etiamsi nullum sit peccatum, confiteri tamen debemus Deo et pro delictis nostris identidem deprecari, gratias agere etiam in malis. Hoc semper obsequium Domino deferamus. Humilitas enim cara et amabilis Deo est, qui quum magis suscipiat peccatorem confitentem quam justum superbum, quanto magis justum suscipiet confitentem, eumque in regnis coelestibus faciet pro humilitate sublimem! Haec sunt quae debet cultor Dei exhibere, hae sunt victimae, hoc sacrificium placabile, hic verus est cultus, quum homo mentis suae pignora in aram Dei confert. Summa illa majestas hoc cultore laetatur, hunc ut filium suscipit, eique idoneum praemium immortalitatis impertit; de qua nunc mihi disserendum est, et arguenda persuasio eorum, qui exstingui animas cum corporibus arbitrantur. Qui quia nec Deum sciebant, nec arcanum mundi perspicere poterant, ne hominis quidem animaeque rationem comprehenderunt. Quomodo enim possent sequentia pervidere, qui summam non tenebant? Negantes igitur esse ullam providentiam, utique Deum, qui fons et caput rerum est, negaverunt. Sequebatur ut ea quae sunt, aut semper fuisse dicerent, aut sua sponte esse nata, aut minutorum seminum conglobatione concreta. Semper fuisse non potest, quod et est et visui subjacet; ipsum enim esse sine aliquo initio non potest. Sua sponte autem nihil nasci potest, quia nulla est sine generante natura. Semina vero principalia quomodo esse potuerunt, quum et semina ex rebus oriantur, et vicissim res ex seminibus? Nullum igitur semen est quod originem non habeat. Sic factum est, ut, quum putarent mundum nulla providentia generatum, ne hominem quidem putarint aliqua ratione generari. Quod si nulla esset in fingendo homine ratio versata, immortalem igitur animam esse non posse. Alii vero ex adverso et Deum esse unum, et ab eo mundum factum, et hominum causa factum, et animas esse immortales existimaverunt. Sed quum vera sentirent, hujus tamen divini operis atque consilii nec causas, nec rationes, nec exitus perspexerunt, ut omne veritatis arcanum consummarent, atque aliquo veluti fine concluderent. Sed quod illi facere non potuerunt, quia veritatem perpetuo non tenebant, nobis faciendum est qui eam cognovimus Deo adnuntiante.

CHAPTER 68

Consideremus igitur quae ratio fuerit hujus tanti tamque immensi operis fabricandi. Fecit Deus mundum, sicut Plato existimavit, sed cur fecerit, non ostendit. 'Quia bonus,' inquit, 'et invidens nulli, fecit quae bona sunt.' Atqui videmus in rerum natura et bona esse et mala. Potest ergo exsistere perversus aliquis, qualis fuerit ἄθεος ille Theodorus, et Platoni respondere: 'Immo, quia malus est, fecit quae mala sunt.' Quomodo illum redarguet? Si quae bona sunt Deus facit, unde igitur tanta mala eruperunt, quae plerumque etiam praevalent bonis? 'In materia', inquit, 'continebantur.' Si mala, ergo et bona; ut aut nihil fecerit Deus, aut si bona tantum fecit, aeterniora sint mala, quae facta non sunt, quam bona quae habuerunt exordium. Finem igitur habebunt quae aliquando coeperunt, et permanebunt quae semper fuerunt. Mala ergo potiora sunt. Si autem potiora esse non possunt, ne aeterniora quidem possunt. Ergo aut utraque semper fuerunt, et Deus otiosus, aut utraque ex uno fonte fluxerunt. Est enim convenientius, ut Deus omnia fecerit potius quam nihil. Ergo secundum sententiam Platonis idem Deus et bonus est, quia bona fecit, et malus, quia mala. Quod si fieri non potest, apparet non ideo factum esse a Deo mundum, quia bonum est mundus; omnia enim complexus est bona et mala, nec fit propter se quicquam, sed propter aliud. Domus etiam aedificatur non ad hoc solum, ut sit domus, sed ut suscipiat et tueatur habitantem. Item navis fabricatur, non ut navis videatur tantum, sed ut in ea possint homines navigare. Vasa item fiunt, non ut vasa sint solum, set ut capiant quae sunt usui necessaria. Sic et mundum Deus ad usum aliquem fecerit necesse est. Stoici aiunt hominum causa factum, et recte; homines enim fruuntur his omnibus bonis quae mundus in se continet. Sed ipsi homines cur facti sint, aut quid in illis utilitatis habeat fabricatrix illa rerum providentia, non explicant. Immortales esse animas idem Plato affirmat; sed cur aut quomodo aut quando aut per quem immortalitatem assequantur, aut quod sit omnino tantum illud mysterium, cur ii qui sunt immortales futuri, prius mortales nascantur, deinde, decurso temporalis vitae spatio, atque abjectis fragilium corporum exuviis, ad aeternam illam beatitudinem transferantur, non comprehendit. Denique nec judicium Dei, nec discrimen justi et injusti explicavit; sed animas, quae se sceleribus immerserint, hactenus condemnari putavit, ut in pecudibus renascantur, et ita peccatorum suorum luere poenas, donec rursus ad figuras hominum revertantur, et hoc fieri semper, nec esse finem transmeandi. Ludum mihi nescio quem inducit, somnio similem, cui nec ratio ulla, nec Dei gubernatio, nec consilium aliquod inesse videatur.

CHAPTER 69

Dicam nunc quae sit illa summa, quam ne ii quidem qui vera dixerunt, collatis in unum causis atque rationibus, connectere potuerunt. Factus a Deo mundus ut homines nascerentur; nascuntur autem homines ut Deum patrem agnoscant in quo est sapientia, agnoscunt ut colant in quo est justitia, colunt ut mercedem immortalitatis accipiant, accipiunt immortalitatem ut in aeternum Deo serviant. Videsne quemadmodum sibi connexa sint et prima cum mediis et media cum extremis? Inspiciamus singula, et videamus utrumne illis ratio subsistat. Fecit Deus mundum propter hominem. Hoc qui non pervidet, non multum distat a pecude. Quis coelum suspicit nisi homo? quis solem? quis astra? Quis omnia Dei opera miratur, nisi homo? Quis colit terram? quis ex ea fructum capit? Quis navigat mare? Quis pisces, quis volatilia, quis quadrupedes, habet in potestate nisi homo? Cuncta igitur propter hominem Deus fecit, quia usui hominis cuncta cessere. Viderunt hoc philosophi, sed illud quod sequitur non viderunt, quod ipsum hominem propter se fecerit. Erat enim consequens, et pium, et necessarium, ut, quum hominis causa tanta opera molitus sit, quum tantum illi honoris, tantum dederit potestatis, ut dominetur mundo, homo agnosceret Deum, tantorum beneficiorum auctorem, qui et ipsum fecit mundum propter ipsum, eique cultum et honorem debitum redderet. Hic Plato aberravit, hic perdidit quam primum arripuerat veritatem, quum de cultu ejus Dei quem conditorem rerum ac parentem fatebatur obticuit, nec intellexit hominem Deo pietatis vinculis esse religatum (unde ipsa religio nominatur), et hoc esse solum propter quod animae immortales fiant. Sensit tamen aeternas esse; sed non per gradus ad eam sententiam descendit, amputatis enim mediis incidit potius in veritatem, quasi per abruptum aliquod praecipitium, nec ulterius progressus est, quoniam casu non ratione verum invenerat. Colendus est igitur Deus, ut per religionem, quae eadem justitia est, accipiat homo a Deo immortalitatem; nec est ullum aliud praemium piae mentis, quae, si est invisibilis, non potest ab invisibili Deo nisi invisibili mercede donari.

CHAPTER 70

Plurimis vero argumentis colligi potest aeternas esse animas. Plato ait, quod·per seipsum semper movetur, neque principium motus habet, etiam finem non habere; animum autem hominis per se semper moveri, qui, quia sit ad cogitandum mobilis, ad inveniendum sollers, ad percipiendum facilis, ad discendum capax, et quia praeterita teneat, praesentia comprehendat, futura prospiciat, multarumque rerum et artium scientiam complectatur, immortalem esse, siquidem nihil habeat in se terreni ponderis labe concretum. Praeterea ex virtute ac voluptate intelligitur aeternitas animae. Voluptas omnibus est communis animalibus, virtus solius est hominis; illa vitiosa est, haec honesta; illa secundum naturam, haec adversa naturae, nisi anima immortalis est. Virtus enim pro fide, pro justitia, nec egestatem timet, nec exsilium metuit, nec carcerem perhorrescit, nec dolorem reformidat, nec mortem recusat; quae quia naturae contraria sunt, aut stultitia est virtus, si et commoda impedit et vitae nocet; aut si stultitia non est, ergo anima immortalis est, et ideo praesentia bona contemnit, quia sunt alia potiora, quae post dissolutionem corporis sui assequatur. Illud etiam maximum argumentum immortalitatis, quod Deum solus homo agnoscit. In mutis nulla suspicio religionis est, quia terrena sunt in terramque prostrata. Homo ideo rectus aspicit coelum, ut Deum quaerat. Non potest igitur non esse immortalis, qui immortalem desiderat. Non potest esse solubilis, qui cum Deo et vultu et mente communis est. Denique coelesti elemento, quod est ignis, homo solus utitur. Si enim lux per ignem, vita per lucem, apparet eum, qui usum ignis habeat, non esse mortalem; quoniam id illi proximum, id familiare est, sine quo non potest nec lux nec vita constare. Sed quid argumentis colligimus aeternas esse animas, quum habeamus testimonia divina? Id enim sacrae literae ac voces Prophetarum docent. Quod si cui parum videtur, legat carmina Sibyllarum, Apollinis quoque Milesii responsa consideret, ut intelligat delirasse Democritum, et Epicurum, et Dicaearchum, qui soli omnium mortalium quod est evidens negaverunt. Confirmata immortalitate, superest docere, a quo, et quibus, et quomodo, et quando tribuatur? Quum certa et constituta divinitus tempora compleri coeperint, interitum et consummationem fieri necesse est, ut innovetur a Deo mundus. Id vero tempus in proximo est, quantum de numero annorum, deque signis quae praedicta sunt a Prophetis, colligi potest. Sed quum sint innumerabilia quae de fine saeculi et conclusione temporum dicta sunt, ea ipsa quae dicuntur nuda ponenda sunt, quoniam, ut testimoniis utamur, immensum est. Si quis illa desiderat, aut nobis minus credit, adeat ad ipsum sacrarium coelestium litterarum, quarum fide instructus errasse philosophos sentiat, qui aut aeternum esse hunc mundum, aut infinita esse annorum millia putaverunt, ex quo fuerit instructus. Nondum enim sex millia completa sunt; quo numero consummato, tunc demum malum omne tolletur, ut regnet sola justitia. Quod quatenus eventurum sit, paucis explicabo.

CHAPTER 71

Haec autem a Prophetis, sed et vatibus futura dicuntur. Quum coeperit mundo finis ultimus propinquare, malitia invalescet, omnia vitiorum et fraudum genera crebrescent, justitia interibit, fides, pax, misericordia, pudor, veritas non erit, vis et audacia praevalebit, nemo quicquam habebit nisi manu partum manuque defensum. Si qui erunt boni, praedae ludibrio habebuntur. Nemo pietatem parentibus exhibebit, nemo infantis aut senis miserebitur, avaritia et libido universa corrumpet. Erunt caedes et sanguinis effusiones. Erunt bella non modo externa et finitima, verum etiam intestina. Civitates inter se belligerabunt, omnis sexus et omnis aetas arma tractabit. Non imperii dignitas conservabitur, non militiae disciplina; sed more latrocinii depraedatio et vastitas fiet. Regnum multiplicabitur, et decem viri occupabunt orbem, partientur, devorabunt; et existet alius longe potentior ac nequior, qui, tribus ex eo numero deletis, Asiam possidebit, et ceteris in potestatem suam redactis et adscitis vexabit omnem terram. Novas leges statuet, veteres abrogabit, rempublicam suam faciet, nomen imperii sedemque mutabit. Tunc erit tempus infandum et exsecrabile, quo nemini libeat vivere. Denique in eum statum res cadet, ut vivos lamentatio, mortuos gratulatio sequatur. Civitates et oppida interibunt, modo ferro, modo igni, modo terrae motibus crebris, modo aquarum inundatione, modo pestilentia et fame. Terra nihil feret, aut frigoribus nimiis aut caloribus sterilis. Aqua omnis partim mutabitur in cruorem, partim amaritudine vitiabitur, ut nihil sit nec ad cibos utile, nec ad potum salubre. His malis accedent etiam prodigia de coelo, ne quid desit hominibus ad timorem. Cometae crebro apparebunt. Sol perpetuo pallore fuscabitur. Luna sanguine inficietur, nec amissae lucis damna reparabit. Stellae omnes decident, nec temporibus sua ratio constabit, hieme atque aestate confusis. Tunc et annus, et mensis, et dies breviabitur. Et hanc esse mundi senectutem ac defectionem Trismegistus elocutus est. Quae quum evenerint, adesse tempus sciendum est, quo Deus ad commutandum saeculum revertatur. Inter haec autem mala surget rex impius, non modo generi hominum sed etiam Deo inimicus. Hic reliquias illius prioris tyranni conteret, cruciabit, vexabit, interimet. Tunc erunt lachrimae juges, luctus et gemitus perpetes, et ad Deum cassae preces, nulla requies a formidine nec somnus ad requiem. Dies cladem, nox metum semper augebit. Sic orbis terrarum paene ad solitudinem, certe ad raritatem hominum redigetur. Tunc et impius justos homines ac dicatos Deo persequetur, et se coli jubebit ut Deum. Se enim dicet esse Christum, cujus erit adversarius. Ut credi ei possit, accipiet potestatem mirabilia faciendi, ut ignis descendat a coelo, ut sol resistat a cursu suo, ut imago quam posuerit loquatur. Quibus prodigiis illiciet multos, ut adorent eum signumque ejus in manu aut fronte suscipiant. Et qui non adoraverit, signumque susceperit, exquisitis cruciatibus morietur. Ita fere duas partes exterminabit, tertia in desertas solitudines fugiet. Sed ille, vecors, ira implacabili furens, adducet exercitum, et obsidebit montem quo justi confugerint. Qui quum se viderint circumsessos, implorabunt auxilium Dei voce magna, et exaudiet eos, et mittet eis liberatorem.

CHAPTER 72

Tunc coelum intempesta nocte patefiet, et descendet Christus in virtute magna, et anteibit eum claritas ignea, et vis inestimabilis angelorum; et exstinguetur omnis illa multitudo impiorum, et torrentes sanguinis current, et ipse ductor effugiet, atque exercitu saepe reparato, quartum praelium faciet, quo captus cum ceteris omnibus tyrannis, tradetur exustioni. Sed et ipse daemonum princeps, auctor et machinator malorum, catenis alligatus, custodiae dabitur, ut pacem mundus accipiat, et vexata tot saeculis terra requiescat. Pace igitur parta, compressoque omni malo, Rex ille justus et victor, judicium magnum de vivis et mortuis faciet super terram; et viventibus quidem justis tradet in servitium gentes universas, mortuos autem ad aeternam vitam suscitabit et in terra cum iis ipse regnabit, et condet sanctam civitatem; et erit hoc regnum justorum mille annis. Per idem tempus stellae candidiores erunt, et claritas solis augebitur, et luna non patietur diminutionem. Tunc descendet a Deo pluvia benedictionis matutina et vespertina, et omnem frugem terra sine labore hominum procreabit. Stillabunt mella de rupibus, lactis et vini fontes exuberabunt, bestiae deposita feritate mansuescent, lupus inter pecudes errabit innoxius, vitulus cum leone pascetur, columba cum accipitre congregabitur, serpens virus non habebit, nullum animal vivet ex sanguine, omnibus enim Deus copiosum atque innocentem victum ministrabit. Peractis vero mille annis, ac resoluto daemonum principe, rebellabunt gentes adversus justos, et veniet innumerabilis multitudo ad expugnandam sanctorum civitatem. Tunc fiet ultimum judicium Dei adversus gentes. Concutiet enim a fundamentis suis terram, et corruent civitates, et pluet super impios ignem cum sulphure et grandine, et ardebunt, et se invicem trucidabunt. Justi vero sub terra paulisper latebunt, donec perditio gentium fiat, et exibunt post diem tertium, et videbunt campos cadaveribus opertos. Tunc fiet terrae motus, et scindentur montes, et subsident valles in altitudinem profundam, et congerentur in eam corpora mortuorum, et vocabitur nomen ejus Polyandrium. Post haec renovabit Deus mundum, et transformabit justos in figuras angelorum, ut immortalitatis veste donati serviant Deo in sempiternum. Et hoc erit regnum Dei, quod finem non habebit. Tunc et impii resurgent, non ad vitam, sed ad poenam. Eos quoque, secunda resurrectione facta, Deus excitabit, ut ad perpetua tormenta damnati et aeternis ignibus traditi merita pro sceleribus suis supplicia persolvant.

EPILOGUS

Quare quum haec omnia vera et certa sint, Prophetarum omnium consonanti adnuntiatione praedicta, quum eadem Trismegistus, eadem Hystaspes, eadem Sibyllae cecinerint, dubitari non potest quin spes omnis vitae ac salutis in sola Dei religione sit posita. Itaque nisi homo Christum susceperit quem Deus ad liberationem misit atque missurus est, nisi summum Deum agnoverit, nisi mandata ejus legemque servaverit, in eas incidet poenas de quibus locuti sumus. Proinde fragilia contemnenda sunt ut solida consequamur, spernenda terrena ut coelestibus honoremur, temporalia fugienda ut ad aeterna veniamus. Erudiat se quisque ad justitiam, reformet ad continentiam, praeparet ad agonem, instruat ad virtutem, ut, si forte adversarius indixerit bellum, nulla vi, nullo terrore, nullis cruciatibus a recto et bono depellatur. Non se substernat insensibilibus figmentis, sed verum et solum Deum rectus agnoscat, abjiciat voluptates quarum illecebris anima sublimis deprimitur ad terram, teneat innocentiam, prosit quamplurimis, incorruptibiles sibi thesauros bonis operibus acquirat, ut possit, Deo judice, pro virtutis suae meritis, vel coronam fidei vel praemium immortalitatis adipisci.

TRANSLATION OF THE EPITOME

PREFACE

Although the seven books of the *Divine Institutes*, which I wrote some years ago, to illustrate the truths of religion, instruct readers in such a way as to avoid a wearisome prolixity and a burdensome excess; yet, my dear brother, seeing you ask for an epitome of those books, presumably that I may write something to you and that your name may be celebrated in my work—such as it is—I shall comply with your wishes though it is no easy task to compress into a single volume matters already dealt with in seven. Incomplete it will be, and reduced in bulk, since a mass of details has to be compressed into a narrow compass; while, owing to its brevity, it will prove less clear, because most of the arguments and examples which serve to illustrate the truth have necessarily to be passed over. Indeed the amount of such material is enough to fill a book in itself. Remove this material, and what will be found either valuable or sufficiently full and clear? Nevertheless I shall try, so far as the subject allows, to abridge what is diffuse, yet in such a way that my book, in which truth must be brought to light, may not appear inadequate or lack clearness for its due understanding.

CHAPTER I

Of Providence

The first question to arise is whether there be a Providence that has made or rules the world. Almost all philosophers—except the Epicureans—declare unanimously that the world could not have been contrived without God for its Designer, nor could it hold together without a Ruler. Accordingly Epicurus is refuted not only by learned men but by the consenting testimony of mankind. For who can doubt of a Providence, when he sees the heavens and the earth so ordered and governed as most fitly to be adapted not only to ornament and beauty but also to the use of mankind and the advantage of all things living? Hence what is in itself rational cannot have a beginning without rationality.

CHAPTER 2

There is but one God

Since it is certain that there is a Providence, a further question arises: whether God be a unity or a plurality—a question involving considerable obscurity. For not only do individual people differ on this point, but even whole peoples and races. But the followers of reason will understand that there can be but one Lord, one Father. For if the God who made all things is both Father and Lord, He must needs be One, as head and fountain of creation. The Universe cannot co-exist, unless all things be referred to One; unless One holds the helm and guides the course; unless as it were one Mind rules all members of the cosmos. If there are many kings in a swarm of bees, they will perish or be scattered, while 'discord with deep passion wars upon the kings'; if in a herd of cattle there are several leaders, they will fight until one be victorious; if there are many commanders in an army, the rank and file cannot obey, since contradictory orders are given; nor can unity be secured by the commanders themselves, because each consults his own interests to the utmost. So in this world-state unless there had been but one ruler (who was also its founder) either the whole structure would have been destroyed, or else it could not have been founded at all. Besides, the entire government could not exist in multiplicity of deities, since they severally possess their own duties and their own powers. So not one of them could be called 'almighty'—the true title of God—since a god can deal with only that which belongs to himself, but what belongs to another he will not venture to handle. Thus: Vulcan will not claim water for his own, nor Neptune fire, nor Ceres skill in the arts; Minerva will lay no claim to harvests, nor Mercury to arms, nor Mars to the lyre, nor Jupiter to medicine, nor Aesculapius to the thunderbolt; he will find it easier to lift a bolt cast by another than to wield it himself. If, then, individual deities cannot do all things, it shows that they have less might, less power. We must count Him as God who can manage the whole, not one who, out of that whole, can control but a very small part.

CHAPTER 3
The verdict of the poets

There is then one God, perfect, eternal, incorruptible, passionless, subject to no circumstance or power; possessing all things, ruling all things, one whom the mind of man cannot assess nor mortal tongue describe. He is too lofty, too great, to be comprehended in thought or word of man. Finally (not to speak of prophets, preachers of the one God), both poets and philosophers testify to one God. Orpheus speaks of a principal God, creator of heaven and earth, of sun and stars, of land and sea. Moreover our poet Virgil calls the supreme God now spirit, now mind, declaring that mind, as though poured into limbs, sets in movement the body of the whole world; that God passes over seas and lands and through the depths of heaven, and that from Him all creatures derive their life. Even Ovid knew that the world was made by God, whom he calls now the framer, now the architect, of all things.

CHAPTER 4
The verdict of the philosophers

But let us now come to the philosophers, whose opinions carry more weight than those of the poets. Plato asserts the sole sovranty of God, that there is one God by whom the world was prepared and perfected by wonderful wisdom. Aristotle, his disciple, admits that there is a single Mind presiding over the world. Antisthenes says that there is one God of nature,[1] director of the whole universe. It would take too long to enumerate what has been said about the Supreme Deity by Thales and Anaximenes in earlier times, or at a later period by the Stoics, Pythagoras, or Cleanthes, Chrysippus, Zeno, or by our own Seneca (a follower of the Stoics) and Cicero himself, since they have all tried to find a definition of God and have affirmed that the world is ruled by Him alone—a God subject to no natural law, seeing that Nature originates with Him. Hermes, justly called Trismegistus, by reason of his virtue and knowledge of many arts, who in the antiquity of his teaching preceded the philosophers, and is worshipped as a god in Egypt, extols with infinite praise the

---

[1] naturalem: could not this mean 'real, genuine'?

majesty of the one God, calling him Lord and Father and declaring that He is nameless, because He needs no personal name, being alone and without parentage, because He exists of Himself and by Himself. Here are the opening words of his address to his son: 'To understand God is indeed hard; but to declare Him in speech is impossible, even for one who is able to understand, for the perfect cannot be comprehended by the imperfect, nor the invisible by the visible.'

CHAPTER 5
Testimony of the Sibyls

It remains to speak of the prophetesses. Varro records the existence of ten sibyls—the Persian, the Libyan, the Delphic, the Cimmerian, the Erythraean, the Samian, the Cumaean, the Hellespontine, the Phrygian, the Tiburtine called the sibyl of Albunea. Of all these there are three books of the Cumaean sibyl alone, containing the destinies of Rome; they are looked upon as secret; those of almost all the others are extant separately and are usually so regarded, but these are entitled 'sibyllines' under a single name, except that the Erythraean sibyl—who is said to have lived in the days of the Trojan war—has her own name inscribed in those books. The books of the others are jumbled together. All these prophetesses, of whom I have spoken (apart from the Cumaean), whom the Fifteen are permitted to read; they all bear witness to the fact that there is one God—Ruler, Maker, Father—unbegotten but self-existing, who has been from everlasting and therefore alone ought to be worshipped, alone feared, alone honoured by all living people. Their testimonies, because I could not abbreviate them, I have passed by; if you greatly wish for these, you must betake yourself to the books themselves. Now let us follow up the subjects that remain to be dealt with.

CHAPTER 6
God is eternal, and therefore is sexless and without succession, unlike the deities of heathenism

These many testimonies plainly teach that there is one sovranty over the world, one power, the origin of which cannot be discovered by thought, nor its might explained. They are fools, then, who imagine deities to exist as the result of sex intercourse, since sexual powers have been assigned to mortals by God, to the end that the human race may be preserved by a succession of offspring. What need have Immortals either of sex or succession, since pleasure and dissolution cannot touch them? Those, therefore, who are deemed gods, since it is certain they were born like the rest of mankind, were in any case mortals; but they were believed to be gods because, when they were once great and powerful kings, they were accorded divine honours after death by reason of the benefits they conferred on humanity; then, when temples and images were erected to them, their memory was preserved and celebrated as though they were themselves immortal.

CHAPTER 7
Concerning Hercules, his evil life and death

Pretty well all nations are convinced that gods exist, but none the less their deeds, the account of which has been handed down by poets and historians, show that they were once men. Who does not know of the date of Hercules, seeing he sailed with the Argonauts and, after the storming of Troy, slew Laomedon for breaking his oath? This is computed to have happened fifteen hundred years ago. Hercules is said to have been of ignoble birth, through his mother's adultery with Jupiter, and to have been addicted to his father's vices; he could never keep his hands off women, but travelled all over the world, not to win glory but to sate lust, not to destroy wild beasts but to beget children. Though unvanquished, he was triumphed over by Omphăle alone, to whom he surrendered his club and lion's skin, while, clothed in feminine garb, he grovelled at a woman's feet, accepting the tasks she enjoined. Subsequently, in a fit of rage, he murdered his wife and children. Finally, after accepting from his wife Deianira a robe, ulcers broke out and unable to bear the pain he raised a funeral pyre on Mount Oeta, whereon he burnt himself alive. The result is that, even if for his courage he might have been credited as a god, he is seen, by reason of his evil deeds, to have been but a human being.

CHAPTER 8
Concerning various deities

Tarquitius states that Aesculapius was of doubtful parentage, and for that reason exposed; he was picked up by hunters, suckled by a bitch, and handed to Chiron for training. He sojourned in Epidaurus, and, according to Cicero, was buried at Cynosūrae, after being killed by a thunder-bolt. His father, Apollo, did not scorn to feed a stranger's flocks in order to win a bride, and, when he had accidentally killed a favourite boy, inscribed a flower with his laments. Mars, a most courageous figure, was guilty of adultery and then chained to his leman for a spectacle to the world. Castor and Pollux ravished other men's wives, and paid for their guilt; to the death and burial of these two Homer testifies, simply and not after the fashion of poets. Mercury, who begat Androgȳnus through an intrigue with Venus, was reckoned a god because he invented the lyre and the wrestling-school. Father Liber, victorious by his conquest of India, after coming by chance to Crete, saw on the seashore Ariadne, whom Theseus had violated and abandoned. Fired with passion, he wedded her and set her crown—so poets tell—among the stars. The Great Mother, while tarrying in Phrygia after her husband's flight and death, old and widowed though she was, fell in love with a handsome youth; but, because he proved false to her, she mutilated him. Hence she now rejoices in having the Galli for her priests.

CHAPTER 9
The scandalous doings of goddesses

Was not Proserpina the illegitimate daughter of Ceres? and was not the same true with Latona and her twins, Apollo and Diana? Venus, exposed to the lusts both of gods and men, while reigning in Cyprus, devised the art of whoredom, and bade women make a gain of it, that she might not be alone in infamy. What of the 'virgins', Minerva and Diana? were *they* chaste? Why did Diana banish Hippolytus to a lonely haunt, or surrender him to a woman, to pass his life solitary amid unknown glades, and—with a change of name—to be called Virbius? What do all these instances imply but unchastity, though the poets do not venture to avow it.

CHAPTER 10
The scandalous life of Jupiter

The king and father of all these deities is Jupiter, who is supposed to hold supremacy in heaven. What filial feeling was his, who drove his father Saturn from the throne and harried him with arms, in his flight? what self-control was his, who was guilty of every form of lust? He slurred the good name of Alcmena and Leda, wives of great men, by his adultery. . . . Why mention his violation of maidens, the great number of whom is proved by the multitude of his sons? In one instance, however, he showed self-control, namely with Thetis; for it was prophesied that her offspring would be mightier than his sire. So he fought against his passion, to prevent anyone being mightier than himself. Well he knew that he was no perfect example of virtue, might, or power, if he feared what he had done to his father Saturn. Why then is he called 'Optimus maximus', seeing that he has defiled himself with sins—which is the part of one who is evil and unjust —and has feared one who should be greater than himself, which is the part of an inferior and a weakling?

CHAPTER II

The emblems under which the poets veiled the foul deeds of Jupiter

But someone will say that these legends are poets' fictions. It is not the function of poetry so to compose things as to turn all to falsehood, but to clothe actions in due shape—so to say, with a parti-coloured veil. Poetic licence has its limits; it must not fabricate the whole (which is the method of a false and foolish writer) but must make changes with some show of reason. We have been told that Jupiter converted himself into a golden shower, by way of deceiving Danae. What is a golden shower? Why, gold coins, by offering quantities of which and pouring them into her lap, he corrupted a frail woman with a bribe. So, too, men speak of an iron shower, when they mean a multitude of war weapons. Jupiter snatched away his catamite on an eagle. What is the eagle? Doubtless a legion, since the image of the bird is the standard of a Roman legion. He transported Europa on a bull. What is the bull? A ship, to be sure, which has as its guardian deity the form of a bull. So the daughter of Inachus did not swim the seas on a cow, but escaped the wrath of Juno in a vessel shaped like a cow. Finally, when she had been carried to Egypt, she became Isis, whose voyage is celebrated, on a fixed day, by way of commemorating her flight.

CHAPTER 12

The poets not simply inventors of these legends

You see then that the poets did not invent all these stories, but that they foreshadowed things in a figure, to the end that, when speaking truthfully, they might nevertheless throw some veil [of divinity] over their so-called gods—as they did respecting their several sovranties. For when they tell us that Jupiter held his realm by lot, they mean either Mount Olympus (where Saturn and afterwards Jupiter dwelt, according to legend) or part of the East which is, they say, higher because light arises there; whereas the western region is lower, and so Pluto was assigned that lower part. But the sea was granted to Neptune because he held the sea coasts with all the islands. Much is thus coloured by the poets, because ignorant people criticize them as false—anyhow in word, for they believe them in fact, since they fashion the images of gods in such a way that, when they make them male or female, and some are wedded, some are parents, some children, they really agree with the poets. Now this cannot happen without sexual intercourse.

CHAPTER 13

The account of Jupiter by Euhemerus

But let us leave the poets and have recourse to history which is based on trustworthy facts and antiquity. Euhemerus was a Messenian, a writer of old days, who gathered from sacred inscriptions in ancient temples information about the origin of Jupiter, his acts and his progeny, together with accounts of the parentage of the other gods—their countries, doings, governments, deaths, even their tombs. His history was translated into Latin by Ennius, whose words are as follows: 'The origins of Jupiter and his kinsmen are as I have written; in this fashion has the tradition been bequeathed to us from sacred writings.' This same Euhemerus informs us, therefore, that Jupiter, after compassing the world five times, and distributing kingdoms to his friends and relatives, and giving laws to mankind, and after many other good deeds, was crowned with immortal fame and everlasting remembrance. He ended his life in Crete and departed into heaven. Furthermore his tomb is in Crete, in the City of Cnossus, and on it are inscribed, in ancient Greek characters, the words *ZAN KPONOY*—that is, 'Jupiter, Saturn's son'. It is certain, then, from what I have recorded, that he was a man and reigned on the earth.

CHAPTER 14
Of Saturn and Uranus

Let us now pass on to an earlier epoch, that we may detect the origin of the whole mistake. Saturn is reported to be the son of Caelus and Terra. This is, of course, incredible. There is a definite reason for the tale, and he who ignores the reason rejects the tale as fabulous. That Uranus was styled the father of Saturn is testified by Hermes and sacred history. When Trismegistus declared that men of perfect learning were very few, he numbered among those few his own kinsfolk, Uranus, Saturn, Mercury. Euhemerus mentions that the same Uranus was the first earthly king; these are his words: 'in the beginning Caelus had supreme rule on earth; he established and made ready that kingdom for himself and his brothers.'

[This chapter is incomplete in MS., and chaps. 15-19 are lost.]

CHAPTER 20
Of the gods peculiar to Rome

I have spoken of religious ceremonies common to all nations. I shall now deal with deities peculiar to the Romans. Who knows not that the wife of Faustulus, nurse of Romulus and Remus—in whose honour the Larentalia were dedicated—was a harlot? Hence her name, Lupa (= harlot); that was why she was represented as a wild beast. Faula and Flora were both prostitutes; one of them became the mistress of Hercules, according to Varius, and the other, after acquiring great riches by the sale of her own person, made the people her heir; so the games, known as the Festival of Flora, were in her honour. Tatius consecrated the statue of a woman, found in the great sewer, and dubbed her the goddess of the sewer! The Romans, when besieged by the Gauls, made catapults out of women's hair, and on that account built an altar and temple to Venus the Bald, and also to Jupiter the Baker, because he had warned them in a dream to turn all their corn into bread, and hurl it against the enemy. This done, the Gauls, in despair of being able to master Rome by hunger, abandoned the siege. Tullus Hostilius made gods of Panic and Pallor. Mind too is worshipped; had men had any mind they would never have imagined that it was an object of worship. Marcellus consecrated Honour and Virtue.

CHAPTER 21
Of the religious rites of the Romans

But the cult of other imaginary gods of this kind the Senate established—Hope, Good Faith, Concord, Peace, Chastity, Piety; all of which, though they should be true in the minds of men, are falsely put within temple walls. Yet I should prefer these deities—albeit outside human nature they are insubstantial—to be honoured rather than Blight and Fever, which are worthy not of consecration but execration; than Fornax, with her ovens; than Stercutus, who was the first to show how to enrich the land with dung; than Muta, mother of the Lares; than Cumīna, who watches over children's cradles; than Caca, who betrayed to Hercules the theft of his oxen, in order that he might slay her brother Cacus. How many portentous absurdities there are besides, of which it irks me to speak! I must not, however, overlook Terminus, because the tale goes that he did not yield even to Jupiter of the Capitol, being himself an unwrought stone. It is thought that Terminus is the custodian of boundaries, and public prayer is made to him that he may preserve the 'immovable stone of the Capitol' and extend the boundaries of the Roman empire.

CHAPTER 22
The religious rites of Faunus and Numa

Faunus was the first in Latium to bring in all these absurdities; it was he that instituted blood sacrifices to Saturn his grandsire; it was he that wanted his father Picus to be worshipped and set Fatua Fauna (his wife and sister) among the gods, calling her the Good Goddess. Then, at Rome, Numa—who loaded untaught rustics with novel superstitions—established priesthoods and divided the gods into families and tribes, by way of diverting the passions of a fierce people from warlike pursuits. That is why

Lucilius, mocking the follies of those who are in slavery to vain superstitions, composed these verses:

> Bugbears and vampires, creatures of man's brain,
> At these he trembles, finds his centre there.
> As children fancy brazen images
> Are living people, so these men hold true
> All fictions; they believe that in the bronze
> There dwells a heart. A painter's gallery!
> That's how it looks—all feigning and no truth.

Cicero, too, in his treatise on the nature of the gods, complains that feigned and imaginary gods had been introduced; hence had arisen false opinions, troublesome errors, and old womanish superstitions. This judgement ought to be deemed the worthier, because spoken by one who was both philosopher and priest.

CHAPTER 23

Barbaric ceremonies

I have spoken of the gods, and shall now deal with their religious ceremonies. In consequence of the ordinance given by Teucrus, a human sacrifice was customarily offered to Cyprian Jupiter. So, too, used the Taurians to sacrifice strangers to Diana; the Latian Jupiter also was propitiated with human blood. Even before this, sexagenarians were, in obedience to an oracle of Apollo, flung from the Milvian bridge into the Tiber in honour of Saturn. The Carthaginians used to offer up to Saturn not only infants; after their defeat by the Sicilians, they sacrificed two hundred sons of the nobility to Saturn, as a piacular offering. The rites of the Great Mother and of Bellona are even to-day equally cruel; at these ceremonies the priests accompany their prayers not with alien blood but their own, hacking their shoulders and sprinkling their vile altars with gore. These are cruel rites; let us come to those of a milder type. The worship of Isis shows nothing else than how she lost and found the body of her little son Osiris. First of all the priests and their attendants shave their bodies, beat their breasts, prosecute their search with loud lamentations, thus imitating the mother's anguish. Subsequently the boy is found by Cynocephalus. Thus ends the mourning with a note of joy.

The mysteries of Ceres are of a like character. On torches being lit, an all night search is made for Proserpine, and when she has been found the whole proceeding ends in congratulations, amid the waving of torches. The men of Lampsacus immolate an ass to Priâpus ... Lindus is a town in Rhodes, where the rites of Hercules are accompanied by imprecations; for, after Hercules had robbed a farmer of his oxen and sacrificed them, the man avenged the wrong done him by revilings, and when he had himself been appointed a priest, it was ordained that both he himself and his successors in the priesthood should celebrate the due rites with the selfsame revilings. The mystery of Cretan Jupiter shows how this god, as a babe, was taken from his father and brought up. Near by is a goat, with whose milk Amalthēa fed the boy. The same thing is shown in the ritual of the great mother of the gods. On that occasion the Corybants had drowned the infant's cries by the clash of helmets and the beating of shields; nowadays this is represented in the ritual ceremony, but instead of helmets cymbals are struck; instead of shields, tambourines; this is done to prevent Saturn hearing the babe's cries.

CHAPTER 24

On the origin of sacred ceremonies and superstitions

Such are the mysteries of the gods. Now let us investigate the origin of religions to find out by whom and when they were instituted. Didymus in his work *A commentary on Pindar* records that Melisseus was King of Crete, his daughters being Amalthea and Melissa who fed Jupiter on goat's milk and honey; that he was the first to bring in novel rites and religious processions with sacrifices to the gods, namely to Vesta—who is called Tellus—whence the words of the poet, 'Tellus, first of the gods'; and subsequently to the Mother of the gods. But Euhemerus, in his Sacred History, tells us that Jupiter himself, after having secured the supreme sovranty, built shrines to himself in many places. For, during his world-wide travels, wherever he went he would unite the chieftains of the peoples to himself in friendship and the law of hospitality. To preserve such a memory he bade shrines to be erected in his honour and annual festivals to be celebrated by his guest friends. By such means he propagated his own cult everywhere. The dates when these deities lived may readily be ascertained. For Thallus tells us in his history that Belus, king of Assyria, whom the Babylonians worship and who was the contemporary and friend of Saturn, lived 322 years before the Trojan war, and since the capture of Troy 1,470 years have elapsed. Hence it is clear that not more than 1,800 years have passed since men fell into error through introducing new cults of the gods.

CHAPTER 25
Of the Golden Age, of images, and of Prometheus

Poets are justified in saying that the Golden Age of Saturn's reign suffered a change. In those days no gods were worshipped: only *one* God was known. When men surrendered to feeble earthly notions, worshipping logs and bronzes and stones, the Golden Age gave place to the Iron Age. All knowledge of the Creator being lost, and this one bond of human society snapped, men began to ravage, prey upon, and subdue one another. Yet would they but lift up their eyes and contemplate God, who has moved men to behold heaven and Himself, never would they abase themselves by venerating earthly objects, whose folly Lucretius inveighs against in these words: 'men bring their hearts low through fear of the gods and bow them down grovelling to earth.' So they give themselves up to idolatry.[1] They do not understand what folly it is to fear what human hands have made, or to hope for protection from things dumb and insensible, which can neither see nor hear the petitioner. What majesty, what divinity can objects possess which it was in man's power not to make, or that these should become something other than they are now? For these [images] can be profaned or stolen, unless protected by law and human guardianship. Can anyone in his senses slaughter victims to such deities as these, or consecrate gifts, or offer costly raiment, as if those that cannot move could make use of them? On good grounds did Dionysius, tyrant of Sicily, plunder and mock at the divinities of Greece, when he had victoriously seized it, and, after acts of sacrilege, returned to Sicily with a prosperous voyage; yes, and kept his throne until old age, nor could the dishonoured gods punish him. How much better to despise lifeless idols and turn to the living God, to preserve that station assigned you by Him, and so uphold your name as 'man'! A man is called ἄνθρωπος because his gaze is upward. He gazes upward who looks to the true and living God,

[1] I adopt here Brandt's conjecture (see commentary).

who is in heaven; who seeks the maker and parent of his soul not merely by feeling and intellect but with uplifted face and eyes.

He who submits himself to the base things of this world, obviously chooses what is beneath him; for, since he is God's handiwork, whereas an image is man's handiwork, the human handiwork cannot be preferred to the divine. And as God is the creator of man, so man is the creator of the image. He is beside himself who adores what his hands have made—of which hateful and stupid handwork Prometheus (son of Iapetus, the uncle of Jupiter) was the author. For at the time when Jupiter, having secured supreme rule, wished to establish himself as a god and found temples, and was looking for someone to express the human shape, Prometheus was alive. And he made the figure of a man out of clay, so lifelike that the novelty and cunning of his craftsmanship seemed miraculous. Finally the men of his day, and the poets after him, proclaimed Prometheus as the maker of a real living man, just as we (whenever we praise fabricated idols) say they are alive and breathe. Prometheus was indeed the inventor of images in earthenware, but posterity wrought them in marble and cast them in bronze; then, in process of time, ornaments of gold and silver were added, so that men's eyes were dazzled not only by the likeness itself but by the glitter of the image. Entranced by beauty and forgetful of genuine majesty, creatures of feeling deemed that objects devoid of feeling, reasonable beings that objects without reason, living beings that lifeless objects, were fit to be worshipped and venerated.

CHAPTER 26

Astrology and element-worship

We may now refute the opinions of those that regard natural phenomena as divinities—to wit the sky, the sun, the moon, whose Maker these men know not while adoring and marvelling at His works. This error is not peculiar to the unlearned; it is accepted also by philosophers. The Stoics, for example, think that all celestial objects should be regarded as divinities, inasmuch as these have fixed and rational motions whereby the changes and vicissitudes of succeeding times are constantly governed. These objects possess no voluntary motions, because they obey preordained laws—not of course by virtue of any understanding of their own, but thanks to the workmanship of the Supreme Maker, who ordained that they shall observe fixed and undeviating periods and courses, thus bringing to pass the alternations of days and nights, of summer and winter. But if men marvel at their courses, brightness, steadfastness, beauty (the results of those laws), how much more should they realize how far lovelier, more excellent, and more powerful, is the Maker and Doer of all these wonders—God Himself! But men have estimated divinity by what comes within the scope of human vision, ignoring the fact that what is visible cannot be eternal, and what is eternal cannot be described by mortal eyes.

CHAPTER 27

Man's creation; his sin and its penalty. Good and bad angels

One subject remains, and the last. Since it generally happens (so we read in histories) that the gods seem to exhibit their majesty by auguries, dreams, and oracles, and also by punishing sacrilege, let me now show why this has come about, to prevent anyone falling into the snares that held the men of old. When God, by virtue of His majestic power, had created the Universe out of nothing and had adorned the heaven with lights and had filled land and sea with living creatures, He then formed man out of clay, in His own image, breathing into him the breath of life; next he placed him in a park which He had planted with fruit-yielding trees of every kind, at the same time bidding him not to taste of one tree wherein He had put the knowledge of good and evil, with the threat that, if he did so, he would lose his life, but that if he obeyed the command he would live for ever. Then the serpent, who was one of God's servants, jealous of the man because he had been made immortal, craftily enticed him to disobey God's laws. And thus man did indeed get knowledge of good and evil, but he lost that life which God had granted him for ever. So God drove out the culprit from the holy place, and exiled him to this world, to win his daily bread by hard toil, to face difficulties and sorrows according to his deserts; and He compassed the park itself with a fiery rampart, that none, right up to the judgement day, might try to creep into that abode of perpetual blessedness.

Then death followed after man, by sentence of God; and yet

his life, though now but transitory, lasted a thousand years: such was its duration for all men until the Flood. For, after the Flood, man's life gradually was shortened and reduced to one hundred and twenty years. But the Serpent, called the Devil by reason of his deeds—that is the false accuser or informer—never ceased to harass the children of him whom he had deceived from the beginning. At length, beset with envy and jealousy, he armed the first man to be born in this world, to kill his brother; that of the two first-born men he might blot out the one, and make the other a murderer. Nor did he cease henceforward from instilling the poison of his malice into the hearts of mankind for generations, from corrupting and perverting them; in short from overwhelming them with crimes so great, that an example of justice became rare, and men lived like beasts. Now when God saw this, He sent His angels to improve men's lives and safeguard them from all evil. He commanded these angels to hold aloof from earthly things, lest they should become spotted with sin and so be shorn of their angelic honour. But that crafty accuser, while they sojourned among men, enticed them too to pleasures, so that they defiled themselves with women. Then, condemned by sentence of God, and cast out by reason of their sins, they lost the name and substance of angels. So, become now the satellites of Satan, that they might possess some assuaging of their own ruin, they betook themselves to destroy men, to protect whom they had originally come.

CHAPTER 28

The daemons and their evil machinations in the world

Now these are the daemons, of whom poets write, and whom Hesiod calls 'protectors of mankind'. So persuasive are they by means of their enticements and lies that men actually believe them to be gods! Socrates used to affirm that he had, from childhood, a guardian, without whose behest he could do nothing. The daemons attach themselves to individual persons, and, under the name of Genii or Penates, take possession of houses. Oratories are assigned to them, and libations made daily to them, as they are to the Lares; respect is paid to them as averters of mischief. From the first it was these daemons who, in order to turn men from a knowledge of the true God, brought in novel superstitions and religious cults; it is they that have taught men to consecrate the memory of dead kings, to build temples, to fashion images—not indeed to diminish the honour due to God, nor to increase their own (which they have lost through sin), but to rob men of life, to take from them all hope of the true light, for fear lest men should win the gift of immortality which they themselves have lost. The same daemons have made known Astrology, Augury, and Divination: these things are indeed fallacious, but the authors of evil so regulate them that people believe them to be true. The daemons have also sleights of magic to cheat the eyes of onlookers. By their devices what is, appears to be non-existent, what is non-existent, to be. They have devised evocation of the dead, the casting of lots, oracles, to deceive men by lying divinations by means of ambiguous results. In all temples and at all sacrifices they are present; and, by exhibiting false miracles to astonish the worshippers, so deceive the people as to make them imagine that images and statues are indwelt by some divine presence. Further, they creep into men's bodies as thin spirits, introducing diseases into the bodies they have contaminated; these diseases they subsequently expel, if duly placated by vows and sacrifices. They send dreams—either terrible dreams to the end they may be invoked, or dreams that may come true: this, that they may be venerated the more. Sometimes they will threaten a measure of vengeance against the sacrilegious, that the beholders may become more timid and more superstitious. So by their deceits they have plunged the human race into darkness, in order that, by suppression of the truth, the name of the great and only God may be forgotten.

CHAPTER 29

The patience and providence of God

But at this point someone objects, 'Why then does the true God allow all this? Why does He not rather abolish evil? Why did He create the Archdaemon at the first, to corrupt and spoil His works?' I will briefly tell you why he willed Satan to be what he is. I put the question: Is virtue a good thing or a bad? Good, undeniably. If virtue is a good, vice is an evil. If vice is evil because it wars against virtue, and virtue good because it casts down vice, virtue as a consequence cannot exist without vice; and if you take vice away, the merits of virtue will also be taken; for there can be no victory without an enemy. Hence good cannot exist without evil. This was plainly seen by Chrysippus, a man of keen intellect, when he was speaking of Providence; and he proved those to be guilty of folly who, while admitting that good was created by God, maintain that He was not the author of evil. Gellius in his *Attic Nights* expounded that philosopher's views thus: 'Those that deny that the world was formed for the sake of God and man, or that human affairs are ruled by Providence, imagine they are using a weighty argument when they say "if there were a Providence there would be no evil". For they assert that nothing is less agreeable to the notion of Providence than that, in a world said to be contrived for mankind, there should be such sorrow and such evil within it.' In his fourth book *Concerning Providence* Chrysippus argued thus: 'Nothing can exceed the absurdity of those that think good would have existed without the presence of evil also. For, as good is the contrary of evil, both must be opposed to each other, yet supported each by reaction to its opposite. Now there can be no opposite without a counter opposite. How can there be a sense of justice, in the absence of wrongs? what is justice but a removal of injustice? Can the nature of courage be understood save by setting cowardice in contrast? Nor can you understand the meaning of self-control save by setting beside it the lack of self-control. Again, how could we possess forethought in the absence of its contrary? In the same way why do fools not long for the presence of truth rather than a lie? Good things and bad co-exist—happiness and misfortune, pleasure and pain. There is a polarity in things, says Plato: take away one of the opposites, and you take away both.'

You see, then, that it is as I say: Good and evil are so closely intertwined that neither can exist without its complement. It was with supreme reason, then, that God placed the 'stuff' of virtue in evil, His aim being to prepare for us a contest, and to crown the victor therein with immortality as his reward.

CHAPTER 30
Of false wisdom

I have shown, I think, that worship of gods is not only wicked but useless, either because they once were men, whose memory has been consecrated after death, or because their images are without feeling and are deaf, seeing they are made of clay, and because men—whose duty it is to contemplate heavenly things—ought not to submit themselves to earthly things; because, too, spirits claiming for themselves religious observances are sinful and unclean, and therefore, being condemned by the judgement of God, have fallen to earth, and you should not come under the sway of those whose superior you are, if you be willing to follow after the true God.

It remains that, as we have spoken of false religion, we should also deal with false wisdom, which philosophers profess, men endowed with great learning and eloquence but far removed from truth, inasmuch as they have recognized neither God nor the wisdom of God. These men are acute and learned; none the less, just because their wisdom is of men, I shall not fear to break a lance with them, that it may be shown that a lie can be easily mastered by the truth, earthly things by heavenly. The nature of philosophy they define thus: 'Philosophy is the love of, or devotion to, wisdom.' Therefore it cannot be wisdom itself, for that which loves is different from love's object. If philosophy is devotion to wisdom, it cannot, even so, *be* wisdom, because wisdom itself is the object sought for, but devotion to wisdom is what seeks it. The definition then, or meaning of the word, is evidence that philosophy is not wisdom itself, and I shall maintain that not even philosophy is a devotion to wisdom, because it does not include the idea of wisdom. For who can be said to be a devotee of something he can never reach? One who devotes himself to medicine, or literature, or oratory may be said to be a devotee of the art he learns; but, once he has learned it, he is spoken of as a doctor, a man of letters, an orator. So ought men who are devotees of wisdom to be called wise after they have learned wisdom. But, since they are called devotees of wisdom in their lifetime, it is obvious that it is not the pursuit that is wisdom, for the plain reason that you cannot arrive at the thing itself—namely the object of devotion—unless perchance those that are devotees all their life long are going to be wise in the world to come!

No right devotion belongs to that which is without end.

CHAPTER 31

Of knowledge, conjecture, and opinion

There are, in addition, two subjects that appear to belong to philosophy—'knowledge' and 'opinion'. Remove these, and philosophy collapses. But note: two of the most eminent philosophers have taken away both: Socrates, knowledge; Zeno, opinion. Let us see whether they were right. Wisdom, as defined by Cicero, is the knowledge of things divine and human. If that be a true definition, wisdom does not come within the competence of man. For who can affirm that he knows the divine and the human? Of things human, I say nothing, because, although intimately connected with the divine, nevertheless, since they belong to man, we must allow that they can be known. Divine things, as they really are, no man can know, because he *is* a man; anyone who knows must himself be divine, and consequently God. But man is not divine, nor is he God; therefore he cannot know, of himself, such matters. Then nobody is wise but God—or, at any rate, one who is taught by God. But these philosophers, being neither gods nor taught of God, cannot be wise—that is, fully cognizant of things human and divine. Rightly, then, was knowledge removed by Socrates and the Academics. Mere opinion is unfitting to the wise, for each person forms an opinion of what he does not know. Now to opine that you know what you do not know is rash folly. So opinion was rightly removed by Zeno. If, then, man has no knowledge, and opinion should have no place, philosophy is severed at the roots.

CHAPTER 32

Of philosophers, their sects, and dissensions

In addition to this, philosophy is not uniform: it is divided into sects and dissolved into conflicting judgements, and therefore it cannot preserve one attitude to the world. Since the sects are always quarrelling with one another, and not one of them but, in the judgement of the rest, is guilty of folly, the result is that, as there is war in its members, the whole body of philosophy is brought to ruin. Hence the origin of the Academic School. For when the heads of that sect saw that philosophy was at the mercy of mutual antagonisms, they declared war against all the sects, in order to annul their several tenets, declaring that only one thing was certain, namely that 'nothing can be known'. So therefore, knowledge being abolished, the old philosophies were overthrown. Even for themselves they did not keep the name of philosophy, but confessed their own ignorance, on the plea that a 'know nothing' attitude is the mark, not indeed of philosophy but not even of a man. Consequently the philosophers, possessing no sort of defence, destroy one another, with wounds on all sides, and philosophy ends by destroying itself with its own weapons.

But, says the objector, it is only *natural* philosophy that falls down; what about *moral* philosophy? Is this firmly founded? Let us see whether philosophers agree in that portion, at least, which concerns the state of life itself.

CHAPTER 33

Of the Supreme Good in life

We must now ask ourselves what is the Highest Good, that all our lives and acts may be directed to that. When enquiry is made concerning the Good, it must be laid down, first of all, that it refers to mankind alone; second that it is the special possession of the mind; lastly that it is to be sought after by Virtue. Let us, then, consider whether this Highest Good, as determined by philosophy, is such that it belongs neither to an animal nor to the body, and can in no wise be attained without Virtue.

Aristippus, founder of the Cyrenaic sect, who placed the Highest Good in bodily pleasure, must be banished from the company of philosophers and common men alike, because he compared himself to an animal. Hieronymus held that the Highest Good consisted in the absence of pain, Diodorus in the cessation of it. But *all* living creatures shrink from pain, and, when they cease to feel it, rejoice. What special privilege belongs to man if his highest good is accounted as shared with the beasts?

Zeno supposed that it meant 'to live in harmony with nature'. But that definition is general, for all living beings live in such a harmony, and each one has its individual nature. Epicurus asserted that the highest good was pleasure of the mind. What is pleasure of the mind but joy, in which the mind, as a rule, delights, and relaxes for play or laughter? But the 'good' affects even dumb animals, which, when satisfied with food, betake themselves to rejoicing and wantonness. Dinomachus and Calliphon approved of noble pleasure, being inclined towards the dictum of Epicurus, implying that mere bodily pleasure is dishonourable; or, if they believed some pleasures to be base and others honourable, it is not the highest good that is assigned to the body. The Peripatetics find the highest good in a combination of the good things of mind,[1] body, and fortune. The good things of the mind may indeed win approval, but, if they need aids to fulfil happiness, they are feeble indeed. Bodily goods and those of fortune are not in man's power, nor is that the highest good which is ascribed to the body or to externals; for even cattle reach this two-fold good, which they need in order to enjoy health and have plenty of food.

The Stoics are supposed to have had a sense of something far better, for they have told us that Virtue is the highest good. But Virtue cannot be this, since, if it enables us to bear ills and toils, it is not of itself blessed but ought to bring to pass the highest good, because it cannot be achieved without great toil and difficulty. Aristotle was wandering far from reason when he united honourable conduct with Virtue, as though this latter could at length be divorced from honourable conduct, or be united to baseness.

Erillus, the Pyrrhonist, made Knowledge the highest good. Knowledge, it is true, belongs to man and the mind alone, but it can exist apart from Virtue. For nobody should be counted as blest who has learned something through hearsay, or has got knowledge by slight reading; nor is knowledge to be defined as the highest good, inasmuch as it may well be a knowledge of evil—at any rate of what is valueless. And, if it be a knowledge of things good and valuable (a knowledge won at the price of toil) yet it cannot be the highest good, because knowledge is not being sought after for its own sake, but for the sake of something else.

That is why the Arts are learnt, to enable us to gain a livelihood, to win fame or even pleasure; and these things certainly cannot be the highest goods. So even in Ethics philosophers do not adhere to the rule, since, in the dispute on which all turns, they quarrel among themselves. Nor can precepts be alike, or equally

---

[1] Latin *animi*: possibly this should be translated 'soul', here and elsewhere in this chapter. See the lexicon.

valid; for some philosophers train their hearers to pleasure, others to honourable conduct; some to nature, others to knowledge; some to the search for, or avoidance of, riches; others to avoidance of pain, and some again to patience under evils; in all which doctrines—as I have shown—they go astray from reason because they know not God.

CHAPTER 34
Of the thesis that men are born to justice

Let us consider now what is that 'highest good' as set before a wise man. Not only sacred scriptures teach that men are born to justice, but even philosophers occasionally admit this. Cicero says: 'Of all philosophical discussions among the learned, nothing is more admirable than the plain conviction that men are born to justice!' Most true. We are not born to iniquity, since we are creatures living in a social community. Wild beasts are born to savagery, for they can support life only by prey and slaughter. Yet these same beasts, even when pressed by hunger, spare their own kith and kin. So do birds, which are compelled to feed on the corpses of others. How much more ought man, linked as he is with man by fellowship in speech and common feeling, to spare and to love his brother man! *That* is what justice implies. But since to man alone wisdom has been granted, to the end that he may know God, and since this alone distinguishes man from the brute creation, justice is itself bound by a double obligation, one that he owes to God as Father, one to man as brother; for we are all children of the same God.

Most rightly is it said that wisdom consists in a knowledge of things human and divine. We ought to be aware of what is due to God and man—namely, worship of God, love of mankind. But the former is the part of wisdom, the latter of virtue, while justice embraces both. If then it is agreed that man is born to justice, the just man must needs be subject to ills, to enable him to employ the virtue which is his birthright. For virtue involves the power to endure ills. Pleasures a man will shun, as evil; riches he will contemn, because they are weak and frail; if he possesses them, he will distribute them to help the wretched; honours he will not seek after, because they are brief-lived and soon fail; he will do no one a wrong; if he has suffered a wrong, he will not requite it, nor will be prosecute one who robs him. He will count it a sin to harm another; and if someone should try to make him revolt from God, he will face tortures and death. The result is he must live poor and humble, despite contumely and even torture.

CHAPTER 35
Immortality is the highest good

What then will be the value of justice and virtue, if the issue is nothing but evil? On the other hand, if virtue (which despises all earthly boons, patiently endures every kind of misfortune, and braves death itself as a duty) cannot go unrewarded, what remains save that immortality is its own reward? If a life of blessedness befalls a man, then, as philosophers insist (and this is their one point of agreement) immortality befalls him also. That alone is blessed, which is incorruptible; that alone is incorruptible, which is eternal. Immortality, therefore, is the highest good, because it is the possession of man, of mind, of virtue alone. Towards this we direct our steps; to win this we are born.

As a consequence God sets before us virtue and justice, that we may secure that eternal prize as the crown of our labours. Of immortality we shall speak later, in its appropriate place. There remains the philosophy of logic, which contributes nothing to a life of blessedness. For wisdom consists not in splendour of language but in the hearts and feelings of men. But if the philosophy of physical nature is needless, as well as the philosophy of logic, in moral philosophy—which alone is needed—philosophers have gone astray, insofar as they have been wholly unable to discover the highest good. What is the result? This, that all philosophy is found to be vain and profitless, because it has proved powerless to understand the faculties of man, or to fulfil its bounden duty and service to mankind.

CHAPTER 36
Of Epicurus and Pythagoras

I have spoken briefly about philosophy, so now I shall say something about philosophers. Primarily the teaching of Epicurus amounts to this, that there is no Providence. He does not deny the existence of gods. Both opinions are irrational. If there are gods, then there is a Providence; otherwise any idea of God is ruled out, for it is His nature and property to *fore*see. He cares for nothing, says Epicurus. In that case He cares nothing for things human or divine; how then can you assert that He exists, or explain His origin? By abolishing Providence and divine care, you ought, consequently, to deny the existence of God altogether. Instead of that, you have left Him in name, but in fact abolished Him. Whence comes Nature herself if God cares for nothing? There are, says Epicurus, tiny 'seeds', invisible and intangible; it is by their fortuitous concourse that all things have come into being, and ever do so. If they are invisible and cannot be perceived by any part of the body, how have you been able to know they exist? Again: if they exist, by what mind-force do they unite to form anything? If smooth, they cannot cohere; if furnished with hooks and angles, they can be cut off; for hooks and angles stand out. But these things are as useless as they are silly. Why does Epicurus represent souls as destructible, when he is refuted not only by all philosophers and by the conviction of mankind, but also by the answers of poets, the incantations of the Sibyls, finally by the divine utterances of the prophets? So that it is surprising that Epicurus stood alone in placing man's lot on a level with that of sheep and wild creatures.

What of Pythagoras—the first to be called a philosopher—who taught that souls were indeed immortal but that they passed into the bodies of sheep, or birds or beasts? Better, surely, that they should be extinguished, together with their bodies, than to be condemned to pass into alien bodies! better, surely, not to exist at all than, after having possessed a human shape, to live on as a pig or a dog! The foolish fellow, to win credit for his statements, declared that in the Trojan war he had himself been Euphorbus, and that, after his death, he had passed into animal shapes, finally becoming Pythagoras. Happy man! to whom alone so great a recollection was vouchsafed; or rather unhappy, who, after changing into a sheep, was not allowed to be ignorant of what he really was. Would he had been alone in his ravings! He actually found some men—men not unlearned—to believe him; these men were to be the inheritors of his folly.

CHAPTER 37
Of Socrates and his reply to objectors

After him, Socrates occupied the chief place in philosophy. He was named the wisest of mankind by an oracle, because he admitted he knew one thing only—that he knew nothing. On the strength of that oracle philosophers were obliged to keep from searching after what they could never know, or from imagining they knew what they did not know. Let us see whether Socrates was the wisest of mankind, as the Pythian deity proclaimed. He often quoted the saying that 'what is above us is no concern of ours'. He had now exceeded the bounds of knowledge, for he who declared he knew one thing (namely that he knew nothing) discovered something else to speak about, as though he did know it: but in vain. For God, who is assuredly above us, ought to be the object of our quest; and religion should be acknowledged, which alone severs us from the brutes. Now this, Socrates not only repudiated but even scorned, swearing by goose or dog—as if forsooth he could not swear by Aesculapius, to whom he had vowed a cock. Lo, a wise man's sacrifice! And because he could not offer it in person, he asked his friends, at the hour of death, to pay that vow after he was dead—doubtless to avoid being imprisoned in the underworld as a debtor! By this he assuredly proclaimed that he knew nothing, and he proved his point.

CHAPTER 38
Of Plato, who gets nearer to the truth. Zeno's errors

Socrates' disciple, Plato, called by Cicero 'the god of philosophers' was the only one who philosophized in such a way as to approximate the truth; yet, because he knew not God, he often lapsed, so that nobody has been guilty of worse errors. This is specially to be noted in the *Republic* where he expressed a wish that all men should possess all things in common. In the case of inheritances, this, though unjust, is tolerable; for it cannot be injurious if a man, thanks to his own industry, has more than his neighbour; nor can it profit him, if, through his own fault, he has less. But, as I have said, this is more or less endurable. Are even our wives and children to be held in common? If so, there will be no blood-distinction, no race certainty, no families, no close relationships; but everything becomes confused and without distinctions, as with flocks and herds; men will prove incontinent, and women immodest. What married love can there be when there is no close, no sure, affection? Who will be dutiful to his father, when he knows not his own origin? Who will love a son, if he believes him to be begotten by a stranger? Nay more: Plato threw open the senate to women, allowing them to serve in the wars, to become magistrates, and to hold military commands. How great will be the unhappiness of that city where women fill the places of men! These questions, however, I shall deal with at another time more fully.

Zeno, master of the Stoics, though he praises virtue, judged that pity (a supreme virtue) ought to be excised as a mental disease, dear though it is to God and necessary for mankind. For what man, finding himself in some misfortune, would decline to be pitied, and not rather long for the helping hand of friends to succour him; friends who are stirred, by feelings of compassion alone, to lend assistance? Though Zeno calls this feeling 'humanity' and 'dutiful conduct' he is merely changing the word, not the thing. Affection—granted only to man—is such that our weakness is alleviated by helping one another; he who robs us of it reduces us to the level of brutes. When Zeno assures us that all faults are equal, it comes from that same lack of humanity wherewith he rails at compassion as if it were a disease. One who finds no difference in faults presumes that light offences ought to be visited with heavy penalties (which is the mark of a cruel judge), or that serious offences should be visited with light penalties (the mark of a lax judge): in both cases the State suffers. If great crimes be lightly dealt with, insolence will increase, leading to yet greater crimes; if an excessive penalty be attached to light offences, many citizens (nobody being without faults) will be in peril—men who, if justly reproved, might well become better.

CHAPTER 39

On various philosophers, and of the Antipodes

These are slight matters, but they arise from the same delusion. Xenophanes declared that the moon was eighteen times bigger than the earth; that within its bosom there is another earth, inhabited by men and animals of every variety. Of the Antipodes we cannot speak or hear without derision. It is asserted, quite seriously, that people there walk with feet opposite to ours! More bearable were the absurdities of those that maintained snow was black. Not merely the words but the acts of certain folk are ridiculous. Democritus surrendered an estate bequeathed him by his father, and let it be turned into common pastureland. Diogenes, with his troop of 'dogs', while professing that perfect virtue consists in despising everything, chose to beg his bread rather than look for it by honest labour, or indeed to have property at all. Surely a wise man's life ought to be an example to others of good living. If all should copy the wisdom of such men, how will states remain standing? But perhaps these Cynics have been able to show an example of modesty, who openly had intercourse with their wives. I do not know how they could defend virtue when they dispensed with any sense of decency. Aristippus was no better; he, I believe, to please his mistress Laïs, established the Cyrenaic school, instructing his followers to place the highest good in bodily pleasure, to lend authority to his faults or to learn his vices. Are these men to be approved the more who, in order to be spoken about as despisers of death, committed suicide—Zeno, Empedocles, Chrysippus, Cleanthes, Democritus, and their imitator Cato? They did not consider that to take one's own life was to be guilty of murder, according to God's ordinance. For God gave us this temporal abode of the body that we should dwell in it for as long as He willed. We must then deem it a sin to wish to depart without the command of God. Violence ought not to be done to Nature: God alone knows how to undo His work. If anyone lays irreligious hands on that work and disrupts the bonds of divine workmanship, he is trying to escape from God, whose sentence no man can evade, living or dead. They are, then, heinous and criminals (I have given their names above) who have taught reasons for a voluntary death; but it was not crime enough that they themselves were self-murderers: they instructed others also to commit the same sin.

CHAPTER 40

On the folly of philosophers

Innumerable are the sayings and doings of philosophers, amply enough to refute their folly. Since I cannot number all their follies, a handful will suffice to enable us to realize that the philosophers were no teachers of justice (of which they were ignorant), no teachers of virtue (to which they falsely laid claim). What can *they* teach who so often confess their own ignorance? (I leave Socrates out of the count: his opinion is familiar.) Anaxagoras affirms that all things are cloaked in darkness; Empedocles that the road to discover the truth of the senses is narrow. Democritus assures us that truth lies deep down in a well; and, because these men can never find it, they maintain that, so far, nobody has even been wise. Since, then, human wisdom does not exist —Socrates says so in Plato—let us follow after divine wisdom, and thank God who has revealed it, and delivered it, to us; and let us congratulate ourselves that, by the mercy of God, we possess both truth and wisdom, which, though sought by so many wits through so many centuries, no philosophy has been able to discover.

CHAPTER 41

Of true religion as contrasted with the false

Now, as we have refuted false religion, which deals with the worship of false gods, and the false wisdom which is embodied in philosophy, let us approach true religion and wisdom. And indeed we must speak of them conjointly, because they are combined. To worship the true God, that, and that alone, is wisdom. God is the Supreme Creator of all things, who has formed man in His own likeness; consequently to him alone of all creatures has He given reason, that he might render honour to Him as Father and fear Him as Lord, and by affection and obedience be rewarded with immortality. Such is the true, the divine, mystery. For the philosophers, because to them these doctrines are untrue, harmony there is none. In philosophy no holy rites are celebrated, nor does philosophy deal with holy things; hence its religion is a false one, because it lacks wisdom; and its wisdom is false because it lacks religion. But where they are joined together, there the truth must be; so that if the question is asked, what is truth? the right reply should be this: a wise religion, or a religious wisdom.

CHAPTER 42
Of religious wisdom: Christ as the Son of God from the beginning

I shall now explain the proper meaning of wise religion or religious wisdom. In the beginning God, before making the world, from the well-spring of His eternity and from His divine and eternal spirit, begat for Himself a Son, incorruptible, and faithfully corresponding to the excellence and majesty of his Father. He is excellent, he is reason, he is the Word of God, he is wisdom. With him as fashioner, as Hermes says; with him as counsellor, as the Sibyl says, God contrived the splendid and glorious fabric of this world. Of all the angels—whom the same God formed from His own breath—the Son alone shared in the supreme power, he alone was called God. Through him all things were made, and apart from him nothing. Plato spoke of a first and a second God, speaking not as a philosopher but a seer, perhaps following Trismegistus in this, whose words I translate from the Greek, and append here: 'The Lord and Maker of all, whom we rightly call God, created a second God, who could be seen and felt. I say "could be felt", not because he is the recipient of feeling but because he causes it, and sight likewise. When the supreme God had created him the first, the only, the One, he appeared unto the Father as supereminently good, and filled with all things good.' The (Erythraean) Sibyl also says that God, the guide of all, was created by God; and another of the Sibyls declared that God, the Son, must be known (as is shown by examples set forth in my books). The prophets, divinely inspired, foretold him, especially Solomon in the Book of Wisdom; and so did his father, David, a writer of heavenly hymns. Both these were famous kings, who antedated the Trojan war by 180 years; they bear witness that he was born of God. His name no man knows, save himself and the Father, as John tells us in the Apocalypse. Hermes says that his name cannot be uttered by human lips. Yet by mankind he is called by two names, Jesus (that is, Saviour), because he is the saving health of all who, through him, believe in God; Christ, because he will himself come down from heaven at the close of this age, to judge the world and, after the dead have been raised, to found a kingdom that shall have no end.

CHAPTER 43
Of the name of Christ and his two-fold nativity

To avoid possible doubt on your side why we call him Jesus, who was born of God before the world was, born of woman 300 years ago, I shall give you the reason. This same Jesus is both Son of God, and Son of Man. He was twice born. First, born of God, ere the world arose; then born in the flesh, during the reign of Augustus. This is a grand and splendid mystery, which involves man's salvation, the religion of the Supreme Deity, and all truth. When impious observances crept in through the craft of daemons, then the religion of the true God rested with the Hebrews, who, ruled by no law but following the custom of their ancestors, kept the form of worship received through succeeding generations until they came out of Egypt, under the leadership of Moses, the first of all the prophets, through whom the Law was imposed upon them by God. Afterwards they came to be called Jews. They served God, therefore, bound by legal chains. But these Jews, straying to profane rites, adopted alien deities, and, abandoning the worship of their sires, sacrificed to senseless idols. So God sent them prophets, filled with a divine spirit, to upbraid them for their sins and to enjoin repentance; to warn them of retribution to follow and to threaten them that, if they persisted in the same sins, He would send yet another prophet, bearer of a new ordinance, and, depriving an unthankful race of their inheritance, would gather to Himself a more faithful people from among the Gentiles. But they not only persisted in their offences, but slew those preachers who were sent. For these iniquities He condemned them, and sent no more prophets to a stiff-necked generation but sent His own Son, to summon all mankind to the grace and mercy of God. Nevertheless, ungodly and ungrateful though they were, He would not exclude them from hope of salvation. Specially He sent His Son, that if perchance they obeyed, they might not lose what they had been given; but if they refused to accept their God, then, the heirs being excluded, the Gentiles should inherit. So the Supreme Father bade His Son to come down to the Earth and take upon him a human body, that, being subject to sufferings of the flesh, he might teach mankind lessons of virtue and of patience, not in words only but in deeds. Therefore Jesus was reborn as man, born of a pure virgin, without a father, so that, as in his first spiritual nativity—being born of God alone—he became a sacred spirit, so now, in his second fleshly nativity, born of a mother only, he might become holy flesh; that, through him, flesh, which had been subject to sin, might be freed from ruin.

CHAPTER 44

The two-fold birth of Jesus foretold in Scripture

The Prophets, as I have explained, foretold that these things would take place. In Solomon we find these words: 'A virgin has conceived, and become a mother in deep pity.' Isaiah wrote thus: 'Lo, a virgin will conceive and bear a son, and his name shall be called Immanuel', that is, God is with us. For he lived with us on earth, when he took upon him flesh; yet was he God in man, and man in God. It was foretold by the prophets that he would be both. That he was God is proclaimed by Isaiah: 'they will adore thee and make prayers unto thee, for God is in thee, and we knew it not—the God of Israel. All they shall be confounded and stand in awe who are thy foes; all enemies will be brought to confusion.' Jeremiah, too, says: 'He is our God, and none shall be accounted of beside Him, who hath found out all the way of wisdom, and hath given it to Jacob his son and to Israel his beloved. Afterwards he was seen in the world, and had his habitation among men.' That he was man we are told by Jeremiah: 'He is man, and who hath known him?' Isaiah, too, spoke as follows: 'The Lord Jehovah shall send them a man, who will be our salvation, and with judgement will he heal them.'

Moses also in the book of Numbers says: 'a Star will arise out of Jacob, and a man out of Israel'. Though he was God, he took upon him our flesh, that, as Mediator between God and men, he might, by conquest over death, by his authority bring man to God.

CHAPTER 45

Of the power and works of Christ, as proved by the Scriptures

We have spoken of the birth of Jesus; now let us speak of his virtue and his doings, for, when he was working majestic miracles among his fellow-men, the Jews, watching them, considered they were wrought by magic, not knowing that all things done by him had been predicted in prophecy. Those that were sick and vexed by various diseases he forthwith strengthened by the might of his word; the weak he restored to health, the lame he set upon their feet, to the blind he gave sight, to the dumb the power to speak and the deaf to hear; the unclean he cleansed; those that were beset by daemons he brought back to sanity; the dead, or those already buried, he summoned to life and light. He fed five thousand with five loaves and two fishes. He walked on the sea, and, during a tempest, rebuked the wind and bade it be still: suddenly there was a great calm. All these wonders we find foretold in Prophets and Sibylline oracles. When a great multitude gathered around him, believing him to be (as he was) the Son of God, and sent by God, the priests, filled with envy, together with the rulers of the Jews, stirred by anger because he inveighed against their sins and injustice, met to slay him. Solomon, in the Book of Wisdom, had declared, rather more than 1,000 years before, that these things would happen, and wrote thus: 'Let us lie in wait for the righteous man because he is hateful to us, and upbraideth us for transgressing the law. He professeth to have knowledge of God, and calleth himself the Son of God. He hath become to us a reproof of our thoughts; he is grievous for us even to behold, because his life is unlike other men's and his ways are strange. We were accounted by him as triflers; he abstaineth from our ways as from uncleanness, and the latter end of the righteous he counts a better lot, vaunting that God is his Father. Let us see if his words be true, and try what his end will be. Let us put him to the test with contumely and torment, that we may learn his meekness and prove his patience. Let us condemn him to a death of shame. Thus they reasoned, and did greatly err, for their own foolishness blinded them. As for the mysteries of God, they knew them not.'

Forgetting these words that they read, the Jews goaded the populace as though Jesus were an enemy of religion. They laid hold of him and led him to judgement, crying out with evil voices that he should be put to death. They counted it a crime because he called himself the Son of God; because, by healing sick folk on the Sabbath, he was breaking the law which he told them he was not breaking but fulfilling. When Pilate (at that time procurator in Syria) saw that his cause did not concern the office of a Roman judge, he sent him to Herod, and allowed the Jews to be themselves judges of their own law; and they, after receiving power to punish his guilt, nailed him to the cross. But first they scourged him and smote him with their hands, crowned him with thorns, spat upon his face, gave him gall and vinegar to taste; yet amid all this he spoke never a word. Then the executioners, having parted his tunic and cloak by lot, nailed him to the cross, though the next day the Passover, the Jewish festival, was to be kept. This crime was followed by miraculous events, that the sin they had committed might be known. For at the moment when he gave up the ghost, there was a great earthquake, and the sun was darkened so that day was turned to night.

CHAPTER 46

The sufferings and death of Jesus foretold by the prophets

All these things were foretold by the prophets. Isaiah says: 'I am not stubborn, nor set myself against any; I gave my back to the scourges, and my cheeks to the smiters; I turned not my face from foul spitting.' The same prophet speaks thus of the silence of Jesus: 'He was brought as a sheep to the slaughter; and, as a lamb before its shearers is dumb, so he opened not his mouth.' David, in the 34th psalm,[1] wrote: 'The scourges were gathered against me, and they knew me not; they were scattered, they put me to the test, they felt no pity, and ground their teeth.' David says, concerning food and drink, in the 68th psalm[2]: 'They gave me gall for food, and in my thirst vinegar to drink.' And of the cross of Christ: 'They pierced my hands and my feet; they counted all my bones; they stared and looked upon me; they parted my garments among them, and upon my vesture they cast lots.' Moses says in Deuteronomy: 'My life shall hang in doubt before thine eyes, and thou shalt be afraid day and night, and shall have no assurance of thy life.' Also, in the book of Numbers: 'God is not holden in doubt as a man, nor doth He endure threats, as the son of man.' Zachariah also says: 'They shall look upon me whom they pierced.' Amos, speaking of an eclipse of the sun, says: 'In that day, saith the Lord, the sun shall set at midday, and the daylight shall be darkened; and I will

[1] In our versions the 35th.
[2] = 69th.

turn your festal days into mourning and your songs into lamentation.' Jeremiah also speaks of Jerusalem where Jesus suffered: 'For her, the sun hath set when it was still midday; she hath been confounded and cursed: her remnants I will put to the sword.' These words were not in vain. After a brief while the Emperor Vespasian overwhelmed the Jews, and ravaged their lands with fire and sword, besieged and subdued them by famine, destroyed Jerusalem, took the captives in triumph, laid an interdict on the residue, forbidding them at any time to return to their native soil. All this was accomplished by God, on account of Christ's crucifixion, even as He declared to Solomon in the Jewish scriptures: 'Israel shall be destroyed, and become a reproach among the peoples, and this house be desolate; and everyone that passes through it will marvel, saying: Why hath the Lord done these evils to this land and to this house? Then will it be said: Because they forsook the Lord their God, and persecuted their king whom God loved, and crucified him with great humiliation; therefore hath the Lord brought upon them these evils.' For what do they not deserve, who slew their Lord, who had come for their salvation?

CHAPTER 47

Of the Resurrection, the sending of the Apostles, and the Ascension

After his crucifixion, Jesus was taken down from the Cross, and laid in a tomb. But, on the third day, before daybreak, there was an earthquake; the stone with which the sepulchre had been closed was rolled away, and he arose. But in the sepulchre nothing was found but his garments. Now the prophets had long ago foretold that he would rise on the third day. David, in the 15th psalm,[1] had said, 'Thou wilt not leave my soul in Hades, nor wilt thou suffer Thine Holy One to see corruption.' So also Hosea: 'This my Son is wise; wherefore he will not now continue in the tribulation of his sons, and I shall rescue him from the hand of the powers beneath. O death, where is thy judgement, where is thy sharp goad?' And again: 'After two days He will revive us on the third day.' So after his resurrection he departed to Galilee, gathering together his disciples, whom fear had turned to flight;

---

[1] = 16th in our versions.

and after giving them commands which he wished to be kept, and having ordained that the gospel should be preached throughout the whole world, he breathed into them the Holy Spirit, and gave them power to work miracles, that they might work for the salvation of mankind by deeds as well as words. Then, at length, on the fortieth day, he was taken up in a cloud and returned to his Father. This, Daniel the prophet had long since put forth: 'I beheld in a vision of the night, and lo, one like unto a son of man coming in the clouds of heaven! And he came unto the Ancient of Days, and those that were standing near presented him. And there was given to him a kingdom, and honour, and authority; and all peoples, tribes, and tongues shall serve him; and his power is for everlasting, which will never pass away, and his kingdom shall never be brought to nought.' Likewise David, in the 109th psalm[1]: 'The Lord said unto my lord: sit at my right hand, until I put thine enemies as the footstool of thy feet.'

CHAPTER 48

Of the disinheriting of the Jews and the adoption of the Gentiles

Since, then, he is sitting at God's right hand, destined to tread under foot his enemies who crucified him, when he comes to judge the world, it is clear that no hope is left the Jews, unless they repent and, washed clean of the blood with which they have polluted themselves, begin to hope in him whom they denied. Esdras therefore says: 'This Passover is our Saviour and our refuge. Bethink you and let it ascend unto your hearts, since we have to humiliate him in symbol; hereafter we shall hope in him.' The Scriptures prove that the Jews have been disinherited, because they rejected Christ, and that we, who are of the Gentiles, have been adopted in their room. Jeremiah says: 'I have forsaken my house, I have cast off my heritage into the hands of her enemies. My heritage is become unto me as a lion in the forest; she hath uttered her voice against me; therefore I have hated her.' Malachi also: 'I have no pleasure in you, said Jehovah, neither will I accept an offering at your hands. For, from the rising of the sun until its setting, my name will be renowned among the nations.' Isaiah says also: 'I come to gather together all peoples and tongues; they shall come and behold my glory.' The same

---

[1] = 110th.

prophet, speaking in the character of the Father to the Son, says: 'I, Jehovah, have called thee to righteousness, and will hold thy hand, and will strengthen thee; and I have given thee for a covenant of my people, for a light of the nations, to open the eyes of the blind, to set free the prisoners from their chains, and them that sit in darkness out of the prison house.'

CHAPTER 49
The unity of God

If, then, the Jews were rejected by God, as the Scriptures testify, but the Gentiles were brought in (as we see), and freed from the darkness of this earthly life and from daemonic chains, the issue is this: no other hope is set before men unless they follow after true religion and true wisdom, which are found in Christ. He that knows not Christ is for ever alienated from truth and from God. Neither Jews nor philosophers must plume themselves concerning the Supreme God. He who acknowledges not the Son cannot acknowledge the Father. This is wisdom, this the mystery of God. It is through the Son that God has willed it that He should be acknowledged and worshipped. For this reason He sent forth prophets aforetime, to foretell his advent, that, when all former predictions had been accomplished in him, he might be believed in by mankind as God, and the Son of God. Yet it must not be imagined that there are two Gods: Father and Son are *one*. For since the Father loves the Son, and assigns all things to him, and since the Son loyally obeys the Father, and wills only what He wills, so great a fellowship cannot be disrupted, so that they can be spoken of as two, in whom substance and will and faith are one—the Son through the Father, the Father through the Son. One honour must be paid to both, as to one God; and it must be so divided through two worships that the very division may be overcome by a bond that cannot be broken. Nothing will be left to him who divides the Father from the Son, or the Son from the Father.

CHAPTER 50
Why God assumed a human body and suffered death

It is left to me to answer those also who think it unsuitable and contrary to reason that God should assume a human body; that he should be subject to men; that he should suffer insults, nay tortures even, and death. I shall give my views, and, as best I can, touch upon a vast subject in a few words. He who teaches anything ought, I hold, himself to do what he teaches, by way of constraining people to obey. Otherwise he will diminish all confidence in his precepts. Examples are needed to strengthen those precepts; and if anyone contemptuously declares that this is impossible, the teacher may convince him by the actual facts. No doctrinal system, then, is perfect when handed down only by words; it becomes perfect when fulfilled by deeds.

Since Christ, therefore, was sent to mankind to teach virtue, he was surely bound to teach and act, that his doctrine might be made perfect. But if he had not put on the body of a man, he could not have practised what he taught—namely, not to be wrathful, not to hanker after wealth, not to be fired with lust, not to fear pain, to despise death. These are clearly virtues, but are impossible apart from flesh. Therefore he was furnished with a body, that, inasmuch as he taught that the lusts of the flesh must be conquered, he might be the first to carry this out, to prevent anyone alleging the weakness of the flesh as an excuse.

CHAPTER 51

The mystery of the cross of Christ

I shall now speak of the mystery of the cross that no one may say: If he had to undergo death, surely it should have been no base and dishonourable death but one possessing something honourable. I know, indeed, that many, abhorring the word 'cross', shrink from the truth, though in the cross there abides great reason and might. For as he had been sent to open the pathway to salvation for the very humblest, he humbled himself in order to set them free. He endured this form of death, which is wont to be laid upon the humble, that all might be given the power to imitate him. Besides this, as he was to rise again, it was not right that his body should be mutilated, or a bone broken, a thing which happens to those on whom capital punishment is inflicted. The cross, therefore, was chosen, for it preserved the body for resurrection, with the bones unharmed. Add to this the fact that, as he had submitted to suffering and death, it was fitting that he should be lifted up. Thus the cross exalted him both in fact and symbol, so that his majesty and excellence, along with the suffering itself, was known to all. Inasmuch as he extended his arms on the cross, he assuredly stretched out his wings eastward and westward, beneath which all nations, from both sides of the world, might meet and find rest.

How wonderful this sign is, and how great its power, is obvious from the fact that the entire host of daemons is driven out and put to flight by this sign. And just as he himself, before he suffered, routed the daemons by the word of his power, so now, by the name and sign of his suffering, the same foul spirits, when they have crept into men's bodies, are driven out; racked and tortured, and admitting themselves to be daemons, they yield themselves to the chastisement of God. What then can the Greeks hope for, from their religions and with all their wisdom, when they see that their own gods, whom they allow to be daemons also, are triumphed over by men through the cross?

CHAPTER 52

Of the hope of salvation that is in the acknowledgement of the true God; and of the hatred of the heathen against Christians

Mankind, then, have but one hope in life, one port of safety, one refuge of freedom, if, abandoning the errors by which they are enslaved, they open the eyes of the mind and recognize God (in whom alone is found the home of truth), despising the things of this world, counting philosophy (which, in the thought of God, is folly) as nothing, and thus adopting the true wisdom—that is, religion—and by such means becoming heirs of immortality.

But, in fact, they are not opposing truth but their own safety; and, when they hear all these things, they hate them as an unforgivable crime. They refuse even to listen; they fancy their ears are violated by an act of sacrilege if they do listen; no longer do they abstain from cursings, but harass their opponents with all scornful words; and these same men, once they secure power, persecute them as public enemies—nay more than enemies—for there is neither death nor slavery nor any more torture awaiting a foe, once arms are surrendered; although they deserved every penalty who even wished to act thus: even amid sword-points clemency has its place. It is unheard-of cruelty when innocence is refused terms granted even to a vanquished foe. What is the cause of this fury? Presumably it is because they cannot contend on the basis of reason that they press their case with violence, and, without understanding the matter in dispute, condemn as criminals those who have refused to rely upon innocence itself. They are not satisfied should those whom they hate so unreasonably die a quick and simple death; no, they mangle them with exquisite tortures, to glut their hatred, which is brought about not by some grave fault but by the truth, which is ever hateful to evil livers. They take it amiss that some men are displeased with their evil deeds. These are they whom they long to destroy, no matter how, that they may be enabled to sin freely, without a witness.

CHAPTER 53
Reasons for hating Christians refuted

Our opponents to-day say they do this by way of defending their deities. First: if gods they be, and possess divinity and power, they need none to defend or plead for them: they can clearly defend themselves. How can we expect gods to defend us if they cannot avenge wrongs done to themselves? It is vain folly to want to defend gods, unless, as a result of this, we evidently mistrust them. For he who undertakes to plead for the god he worships admits that such a god is valueless; but, if he worships because he believes that God is powerful, surely he ought not to wish to defend one by whom he ought himself to be defended. So we act rightly. For when those defenders of false gods, rebels against the True, persecute His name in us, we do not attack in deed or word, but in gentleness and patience bear whatever cruelties are devised against us. For we have confidence in God, by whom we expect to be avenged forthwith. This is no idle confidence. We partly know, partly have seen, what a miserable end awaits these sinners. No man has ever offended God without paying the penalty; but he that has refused to learn through the *word* who the true God is, has learned this through his own *punishment*. I should like to know, when men force the unwilling to sacrifice, what reason they entertain by so doing, or to whom they are presenting that offering. If to the gods, that is no worship, nor an acceptable sacrifice, which is wrested from them by wrongdoing, and extorted by suffering. If men act through compulsion, clearly no benefit accrues; who would accept such a benefit? he would sooner die! If that be a good thing to which you summon me, why invite me with evil? why with blows instead of words? why with physical torments and not by dint of reasoning? Obviously that is evil to which you do not entice me in *accord* with my will, but hale me *against* my will. What folly it is to trust a man against his will! Tell me: does anyone try, under pressure of misfortunes, to flee towards death? Can you, if you wrench away the sword, or break the net, or drag a man back from a precipice, or spill the poison-draught—can you, I say, boast yourself as that man's preserver, when he (whom you imagine you have saved) offers you no thanks, but thinks you have done him an ill turn? And that, because you have hindered him from dying as he wished, and because you have not allowed him to reach his end, and to rest from his labours? A blessing should be weighed not by the quality of the thing itself, but by the wishes of the receiver. Why count what is a crime to me as a blessing? You want me to worship your gods, a thing I regard as bringing death to myself. If it is a good thing, I envy it not. Enjoy your blessings alone, by yourself. There is no need to support my error, which I have adopted by my own deliberate judgement and wish; if it is an evil thing, why force me to partake in evil? 'Make use of the lot that is yours.' I prefer to die in a good cause rather than live in an evil one.

CHAPTER 54

Of religious freedom, and the cruelty of the persecutors

All this may be said with justice. But who will listen when angry and violent men think their supremacy is being diminished if freedom be granted in human affairs? And yet it is religion alone in which liberty has established her dwelling place. Beyond everything else religion is a matter of free choice, nor can anyone be compelled to worship what he dislikes. Freedom may perhaps be pretended, but never wished. Whenever some, overcome by fear of torture, or mastered by agony, have consented to offer detestable sacrifice, they never do of their own accord what necessity has forced upon them; but, once they are given the opportunity, on liberty being restored they revert to God, and placate Him with tears and supplications, repenting not of the will which they had not, but of the compulsion to which they were subject. Nor is forgiveness denied when they offer due satisfaction. What does he gain who defiles the body, since the will he cannot change? But persecutors, void of understanding, if they have driven some strong man to offer libations to their gods, exult insolently, with amazing speed, rejoicing as if they had sent a foe beneath the yoke.

If, however, someone, terrified neither by threats nor torments, prefers his faith to his life, against such a man cruelty puts forth all its strength, contrives torture unspeakable, unbearable; and just because it is known that death for God's sake is glorious, and that victory consists in rising superior to torment, and in laying down life itself for faith and religion—why, then, these men too strive to win a victory. Not by death do they afflict us, but devise new and unheard of cruelties, to compel human frailty to succumb to bodily anguish. Should this fail, they defer things; they apply to wounds every care, that reiterated torture may increase the pain in scars still raw, plying the rack against the innocent. They actually consider themselves pious, just, and religious (for with such rites their gods are well pleased), while they speak of the martyrs as impious and beyond remedy. What perversity is this, to call an innocent and tortured victim a desperate and impious creature, while the tormentor is called just and pious!

CHAPTER 55

The heathen regard the loyal following of God as impiety

It is said that men are rightly and deservedly punished who revile the religious observances of the State, which have been handed down by their ancestors. What if those ancestors were fools in adopting vain rites (as we have already shown), are *we* to be hindered from pursuing a true and a better course? Why abandon our liberty and become slaves to alien errors, as though we were sold to them? Allow us to be wise and to search after truth. Yet, should they elect to defend ancestral religions, why are the Egyptians exempt, who worship cattle and creatures of every kind as deities? Why do actors on the comic stage ridicule the gods themselves? and why is he honoured who has mocked these gods with the greater wit? Why are philosophers listened to, when they affirm either that there are no gods, or that, if they do exist, they have no care or regard for human affairs, or argue that there is no providential order in the world? Of all mankind those alone are judged irreligious who follow after God's truth! Since this truth is both justice and wisdom, these men brand it as a crime, counting it irreligion or folly; they obviously do not understand the nature of what is deceiving them, when they call evil good, and good evil. Many philosophers, particularly Plato and Aristotle, have spoken much about justice, asserting and extolling that virtue in laudatory terms, on the ground that it gives to each his due, because it promotes equity everywhere; and since all other virtues are silent, and kept shut within us, they hold that justice is the one quality that is not devoted to its own interests, and is not secret, but openly walks abroad and is keen to benefit and help as many people as possible —as though forsooth justice should belong to judges alone and to those in high power and place, and not to all men everywhere!

Nevertheless there is no one, not even among the weak or poor, who is without a sense of justice. But because they did not know its character, its source, or its sphere of activity, those philosophers assigned to but few this supreme virtue (namely the universal Good) declaring that its object was no special advantage for itself but solely for the advantage of others. Not without good grounds did Carneades—a man of great insight and intelligence —stand forth to refute such doctrines and to overturn a justice that had no solid foundation; not because he felt it should be disparaged but to demonstrate that its defenders had no fixed or sure principles on which to base an argument.

CHAPTER 56

Concerning justice, which is worship of the true God

If justice is worship of the true God (for what is so just in equity, so faithful in honour, so necessary for salvation as to recognize God as Father, to reverence Him as Lord, and to obey His law and behests?), then philosophers have not known justice, because they have neither recognized God Himself nor kept loyal to His worship and law. For that reason they might have been refuted by Carneades, whose argument was this: 'There is no natural right or justice, and so all living creatures, at the bidding of Nature herself, defend their own interests; and, as a result, if justice consults the interests of others, but neglects its own, it ought to be called folly. But if all nations that hold sovran sway, and if the Romans themselves, who dominate the world, desire to follow justice, and to render to each what they have won by force of arms, they will be returning to primitive conditions and to poverty. Were this done we should be obliged to count as fools, though just, those who, in order to benefit others, contrive to harm themselves. Hence if we should find anyone prepared, through a blunder, to sell gold for brass, silver for lead; and if necessity should compel the purchase, will he dissemble and buy at a low price, or will he rather point the matter out? If he does, he will be called just because he practised no deceit; but he will be a fool for enriching another to his own loss. Judgement, where a loss is concerned, is easy. Suppose a man's life is in peril, so that the alternative is whether to slay or be slain, what course is he to adopt? It may happen that, in a shipwreck, a man finds some feeble person clinging to a plank; or his army has been defeated and, during his flight, he may discover a wounded comrade riding a horse: is he to drag the one from his plank, the other from his horse, to enable himself to get away safely? If he wants to be just, he will not do it, but he will be deemed a fool; for in sparing another's life, he gives up his own. By such an act, he will appear to be wise indeed, because he will be consulting his own interests; but he will also appear base, because he will be perpetrating a wrong.'

CHAPTER 57
Of wisdom and of foolishness

A clear-sighted view, this of Carneades; but a reply is easily given. It is the change of names that makes it appear so. Justice has the semblance of folly, but it is not folly; and ill-will has the semblance of wisdom, without the reality. Just as this ill-will, clever in maintaining its own interests (and shrewd too), is not wisdom, but craftiness and subtlety; even so justice should not be termed folly but innocence; inasmuch as a just man is bound to be wise, and a fool unjust. Neither reason nor nature allows the just man to be unwise, since the just does only what is right and good, and always shuns what is depraved and wicked. Who can discern between good and evil, depravity and correct conduct, except the wise? A fool does wrong because he knows not what good and evil are; he sins because he confuses right and wrong.

Justice, then, is unsuited to a foolish man, and wisdom to an unjust man. He is not a fool who does not pull the shipwrecked man from his plank, or the wounded man from his horse; and that, because he has refrained from doing him an injury—which is a sinful act; and a wise man will shun sin. That, at first sight, he appears to be foolish arises from the fact that philosophers imagine the soul to perish along with the body; consequently they ascribe all advantages to the present life. If death ends everything, surely he is acting foolishly who spares another's life at the cost of his own, or who consults another's gain rather than his own. If death extinguishes the soul, we must do our best to live all the longer and the happier; but, if death is followed by a life of eternal blessedness, the just and wise man will assuredly scorn this corporeal life along with this world's goods, knowing what sort of reward he will receive at the hands of God. Therefore let us hold fast to innocency, hold fast to justice, submit to the semblance of folly, that we may possess true wisdom. If some men think it stupid folly to choose torment and death sooner then offer libations to gods, and by so doing escape unharmed, let us at least with all virtue and patience endeavour to show fidelity towards God. Let no death alarm us, nor pain break down our resolution; rather let us preserve, unshaken, both strength of mind and constancy. They may call us fools, while they are themselves utter fools, blind and stupid, like the beasts; such men do not comprehend how deadly it is to abandon the living God, and bow down in adoration before earthly objects, knowing not that eternal punishment awaits those who have worshipped senseless idols; whereas those that have braved torture and death for the worship and honour of the true God shall win everlasting life. This is faith at its highest; this is true wisdom, this is perfect justice. It is no concern of ours what poor foolish men think. We must await God's judgement, that hereafter we may judge those who now inflict judgement upon us.

CHAPTER 58

Of the true worship of God, and sacrifice

I have described the character of justice. I must now demonstrate what true sacrifice to God implies, in what the right ritual in worship consists, to prevent any from supposing that sacrificial victims, incense, or costly gifts are longed after by God, who knows neither hunger nor thirst nor cold nor desire of earthly objects, and so has no use at all for offerings in temples to deities of clay; but as corporeal sacrifices are needed for corporeal deities, so indeed an incorporeal offering is required for an incorporeal God. He Himself needs not things He has granted for man's use, since the whole Universe is under His domination. He needs no temple, whose dwelling place is the Universe; He needs no image, who is invisible and beyond all our understanding; He needs no earthly lights who has kindled the light of sun and stars for man's use. What then does God ask of mankind save a worship of the mind, a worship both pure and holy? The workmanship of men's hands, that which is outside of man, is foolish, weak and unthankworthy. True sacrifice is fetched not from a box but from the heart, and such sacrifice is made not by the hand but the mind. That victim is worthy of acceptance which the mind freely sacrifices. Sacrificed victims, sweet odours, silver and gold, precious jewels—what value have these, if the worshipper's mind is impure? Righteousness alone is what God seeks after. It is there that sacrifice and the true worship of God are to be found. Concerning these matters I have now to speak, and show the sphere wherein justice and righteousness must, of necessity, operate.

CHAPTER 59

Of life, and its ways, in the early history of the world

That there are two ways in human life was not unknown either to philosophers or poets; both brought them to notice in divers fashions. The philosophers determined that one road was that of diligence, the other of idleness—an incorrect view, because they referred these to the blessings of this life alone. The poets were wiser: they said that the one way was that of the just, the other of the unjust; but they err in maintaining that these roads do not belong to this life but to the underworld. We have a truer belief, for we hold that the one way is that of life, the other of death; that these two ways are here, that the right hand way by which the just walk, leads not to Elysium but to Heaven; for the just become immortal. The left hand way leads to Tartarus, because the unjust are doomed to everlasting torments. We, then, must keep to the way of justice, leading to life. Now it is the primary business of justice to recognize God as ever present, to fear Him as our Master, to love Him as our Father. He that has made us, breathed into us the breath of life, who nurtures and holds us in His keeping, not only as Father but Master, has the right of chastening us, in whose hands is the power of life and death. Hence men are bound to yield Him a twofold honour, namely their love and fear. The second duty is to recognize our fellow man as a brother. For if the same God made us and begat men on equal terms for righteousness and for life eternal, surely we are linked together by ties of brotherly affection; he who will not admit this is unjust. But the cause of this evil whereby human society and the bond of amity are broken, comes from ignorance of the true nature of God. Anyone who knows not that well-spring of loving kindness cannot, on any terms, be counted good.

Ever since a multitude of deities began to be honoured and worshipped by mankind, justice (so the poets tell us) was put to flight; every covenant was annulled, the bonds of human society snapped. Everybody thought but of his own interests, made might the measure of right, injured his neighbour, defrauded, enlarged his own comfort at the expense of others, spared neither kindred, nor children, nor parents, prepared poison cups for murder, waylaid men by force of arms, infested the sea with piracy, gave free course to lust wherever passion led him; in fact, deemed nothing sacred which his unspeakable greed did not violate. Consequently men established laws for the common good, to protect one another meanwhile from wrongs. But fear of the laws did not crush out crime, though it checked unrestrained freedom; for, though legal enactments could punish offences, they could not punish conscience. So what was once done openly now began to be done in secret. Laws were evaded, seeing that the ministers of those laws were corrupted and bribed; or else they sold judgement to set free evil doers and ruin the innocent. Add to all this, discord, war, plunderings; and, the laws once overthrown, the forces of violence usurped without let or hindrance.

CHAPTER 60

Of justice and its duties

In this condition of human affairs God had pity on us by revealing Himself to us, that in Him we might learn religion, faith, chastity, compassion; that, casting off the error of our former life, we might know our own selves (whom irreligion had alienated from God) and might adopt that divine law which united the human and the celestial, delivered by the Lord Himself, and so be rescued from those snares in which we were all entangled, along with vain and wicked superstitions. The obligations to our fellow men are set forth in that same law which teaches that whatever you render to your fellows is rendered to God. But the taproot of justice and the entire foundation of equity consists in not doing to another what you would not endure yourself, measuring your own feelings by those of your neighbour. If it is bitter to tolerate a wrong, and the doer appears unjust, transfer to another what you are yourself feeling, and to yourself what you judge concerning another; you will then understand that you are acting as unjustly if you hurt another as another if he hurts you. If we ponder this, we shall hold fast to innocence, which is the first stepping-stone of justice. The first stone is 'hurt not'; the next 'be helpful'. And as in untilled fields, before you sow the seed, you must pluck up the briars and cut away all roots and stumps before you can cleanse the tilths; so it is with our own souls; first extirpate the vices, then implant the virtues, from which the fruits of immortality sown by the word of God may spring.

CHAPTER 61

Concerning human passions

There exist three passions or, if I may say so, three furies that cause such commotions in man's minds, and at times bring such pressure to bear, that they tolerate no regard for their personal honour or safety. For instance, anger longs for revenge; desire for gain hankers after wealth; lust aims at pleasure. These vices must be strenuously resisted; these evil roots must be dug up, to allow virtues to be planted in their room. The Stoics suppose that they should be clean cut off, the Peripatetics that they should be curbed. Neither party is right, because the passions cannot be removed wholly, for, being implanted by nature, they have good and sure reasons for being what they are; nor can they be lessened, since, if they are evil, men must do without them even when kept within due bounds. If, on the other hand, they are good, they must be used in their entirety. Now *we* assert that they should neither be withdrawn nor diminished. They are not of themselves evil things, for God has planted them in man with good reason; yet though good by nature—since they are given to protect life—they become evil through ill use of them. Just as courage, if you be fighting for your fatherland, is a good thing, if against it, an evil thing; so too the passions, if put to a good purpose, will be virtues; if to bad uses, they will be termed vices. Anger has been given us for the checking of offences; that is, it is meant to discipline those in subjection, that fear may repress licence and control insolence. Those who are ignorant of its limitations are angry with their equals, even with their superiors. Consequently men burst out into dreadful crimes, rise up to kill, and wage wars. A desire for gain has been granted, that we may seek earnestly for life's necessities; but those who know not its limits are insatiable in their desire to pile up riches. Hence break out poisonings, fraudulent dealings, false wills—in fact every kind of deception. Lust itself is inborn that we may beget children; but 'those that overpass its limitations employ it for mere pleasure alone. What is the result? illicit loves, adulteries, fornication, and every sort of corruptness. The passions need to be controlled and directed aright; then, even when men are ardent, they cannot be charged with guilt.

CHAPTER 62

Our duty to hold in check all sensual desires and wrong ambitions

We must restrain anger when suffering a wrong, that the evil may be crushed which a contest threatens, and that we may cling to those two mightiest of virtues, innocence and patience. Avarice must be broken when we possess a sufficiency. What madness is it to toil in piling up wealth which, through robbery, theft, confiscation, or death, must pass to others! Lust must not step beyond the marriage bed, but serve for the begetting of children.

Too great an appetite for pleasure is perilous and causes disgrace, and (what is mainly to be guarded against) incurs everlasting death. Nothing is so hateful to God as an unchaste mind and an impure heart. Nor should anyone think he ought to refrain from merely sexual delights, but from all other sensual pleasures as well, because they are themselves corrupt, and to despise them is a mark of the same virtue. The pleasure of the eyes is experienced by the beauty of things seen; of the ears by suave and harmonious sounds, of the nostrils by exquisite odours, of the taste by pleasant food; but against these virtue should contend stoutly, lest the soul, drawn on by these allurements, should descend from heavenly to earthly, from eternal to temporal things, from life immortal to perpetual punishment.

In the pleasures of taste and smell lies this danger: they can entice to riotous living. The man who is given over to these charms will never possess property; or, if he does, he will squander it and afterwards lead a wretched existence. He that is ravished by what he hears (to say nothing of songs that so often soothe our deepest feelings that they can disturb our peace of mind with frenzy through cunningly prepared speeches, by melodious songs, by lively discussions) is easily tempted to unholy forms of worship. Hence men of eloquence, or those that prefer to read eloquent books, have little belief in holy writings, because these appear artless and rude; they seek not the true but the agreeable; nay, those writings seem truest which flatter the ear. Thus they reject truth, caught by the charm of the spoken word. But the pleasure that comes of things seen consists of many and various shapes; what is perceived through the beauty of precious objects kindles greed, which should be hateful to a wise and a just man; while the pleasure derived from the looks of women hurries men to another pleasure, of which I have already spoken.

CHAPTER 63

Of sensual pleasures, and how they must be restrained

It remains to speak of the popular shows, for, as they are so powerful in debasing men's minds, they should be rigorously eschewed by the wise; they were originally celebrated because held to do honour to the gods. These exhibitions are festivals of Saturn; the stage is the property of Bacchus. But the games in the Circus are supposed to be sacred to Neptune, so that he who takes part in these spectacles seems to have abandoned the worship of God, and betaken himself to unholy rites. But I would rather speak of the fact itself than of its origin. What so horrible, so foul, as the butchery of a human being? That is why our lives are protected by strict legislation; that is why warfare is so hateful. Yet custom has found a way to enable murder to be done apart from war, and without the law; and its pleasure consists in the avenging of crime. But if one's presence at manslaughter involves a consciousness of guilt, the spectator is equally guilty with the doer of the deed; consequently in these gladiatorial butcheries the onlooker is no less sprinkled with blood than the butcher; nor can he be free from blood who has wanted it shed, nor can he appear not to have shared in the death-blow who has cheered the slayer and demanded for him a reward.

What of the stage? is it less vile? there comedy discourses of debaucheries and illicit loves, tragedy of incest and parricide. The lewd gestures of actors, whereby they imitate loose women, actually teach the lusts expressed in their dances. The farce too is a school of iniquity, in which shameful things are done by representation, so that things that are true are accomplished without any sense of shame. These plays are watched by the young, whose critical years—which should be rigorously controlled—are actually trained by these representations to vice and sin.

The Circus, indeed, is considered comparatively harmless; but here the excitement is even greater, since the minds of the onlookers are so carried away by madness that, as a result, not merely abusive words, but quarrels, nay even battles and fierce struggles arise. All shows, then, are to be shunned, that we may be enabled to enjoy a peaceful state of mind. Harmful pleasures we must renounce, lest, captivated by their baleful sweetness, we fall into the snares and traps of death.

CHAPTER 64

The passions to be subdued, and forbidden things disallowed

Let virtue alone comfort us, the wages of which is immortality when it has overcome pleasure. But the passions once quelled, there is no difficulty in mastering other faults, at least for one who is a follower of God and truth. Such a man will not give way to slander, if he hopes for God's blessing; he will not forswear, lest he make a mock of God; nay, he will not even swear, lest by necessity or by custom he should be guilty of perjury. He will use no deceit in his tongue, nor speak to deceive; nor will he refuse to admit a pledge once made, or promise what he cannot fulfil; he will envy no one, inasmuch as he is content with what he has; nor will he rob or wish ill to another on whom, may be, God's blessing is more abundant. He will not steal, or covet another's goods, nor will he give his money upon usury (for this means making profit out of others' misfortunes); yet he will agree to lend, if necessity compels any man to borrow. He should not be harsh to son or to slave, for he must bear in mind that he, too, has a Father and a Master. So let him treat these as he would like others to treat him. He should not accept extravagant gifts from people with slender means, because it is unjust that the possessions of the rich should be increased through the losses of the wretched.

It is an old commandment, 'thou shall do no murder'; but this must not be taken as though we were bidden to abstain from homicide alone—a thing that is punished even by public law. Thanks to this enactment we cannot be allowed to imperil life even by word, or kill or expose an infant; nor must we condemn ourselves by suicide. Yet more: there is the old commandment, 'thou shalt not commit adultery'; but, by this rule, not only are we forbidden to violate another's marriage rights—a practice condemned by the common law of the world—but we are required to abjure any dealing with harlots, for, transcending all human laws, is the law of God, which forbids even those acts which are counted legitimate. And this, that justice may be fulfilled. It is part of the same law not to speak false witness; and this has a rather wide scope. For if false witness, by lying, harms him against whom it is uttered, and deceives him in whose presence it is given, we must therefore never lie, because a lie always deceives or harms. No just man is he who, without actually causing an injury, speaks a lie during some idle conversation. The just man indeed must not cringe and flatter, for flattery is deadly and deceitful; no, he will everywhere guard the truth. And though, for the moment, truth may prove disagreeable, none the less, when its fruitful results are witnessed, it will bring, not hatred (as the poet writes) but thanks.

CHAPTER 65

Various precepts. Of compassion as a Christian virtue

I have spoken of what is forbidden; I shall now tell briefly what is bidden. Compassion is close akin to innocence, for as the former does not work evil, so the latter works good; the former is the beginning of justice, the latter its end. Since man is by nature weaker than all other creatures which their maker, God, has endowed with means to deal injury, and powers to repel it, to us He has given the feeling of compassion, that our lives might be safeguarded by mutual aids. For if we have been created by one God, and sprung from one man, and are linked together by the law of blood-kinship, we ought, in consequence, to love all mankind. Not only should we refrain from causing injury; we must not even avenge it when done to us, that in us innocence may be perfect. So God enjoins on us to pray, always, even for our enemies. We ought to be creatures living in society, sharing in a common life, that we may protect ourselves by giving and receiving help. For we are frail and subject to many changes and chances in this mortal life. Anticipate that what you see has befallen your neighbour may equally well befall you. As a result, you will be roused at last to lend a helpful hand, if only you put yourself in the position of him who, finding himself in sore straits, asks for your assistance. If anyone needs food, let us give it; if anyone comes to us naked, let us clothe him; if anyone has been wronged by another more powerful than himself, let us deliver him. Our doors should be open to the stranger, or to those needing a roof for shelter. It should be ours to safeguard wards, and protect widows.[1]

The ransoming of captives is a great work of pity, even as it is to visit and console the sick and needy. If the poverty-stricken or strangers die, we must not suffer them to remain unburied. Such are the works of compassion, such its duties; and, if these be carried out, a true and acceptable sacrifice will be offered to God. With such sacrifice God is well pleased; not with the blood of a sheep, but with the godly affection of man, whom God, because He is just, accompanies with His own law and on His own terms. He has pity on one whom He sees to be pitiful, but inexorable to one whom He finds pitiless to the prayers of others. To enable us to accomplish all these things that are pleasing to God, we must despise money, and transfer it to treasures in Heaven, where no thief can break through, nor rust corrode, nor tyrant steal; but where it may, under God's guardianship, be kept to enrich us for ever.

---

[1] 'Viduis' might equally well mean those who are without defence, men or women.

CHAPTER 66

Of faith, of courage, and of chastity

Faith, too, is a large part of justice[1], and we, who bear the name of Christian, must cling to it, especially in matters religious, because God is prior to, and mightier than, man. Though it is glorious to lay down life for friends, parents, children (that is, for man), and he that does this wins lasting remembrance and praise; how much more glorious for the sake of God, who can dower us with life eternal in place of death in time! When forced of necessity to turn aside from Him and have recourse to heathen rites, no fear, no terror, can hinder us from guarding the faith delivered to us. Let God be ever in our eyes, in our hearts, by whose inward help we may master bodily pain, and agonies inflicted on our persons. Let us bethink us of nothing save the prize of immortality. Even if our limbs are to be hacked asunder or burnt, we shall endure whatever is devised by the insanity of tyrannic cruelty. Lastly, let us strive to bear death itself, nor grudgingly nor with faint hearts, but freely, unterrified, as knowing what glory shall be ours to enjoy in the presence of God, triumphant over this world and attaining the promises. What good things, what blessedness, shall be ours in exchange for our brief afflictions and the losses of our present life! Even if we be denied this splendid chance, yet will faith have its reward in the day of peace.

Let faith, then, be observed in all life's duties, and in marriage. It is not enough to abstain from another's couch, or from a brothel. The man with a wife should not go in quest of aught further, but rest content with what he has, and safeguard the mysteries of a wedlock pure and undefiled. He is an adulterer and impure in the sight of God who, flinging aside the yoke of matrimony, wantons with a free woman or a slave. As a wife is restrained by the ties of chastity from lusting after another man, so let the husband be subject to the same law, because God has united man and wife in one flesh. He has commanded that a wife be not divorced, unless guilty of adultery, that the marriage bond may never be broken—unfaithfulness apart. For the perfecting of purity, there is this further obligation: we must abstain not only from the act of adultery, but from the thought of it.

---

[1] Or 'righteousness.'

For the mind, as is evident, is sullied by the bare desire; and a righteous man should neither do nor will what is contrary to right living. Conscience must be purged, for the eyes of God—who cannot be deceived—are upon it. Let the breast be cleansed of every stain, that it may become a temple of God, illuminated not by the sheen of gold or ivory, but by the brightness of faith and purity.

CHAPTER 67

Of repentance, the soul's immortality, and of Providence

But indeed all this is hard for man, nor does his natural frailty allow anyone to be unblemished. The final cure is to betake ourselves to repentance—not the least of the virtues, because it involves self-correction, to the end that, when we happen to slip in word or deed, we may without delay return to our truer selves and confess our fault, praying God for forgiveness, which He will not refuse unless we persist in our transgression. Great is the help, great the comfort of penitence: it is the balm for wounds and sin; it brings hope; it is the port of safety; and he who abolishes this, cuts himself off from the way of life, because nobody can be so just as never to need repentance.

Even though we have not fallen into sin, we are bound to make confession to God, and pray to Him continually to forgive us our trespasses, and to yield Him thanks even in misfortunes. Let us ever show ourselves obedient to the Lord. For humility is dear and acceptable to God. He accepts the sinner that confesses rather than the just man in his pride; how much more, then, will He accept the just man who confesses his faults, and, in proportion to his humility, will exalt him in His heavenly kingdom! These are the characteristics that the genuine worshipper should exhibit; these are the offerings, this the sacrifice, with which God is well pleased; this is real worship when a man brings to God's altar the pledges of his heart and soul. In such a worshipper the Most High delights; He welcomes him as a son, and grants him the due reward of immortal life. And this latter I must now discuss, refuting the views of those thinkers who assert that the soul is destroyed along with the body. These men, ignorant of God and unable to perceive clearly the mystery of the Universe, have not even understood the nature of man and of the soul. How could they, who did not hold fast the supreme Reality, discern the results? By denying the being of a Providence, they obviously denied the being of God. What followed? they asserted that what exists has always existed, or else arose spontaneously, or was brought to pass by the gathering together of tiny seeds. But what exists, and is visible, cannot always have existed, for without a beginning no existence is possible. Nothing can come into being spontaneously, because, without a Generator, there is no such thing as Nature. How could there be primordial seeds, seeing that seeds spring from objects and objects from seeds? Thus then there is no seed without an origin. So when men imagined that the Universe was brought about without a Providence, they believed that even man himself was produced without a plan. Now if mankind were created without a plan, the soul itself cannot be immortal. Some, on the contrary, held that there is one God, and that the Universe was formed by Him for man's sake, and that souls are immortal. They reasoned aright, but could not plainly see the causes, the reasons, or the results of this divine work and counsel, so as to consummate the entire mystery of truth, and bring it to some final conclusion. Yet what these thinkers could not do, because they did not hold the truth consistently, must be done by us who have knowledge of that truth by divine revelation.

CHAPTER 68
Why God made the world

Let us know what was God's scheme in creating this vast Universe. Plato thought it was the work of God, but never explained why He made it. 'God', he said, 'is good, and jealous of no man; consequently He made what was good.' Yet we see that, in Nature, there is a commingling of good and evil. Some perverse fellow, like Theodorus 'the Atheist', may answer Plato after this fashion: 'No! because God is evil, He is the author of evil.' What refutation is possible? If God made what is good, whence comes that uprush of so many evil things which generally overcome the good things? 'Why, they were', says he, 'included in Matter.' If there is evil, there is consequently good, so that God either made nothing, or, if He made only what is good, the evil things which were not made are more eternal than the good things which had a beginning. Hence those things which began at some time or another will have an end, while what has always existed will remain constant. Therefore evil is superior to good. If, however, evil cannot be superior, neither can it be more eternal. So either both qualities, good and evil, have existed for ever, and God is superfluous; or else good and evil alike have issued from a single source; for it is more rational to hold that God should be the author of all than that He made nothing. In Plato's belief, the same God is good because He is the author of what is good, and evil because He is the author of evil. If this be impossible, it stands to reason that the Universe was not made by God, because the Universe is good. For He embraced all things, good and bad, and nothing will come into being for its own sake but for the sake of something else. A house is built not to be merely a house but to receive and protect the dweller in it. Likewise a ship is constructed not to be a ship only but that people may sail in it. Dishes, too, are made not to be dishes and nothing else, but to contain what is needed for use. So God must have made the Universe to serve some purpose. The Stoics aver that it was made to serve mankind: and rightly so, for men enjoy all the good things contained therein. But why men themselves were made, or what value Providence (the maker of all things) finds in them—this is left unanswered. Plato also maintains that souls are immortal; but why, how, when, or through what agency they achieve immortality, or what this great mystery signifies; why those that are destined to be immortal are first born mortal, and then, their course in this temporal life ended, and the trappings of their frail bodies laid aside, are carried to that eternal blessedness—of all this Plato understands nothing. Finally, Plato did not expound God's judgement or the difference between the just and the unjust man; but, as he supposed that souls which plunged in crimes are so far condemned as to find themselves reborn as animals, and so atone for their sins until once again they return to human shape, and that this process is ever going on, and that of transmigration there is no end—well, in my view, Plato is introducing a piece of play-acting, not unlike a dream, in which there is no semblance of an ordered scheme, no divine government, and no purpose whatsoever.

CHAPTER 69
The world made for man, and man for God

I shall now explain what that main conclusion is, which even truth-tellers have not been able to connect logically with causes and reasons brought to unity. The world was made by God for the birth of mankind; now men are born that they may acknowledge Him as Father, in whom dwelleth wisdom. They acknowledge Him that they may worship Him, in whom dwelleth righteousness; they worship Him that immortality may be their reward; they are dowered with immortality that they may serve Him for ever. Do you mark how closely these things are interconnected—the first with the middle, the middle with the last? Let us examine them severally, to see whether they are consistent with reason.[1]

God made the world for man: anyone who fails to recognize this fact is little better than an animal. Who gazes heavenward but man? who marvels to behold sun, and stars, and all the works of the Creator but man? who tills the earth and takes the fruit therefrom? who sails the ocean? who has dominion over fishes, and flying creatures, and four-footed things, but man? It was for man's sake that God made all things, because they have served man's advantage. Philosophers have observed this, but its sequel, that God made man for His own sake, this they have not seen. Hence it was right and necessary (since God accomplished such mighty works for man, when He bestowed upon him such glory and power as to be lord of the world) that man should acknowledge God, the Author of all these blessings, who made the world itself on his account, and should moreover pay Him the worship and honour that is due to Him. It was here that Plato went astray: he lost the truth which he had seized on at the first, for, as touching the worship of that God whom he admitted to be the Architect and Parent of the Universe, he was silent. He failed to comprehend that man was bound to God by links of loyal affection (hence the origin of the word 'religion'), and that this is the one and only ground for souls becoming immortal. Yet Plato felt instinctively that they are eternal, but he did not come to that belief, step by step. The central reasons being cut away, he *fell* into the truth by accident, as though over some steep

---
[1] or 'design'.

precipice; nor did he ever make any advance further, because he had hit upon the truth by chance, not by process of reasoning. So we conclude: God must be worshipped that, through religion —which is righteousness—man may receive immortality at the hands of God. There is no other reward of a godly mind, which, in itself invisible, can receive, from an invisible God, only an invisible reward.

CHAPTER 70
Proof of the soul's immortality

Many arguments may be adduced to prove the immortality of the soul. Plato says that what always is self-moving, without any beginning of motion, also has no end; but that the mind of man is ever moved by itself, and because it is swift to reflect, adroit to invent, easy to perceive, apt to learn, holds the past, apprehends the present, discerns the future, and grasps a knowledge of many subjects and arts, it is therefore immortal, for it contains nothing commingled with the flaws of earthliness. Furthermore, the soul's eternity is perceived from virtue and pleasure. Pleasure belongs to all living creatures, virtue to man alone; the one is faulty, the other honourable; the one is in harmony with nature, the other contrary—unless the soul is immortal. For virtue, struggling for faith and right, fears no poverty nor exile, nor does it shrink from prison; it is not affrighted by pain, nor does it refuse to die; but in so far as these things are opposed to nature, either virtue is folly if it impedes our comforts and harms our lives; or else, if it is not folly, the soul is itself immortal, and scorns the delights of to-day because there are other and better things to be won after the dissolution of the body. Here lies the supreme proof of immortality, that man alone has a knowledge of God. In dumb brutes there is no idea of religion, for they are creatures of earth and are bent earthward. Man, who stands upright, gazes to heaven that he may seek after God. So he cannot be other than immortal, if he longs for One that is immortal. He cannot pass into nothingness, when he is united to God alike in appearance and mind. Lastly, only man employs the celestial element, which is fire. For if light comes to us through fire, and life through light, clearly he that employs fire is not mortal, since this is closely connected with Him apart from whom there is neither life nor light.

But why marshal arguments to prove that souls are eternal when we have divine assurance to this effect? The sacred Scriptures, the voices of prophet and seer, all testify to that truth. If anyone deems this not enough, let him read the Sibylline oracles, and ponder the responses of Milesian Apollo; he will then understand that Democritus, Epicurus, and Dicaearchus have all doted when, alone of mortals, they denied the obvious. Having established the doctrine of immortality, we have now to show by whom, to whom, how and when, such doctrine is imparted. Since divinely determined times have begun to be fulfilled, there must inevitably be an end and consummation of all things, that the world may be renewed by God. That period is very near, so far as we can estimate from the number of years and from signs foretold in prophecy. But since the forecasts of the end of the age and the final consummation of all things are innumerable, what has been declared must be set forth in its nakedness, for it would involve immense labour to make use of the entire prophetic witness. Yet, if any so desire or have no confidence in us, let them have recourse to the very Shrine of heavenly records, trusting to which they will feel how philosophers have gone astray in supposing this present world to be eternal, or that infinite time has elapsed since its creation. Six thousand years are not yet ended; but, when that number is completed, then all evil will be removed that righteousness alone may hold sway. How this will come to pass I shall now briefly state.

CHAPTER 71

The close of the present dispensation

These are the things that both prophets and seers declare will come to pass. When the final scene is approaching, wickedness will predominate, every sort of crime and deceit will increase, justice will perish; faith, peace, compassion, modesty, and truth will cease; violence and presumption will prevail; nobody will possess anything, unless won by force and guarded by a strong hand. If any good men are to be found, they will be regarded as a prey and for mockery. The child will be undutiful to its parents, no one will show pity to an infant or to an old man; greed and lust will corrupt universally. Murder and bloodshed will abound.

Not only will wars be fought against enemies abroad and neighbouring peoples, but civil strife will arise. Cities will war with one another; arms will be taken up by all, irrespective of age or sex. The dignity of Empire will be lost; armies will become undisciplined; plundering and destruction, after the ways of brigandage, will be done. The imperial power will be enlarged, and ten men will capture the whole world, dividing it up and swallowing it; but yet another will arise, far mightier and more iniquitous than the ten, who, after destroying three, will seize Asia, and, bringing the remainder into his power, will ravage the earth. This potentate will establish new laws after abrogating old ones, thus securing the commonwealth for his own possession, and will change the name and place of government. Then will be witnessed a time unspeakably vile, in which no one would desire to live.

Finally, things will reach such a pass that lamenations will follow the living, and greetings the dead. Cities and towns will be destroyed, now by sword, now by fire; now by earthquakes in divers places, now by deluge, now by pestilence and famine. The earth will cease to yield its harvests, for it will have been made barren by excessive cold or heat. All water will be partly turned into blood, partly spoiled by bitterness, so that nothing will be left fit for food or safe to drink. To these plagues will be added also miraculous signs from heaven, that everything may combine to increase human alarm. Comets will frequently be seen. The sun will be darkened with perpetual gloom; the moon will be dyed in blood, nor will it renew its lost light; all the stars will fall, nor will the seasons observe their proper course, for winter and summer will be confounded. Year and month and day will be shortened. That this is the old age of the world, and its declension, has been foretold by Trismegistus.

When these things come to pass, know that the time is at hand when God will return to transform this age. Now among all these evils there will spring up a wicked king, an enemy not only of the human race but even of God Himself. Those who had been left alive by the previous despot this King will crush, torture, persecute, and destroy. Then will tears flow unceasingly, with lamentation and perpetual groanings, and supplications to God—in vain; there will be no respite from alarm, no sleep for repose. Day will add to the calamity, night will enlarge fear. So the whole earth will be brought wellnigh to a solitude and its inhabitants be diminished. This unrighteous man will persecute the righteous and all who have been dedicated to God; he will summon all men to worship him as a God, for he will call himself Christ, whose adversary he will be. To win credence, he will receive power to work miracles, so that fire will come down from the sky, the sun be stayed in its course, and his image (which he has set up) will speak. By such prodigies he will allure many to adore him, and to receive on hand or brow his mark. Those that refuse him worship, and have not received the mark, will be put to death with exquisite tortures. Thus he will exterminate two parts of mankind; the third will fly for refuge to desert places. Void of reason, frenzied with implacable rage, he will bring his army to besiege the mountain where the saints have fled, and when they see themselves hemmed round, they will cry aloud in supplication to God for His aid; and He will give ear to their cry, and send down a Deliverer.

CHAPTER 72

Christ's descent from Heaven; the last Judgement, and the Millennial reign

Then shall the heavens be opened in the dead of night, and Christ descend with great power; before him will go a fiery brilliance and an innumerable company of angels; all that multitude of sinners will be blotted out, torrents of blood flow, and the chief ruler will flee away; and, when his hosts have often been reinforced, he will do battle for the fourth time, in which, after being taken captive along with all other tyrants, he will be delivered over to the flames. Nay, the very Prince of the daemons, author and deviser of evils, will be bound with chains and cast into a dungeon, that the world may have peace, and the earth, tormented through so many ages, be at rest. Peace once secured, and all evil overthrown, the righteous and victorious prince will execute judgement on the living and the dead over all the earth; to the living righteous he will assign all nations for servitude, but the dead he will raise to eternal life, and will himself reign with them on earth and found a Holy City. This kingdom of the saints will last a thousand years. During that same time the light of the stars will be magnified, and the sun's brightness be increased and the light of the moon no longer suffer diminution [or 'eclipse']. Then will come down from God showers of blessing, both morning and evening, while the earth will yield her fruits without toil on the part of mankind. Honey will drip from the rocks, fountains of milk and wine gush forth, wild beasts—laying aside their ferocity—will grow gentle, the wolf wandering harmless amid the flocks, the calf feeding with the lion, the dove consorting with the hawk, the snake losing its venom; no creature will then live by blood. For God will bestow upon all creatures innocent food in abundance. But, at the close of the thousand years, when the Prince of the daemons is unchained, the nations will renew warfare with the righteous and an innumerable multitude will come to storm the city of the Saints. In that hour shall the Last Judgement of God be executed upon the nations, for He will smite the Earth from its foundations, the cities will fall as one, and upon transgressors He will rain fire and brimstone and hail; they will be burned with fire and will murder one another. For a brief while the righteous will lie hidden underground, until the nations come to perdition; then, after three days, they will issue forth and behold the plains covered with dead bodies. There will be an earthquake; mountains will be riven, and the valleys sink into the depths, while the bodies of the dead will be cast together into a place called Polyandrion. After this, God will renew the world and change the righteous into angelic shapes, that, being clothed with the garment of immortality, they may serve God for ever. And this will be the Kingdom of God, and of that Kingdom there shall be no end. Afterwards the wicked will rise again, not unto life but to condemnation. These also will God summon, after the second resurrection, that, doomed to perpetual torments and delivered to undying fires, they may pay the due penalties for their crimes.

EPILOGUE

Since these events are true and certain of fulfilment, being in agreement with prophecies uttered by the seers, and since Trismegistus and Hystaspes and the Sibyls have foretold the same destinies, it is indisputable that all hope of life and salvation rests on the religion of God alone. Accordingly, unless a man accepts Christ, whom God has already sent to free mankind from sin— yes, and will send yet again; unless man acknowledges the

Supreme God and keeps His commandments and His law, he will suffer those penalties of which I have already spoken. We must despise what is weak and frail, that we may attain what is surely established; we must make light of earthly things, to become ennobled by heavenly things; we must flee from the lures of time that we may win the joys that are eternal. Let each instruct his own heart unto righteousness, conform to self-control, be prepared and ready for the contest, learn the lessons of virtue; so that, if maybe an adversary declares war, each may not be turned aside from the strait and goodly path by any violence, or terror, or suffering; that he may never bow and submit to senseless fancies, but with upright heart acknowledge the true and only God. Let him thrust aside the pleasures of sense, by the enticements of which the lofty soul is driven earthward; let him hold fast innocency, be serviceable to all men, and by his good works obtain incorruptible treasures, to the end that, with God as his judge, he may win for his virtuous deserts either the crown of faith or the prize of immortality.

After reading Lactantius

Lactantius, quasi quidam fluvius eloquentiae Tullianae.—
Jerome, Ep. 58, §10

Lactantius, once pagan, then brought home
To Christ's own flock—may we not greet thee, now
That sixteen hundred years have passed since thou,
Obedient to the Galilean call,
Didst honour to His name before the hosts
Of heathendom? How oft must thou have known
The martyrdom of thousands in that last
Fierce persecution! Yet thou livedst to watch
That final triumph, when the Church rose free.
Perchance within thy page we shall not find
Augustine's deep-set knowledge of man's heart,
Tertullian's fiery eloquence, or the ripe
Persuasive words of mighter souls than thine,
Drawn from the secret armoury of heaven.
Yet much abides. We prize thy writings, hail
Their calm good sense, the faith that guided them,
Their purity of style, and, mixed therewith,
Those loftier thoughts that shadow forth the truth.
Thanks for thy message; it has power to wake
A salutary joy, a hope serene
Tho' touched with mortal warning, while we tread
The appointed path of life—made lovelier
By one great Light that breaks thro' clouded days,
Far-shining from the Paradise of God.

E. H. BLAKENEY.

COMMENTARY

PREFACE

The purpose of the *Epitome*, and its scope **in unum conferre.** Suetonius, *Nero* 19 (these acts of his) 'in unum contuli'.

The usual reading is 'fit enim totum et minus plenum'; what seems required is 'fiet enim mutilum (curtailed) . . .'

substringere. Cf. chap. 50, 'rem immensam paucis substringam'. Just above there is a small gap in MS. after 'poterit'. Perhaps it may be filled with (*a*) 'utile,' (*b*) 'satis plenum,' (*c*) 'perspicuum'; any one of these conjectures will make sense.

breviare. A post-Augustan word, but found as early as Quintilian and Manilius. Again, chap. 5.

CHAPTER I

[*Inst. i.* 2]

scholam Epicuri. This philosopher eliminated (or tried to eliminate) all belief in a supernatural order of the world. So argues his disciple Lucretius in the *de rerum natura*.

For a brief discussion of the Epicurean system, see Gilbert Murray, *Five Stages of Greek Religion*; Wallace deals at length with it in his *Epicureanism* (S.P.C.K.). Cf. Tennyson's *Lucretius*. For an enumeration of the secondary causes which led to the adoption of Epicureanism in ancient times, see Lactantius, *Institutes*, iii. 17, and the many references to it in Cicero, *de Finibus*; *Academica*; *de natura deorum*. This philosophy was destined, ultimately, to have a fatal influence on belief and morals.—See more on chap. 36 n.

nec fieri sine artifice Deo . . . constare. Cf. Cic. *de nat. deor.* ii. 35, § 90 (philosophers ought to have understood that there was in the universe) 'rectorem et moderatorem et tanquam architectum tanti operis tantique muneris'.

omnium mortalium. The old argument 'e consensu gentium', met with in Cicero, and emphasized by the Stoics; it is constantly appealed to by Aristotle. Similarly by Seneca. The analogous ecclesiastical doctrine is set forth in the famous canon of Vincent of Lerins—'quod ubique, quod semper, quod ab omnibus creditum est'. See Flint's *Theism*, App. viii. The equally famous maxim of Augustine, 'securus judicat orbis terrarum' is not a true parallel, though too often quoted as such, for 'securus' there = free from anxiety.

The argument from design, which is the central thought of Aristotle in his philosophy; cf. J. H. Stirling's *Philosophy and Theology*, pp. 93–6, 127–37. The vast expansion of our knowledge (wrote

Prof. A. E. Taylor in his last book, *Does God exist?*), so far from weakening the traditional 'argument from design', has made it much stronger. See the remarkable book, *Man does not stand alone*, by A. C. Morrison.

caelos. The masc. pl. for *caelum* was a Hebraism used by patristic writers.

ratione. 'according with a plan', perhaps; but *ratio* is a difficult word to translate: Cicero uses it with many shades of meaning; so does Lucretius—e.g. reason, reasoning, system, law, opinion, plan, philosophy, general principle. A good example in chap. 68 (init) where = plan. Sometimes almost = 'influence', as in Cic. *pro Rabir.* § 2 'humanitatis ratio'.

CHAPTER 2
[*Inst. i.* 3]

unus Deus . . . idem Pater. Cf. Eph. 4. 6, εἷς Θεὸς καὶ Πατὴρ πάντων ὁ ἐπὶ πάντων καὶ διὰ πάντων καὶ ἐν πᾶσιν.

apum reges. The ancients regarded what we term the *queen* bee as male. It is well known that two queens cannot exist in one hive. The line quoted is from Virg. *Geor.* iv. 68. Cf. the argument in Minuc. Fel. xviii.

pro viribus. So Davies for *moribus*: rightly.

quod in ipso, viz. his own special prerogatives.

Minerva fruges. Routh's conj. for *frugum*.

quam qui . . . , i.e. potius quam qui . . .

CHAPTER 3
[*Inst. i.* 3—5]

impassibilis. Non-class., but found in Tertullian, Jerome, Prudentius, and others. Cf. the wording of the first Article in P.B., 'There is but one living and true God, *everlasting*, without body, parts, or **passions**'.

singulari = uni, unico. A favourite use of the word in Lactantius.

Orpheus, a legendary poet of pre-Homeric times, famed for his wonderful gift of music: cf. Shakespeare, *Henry VIII*, Act iii. sc. 1; and Milton, *Il Pens.* 105. The lovely story of Orpheus and his wife Eurydice is told by Virgil at the close of his 4th Georgic.

noster Maro. In *Aeneid,* vi. 726f.; *Georg.* iv. 221f.

Ovidius. See *Metam.* i. 79.

opificem . . . fabricatorem. Contrast with this the Epicurean arguments in Cic. *de nat. deor.* I. viii. f.

COMMENTARY   131

CHAPTER 4
[*Inst.* i. 5, 6]

auctoritas has several shades of meaning—influence (due to high position); authority; moral influence; personal weight; opinion (or decision, as in 'senatus auctoritas').

Plato monarchiam adserit. Still more strong are the words in the *Inst.*, 'Plato m. plane aperteque defendit'. So Plato does, in many places, but associates with the supreme God the usual deities of the popular religion, associating these again with δαίμονες of a lower rank.

Antisthenes, generally counted as founder of the Cynic school (*fl.* 380 B.C.), maintained that the gods of the people were many, but that the God of nature was one only: Cic. *de nat. deor.* I. xiii. 32. For Aristotle's views, see the magnificent passage in the 11th book (called by some the 12th) of the *Metaphysics*, which closes thus: 'God is a living being, perfect and eternal. Life eternal and enduring being belong to Him; and God is that'—the infinite I AM. For Thales and the rest, see any good classical dictionary, and Cicero's *de nat. deor.* I. ii. 10f.

nostrorum Seneca. Jerome speaks of 'noster Seneca', and so does Tertullian; while Lactantius styles him (*Inst.* i. 5) 'the keenest of Roman Stoics'. Seneca was frequently regarded as approximating to the Christian faith. Consult Lightfoot's excursus in his *Philippians*.

Hermes . . . Trismegistus (= thrice great). From the third century A.D. the name was attached to the author of various Neoplatonic writings, many of which are still extant. The Hermetic discourses are constantly referred to by the Christian Fathers, but are of no real philosophic value: they have been collected and edited, with amazing erudition, by W. Scott, *Hermetica* (4 vols., 1924–36). Lactantius, like most of the patristic writers, wrongly ascribed a great antiquity to 'Hermes'.

vocabulo non indigeat. Cf. Hermetica, *Lib.* v. 10, οὗτος ὁ Θεὸς ὀνόματος κρείττων . . . αὐτὸς ὄνομα οὐκ ἔχει ὅτι πάντων ἐστὶ πατήρ; and Tennyson, *The Ancient Sage* (in the lines beginning 'Thou canst not prove the Nameless').

ex se et per se. Cf. the closing words of Abailard's great hymn (*O quanta qualia*), God—'ex quo sunt, per quem sunt, in quo sunt omnia', words which recall Rom. **11.** 36, ἐξ αὐτοῦ καὶ δι' αὐτοῦ καὶ εἰς αὐτὸν τὰ πάντα.

CHAPTER 5
[*Inst.* i. 7]

Varro (116–27 B.C.)—'vir Romanorum eruditissimus', according to Quintilian, x. 95—was a monotheist, and is constantly referred to by

the Fathers of the Church, especially by Augustine, mainly in the *de civitate Dei*, e.g. iii. 4, iv. 31, vi. 3–6. Of his encyclopaedic learning little now remains. Cicero treated him with great respect (see the *Academica*).
Cf. Mommsen, *Hist. Rome*, vol. v; Sandys, *Hist. Class. Scholarship*, vol. i; *Cambridge Ancient Hist.*, vol. x. p. 470; and, for his attitude to religion, Warde Fowler, *Social Life in Rome*, chap. xi; for a general review of his work, H. J. Rose, *Latin Literature*, pp. 220f.

Sibyllas. 'Inspired' prophetesses of ancient times, of whom one of the most famous was she of Cumae (see Virg. *Aen.* vi). The story of the Roman 'books' is too well known to be repeated here: they have now all perished. Yet they managed to survive the great fire of A.D. 363, according to Ammianus.

These books are not to be confused with the SIBYLLINE ORACLES of Jewish-Christian origin, many of which are still in existence. They are for the most part forgeries, though often quoted by certain patristic writers as if inspired. They are still accepted, says Reinach, as such in the Roman Catholic funeral service ('teste David cum Sibylla', in the *Dies Irae*). These medleys have for their object the maintenance of belief in the unity and sovereignty of the Deity; hence the liberal use of them by Lactantius in his onslaught on paganism.

See vol. ii of Charles' *Apocrypha and Pseudepigrapha*, where a translation of these medleys, with notes, is given from the original Greek hexameters. See too an article by Rendel Harris in vol. 5 of Hastings' *D.B.*; Bousset, *The Antichrist Legend* (E.T.); Cruttwell, *Lit. Hist. of Early Christianity*, p. 159, the references given by Mayor in his note on Tertullian, *Apol.* p. 273, and the notes of Welldon on August. *de civ. Dei*, xviii. 23; in the course of this chapter A. twice refers to Lactantius. In these 'Oracles' there appear to be several passages based on the Preaching of Peter: cf. Armitage Robinson on the *Apology of Aristides*, where he gives quotations.

Quindecimviris (sacris faciendis). At Rome, a board of fifteen commissioners who had the sole charge of the old *Sibylline books* and the privilege of interpreting them.—For *Albuneae*, cf. Hor. *Od.* I. vii. 12; Virg. *Aen.* vii. 81f.

CHAPTER 6

[*Inst. i.* 8]

ipsi sexus. Cf. *Inst.* I. viii (pagan deities of merely human origin because) 'sunt ex duobus sexibus nati'.

mortales utique. Lactantius adopts the doctrine of Euhemerus; see, below, chap. 13.

COMMENTARY 133

CHAPTER 7
[*Inst. i.* 9]

Chapters 7–23 deal with the Pagan pantheon, and should be compared with the elaborate account of the gods of Rome given by Augustine in the 7th book of his *de civitate Dei*. The breakdown of the old pagan cults was largely owing to one thing: men worshipped and served the creature rather than the Creator, whom they almost ignored (Rom. 1. 25). As the old legends had ceased to be taken seriously by all educated people, the onslaughts of Lactantius (and others) had become outmoded long before his time. Moreover, as the official Roman cults had exhausted their vitality—though on formal occasions they long served as an expression of politico-religious unity—any genuine faith found a natural home in the so-called mystery religions (see the bishop of Birmingham's recent volume *The Rise of Christianity*, chap. iii).

Hercules (Gk. Heracles). His legendary doings and his Twelve Labours are recounted at immense length by Apollodorus (consult Frazer's edition in the Loeb series, and the ample notes there: vol. i). The story of the **Argonauts**, one of the most celebrated in antiquity, is the subject of the epic poem by Apollonius Rhodius, and of Pindar's fourth Pythian ode. It has been given in a modern shape by W. Morris, *Life and Death of Jason*. **Laomedon,** a mythical king of Troy. Cic. *Tusc.* I. 26, 'non justa causa cur Laomedonti tanta fieret injuria'. · He violated the pledge given to Poseidon and Apollo and to Hercules: August. *de civ. Dei*, iii. 2. **Omphăle,** mistress of Hercules; Deianira's part in the death of Hercules is told us in the *Trachiniae* of Sophocles. The shirt she innocently gave him as a love-charm had been previously smeared with the blood of the Hydra: hence the 'ulcers', the agonizing pains of which led to his suicide.

cernatur. Davies' conj. for 'credatur'.

CHAPTER 8
[*Inst. i.* 10]

Aesculapium, the Greek Asclepius, god of medicine, to whose temples sick folk resorted for the serpent cure: see Apollodorus (vol. ii in Frazer's edition), and Frazer's *Pausanias* (index). No one could forget the ever memorable last words of Socrates—'Ἀσκληπιῷ ὀφείλομεν ἀλεκτρυόνα (Plato, *Phaed.* 118). **Chironi,** the centaur, legendary tutor of Achilles. Epidaurus was in Argolis: for the reference to Cicero, cf. *de nat. deor.* III. 22. **datum.** Brandt adds here 'didicisse medicinam', referring to *Inst.* I. x. 2.

alienum, i.e. Admetus: cf. Eurip. *Alcestis.* **gemitus in flore,** Ovid. *Metam.* x. 215. The story of the slain boy, Hyacinthus, is told, ibid. 183f.

Marti, putative father of Romulus and Remus; for the doings of **Castor** and **Pollux** (the 'Dioscuri' of the Greeks), see *Pausanias,* i. 18, 1.

For **Mercurius** as inventor of the lyre, cf. Hor. *Odes,* i, 10, 6; Ovid, *Fast.* v. 104.

Liber = Bacchus (Dionysus). His conquest of India is referred to in Ovid, *Fast.* iii. 465 (where see Frazer). For Ariadne's crown, cf. Hor. *Odes,* ii. 19, 13; Ovid, *Fasti,* iii. 459–end; *Met.* viii. 177; Catull. xvi. 59; Apoll. Rhod. iii. 1003, ἀστερόεις στέφανος, τόντε κλείουσ' Ἀριάδνης. For Ariadne's lamentations on her desertion by Theseus, see Ovid, *Heroides* x.

mater [magna] **ipsa** should, I think, be read, viz. Cybele. The Galli were her eunuch priests often referred to in classical literature. The youth was Attis: see the famous 63rd poem of Catullus, where the ugly story is told.

CHAPTER 9

[*Inst. i.* 17]

For the touching legend of Ceres in her search for her lost Proserpina—a favourite with poets, both ancient and modern—see the fine study by Pater, under the title of *Demeter and Persephone,* the Greek names for the two goddesses. Robert Bridges wrote a masque in 1904, *Demeter*; Milton's lines are well known (in *P.L.* iv. 268, 'That fair field of Enna, where Proserpin, gathering flowers, Herself a fairer flower, by gloomy Dis was gathered—which cost Ceres all that pain To seek her through the world'). The Mater Dolorosa of paganism.

Cypro. Hor. *Odes,* i. 3, 1; i. 30, 2.

Hippolytum. There are variants of his story, one given by Euripides in his play, another by Virgil, *Aen.* vii. 774–7, and this Lact. follows:

> At Trivia [= Diana] Hippolytum secretis alma recondit
> Sedibus, et nymphae Egeriae nemorique relegat,
> Solus ubi in silvis Italis ignobilis aevum
> Exigeret, versoque ubi nomine Virbius esset

Virbius, viz. a man who had two lives. Diana is the Greek Artemis. One thinks of the scene in *Acts,* and the reiterated cry, 'Great Artemis of the Ephesians!'

CHAPTER 10

[*Inst. i.* 11]

Augustine, in the *de civitate Dei* (e.g. II. vii), castigates the criminal conduct of the Olympians, with Jupiter as prime offender at their head,

COMMENTARY

as depicted by heathen writers: cf. Minuc. Fel. xxii; Tertull. *Apol.* xxi with references in Mayor's edition. It is little wonder that Plato indignantly attacked these writers, who had contrived to degrade the very notion of Deity.

Saturnum, originally an Italian god of agriculture, later identified with the Greek Κρόνος. **Alcmena,** wife of Amphitryon; by her Jupiter begat Hercules. **Leda,** wife of Tyndareus. Jupiter, in the guise of a swan, approached her and so became the father of Castor and Pollux.

Thetis, the sea goddess; mother of Achilles. For **Optimus Maximus,** see Cic. *de nat. deor.* II. 25, 64.

CHAPTER 11
[*Inst. i.* 11]

Danaen. Danäe was a daughter of king Acrisius, and became the mother of Perseus who slew the Gorgon. The story is given in a poem by Simonides (part of which we still have); and there are references to that story in Soph. *Ant.* 944f.; Hor. *Odes*, III. 16, 1-8; August. *de civ. Dei*, xviii. 13, and elsewhere.

catamitum, viz. Ganymede, who became the cupbearer of Jupiter. See the stern words of Justin M., *Apol.* xxi.

aquila. The standard was worshipped by the Roman soldiery, because it symbolized Jupiter.

Europam. Cf. Ovid, *Met.* ii. 836f.; Hor. *Odes*, iii. 27, 25f. (Orelli). The Europa legend was a favourite in antiquity, and Tennyson refers to it in his *Palace of Art*.

tutelam, i.e. the painted image of a protecting deity on a ship. Cf. Virg. *Aen.* x. 171; Hor. *Odes*, i. 14, 10; Ov. *Trist.* i. 10, 1; Persius, vi. 30; Seneca Epp. 76, § 13. See Rich, *Dict.* s. v.

Inachi filia, Io. Cf. Ovid. *Met.* i. 583f. She appears as one of the dramatis personae in the *Prometheus* of Aeschylus. **Isis,** one of the chief deities of Egypt, and spouse of Osiris (see Plutarch, *de Is. et Os.*). It is noteworthy how often she is referred to in imperial times, when her cult had established itself in Rome, so much so that Domitian raised a temple to her. For a few out of many references, see Juvenal, Tibullus, Ovid, Lucian (dialogues of the gods), Apuleius (in his *Metamorphoses*), Augustine.

The student is advised to consult the admirable work by the late S. Dill (*Roman Society from Nero to Marcus Aurelius*) for a full account of Isis-worship. It is remarkable that as late as A.D. 394 her festival was celebrated in Rome. There is a brief but useful account of Isis in Inge's *Phil. of Plotinus*, vol. 2. Cf. Frazer, *Golden Bough* (Adonis, Attis, Osiris); Cumont, *Oriental Religions*, chap. iv. See further in chap. 23.

CHAPTER 12
[Inst. i. 10, 11]

praefigurasse. A word unknown in classical authors.

aliquid tamen. So I would write for 'aliquid *tale*'.

Olympum. A lofty range on the borders of Thessaly and Macedonia.

dumtaxat. A curious word, legal in origin, qualifying a previous statement: (*a*) at all events, (*b*) merely. Munro, Lucr. ii. 123; Reid Cic. *de Fin.* ii. 21.

CHAPTER 13
[Inst. i. 11]

Euhemerus held, as a result of documentary evidence which he pretended to have discovered, that the gods of mythology were deified kings or heroes. See the remarks of Cicero, *de nat. deor.* I. 42, 119; Euseb. *Prep. Evang.* 59; August. *de civ. Dei,* vi. 7. This theory was revived in part by Herbert Spencer, and by John Locke before him, and it is interesting to note how Lactantius was equally prepared to rationalize the old myths. Cf. too Plut. *de Is. et Osir.* 360.

Ennius (209–169 B.C.), 'the father of Latin poetry'. Fragments of his *Annales* are extant, and are frequently quoted by Latin authors. As the inventor of the Latin hexameter, his influence on subsequent poets was considerable: see Munro, *Lucr.* vol. ii. pp. 12–13. According to Cicero he not only translated but explained Euhemerus, as was natural, both being rationalists.

sepulcrum in Creta. The Cretans declared that Jupiter (Zeus) both died and was born in their island; cf. Lucian, *de sacrif.* 10. There are references to this in the Sibylline Oracles, Callimachus, Cicero, and Origen.

hominem fuisse. The student should read here chapters xxii, xxiii in Minucius Felix, for a similar line of argument.

CHAPTER 14
[Inst. i. 11, 12, 13]

Caelo et Terra. Caelus is of course the Gk. Οὐρανός, the sky personified; Terra (or more often Tellus), the personified Earth (Γῆ). Apollodorus begins his treatise thus: 'Sky was the first to rule over the whole world, and was the husband of Earth.'

Hermes Trismegistus. See on iv, § 4. There is a gap in the manuscripts after the word 'paravit'. I have mended this gap by adding a few words, to make the general meaning clear.

CHAPTER 20

[*Inst. i.* 20]

Larentinalia. Perhaps this should be corrected to Larentalia. Her festival took place in December: see Ovid, *Fast.* iii. 55f., with Frazer's notes. Larentia, the wife of Faustulus, was reputed to be a harlot (vulgati corporis). **Lupa** means both she-wolf and harlot.

Of the various curious deities mentioned in this and the next chapter, Augustine has something to say in the *de civitate Dei* (IV. viii, xxiii and elsewhere, e.g. VI. x.) Cf. Cyprian, *de idol. vanit.* 5.

Cloacinam. Really a title of Venus, meaning The Purifier, from *cluare* or *cloare* = to cleanse. But Augustine, like Lactantius, apparently takes the word to mean 'sewer goddess'. See Min. Fel. xxv. For the Floralia, just above, see Frazer on Ovid. *Fast.* iv. 945.

obsessi, in 363 B.C. Rome was sacked but not vanquished. Livy gives a lengthy account in book v of his history.

Pistori Jovi. Ovid says he can explain the story: *Fast.* vi. 350 (where see Frazer's notes). **Pavorem, Pallorem:** Livy, I. 27.

Marcellus, conqueror of Syracuse, 212 B.C. Livy devotes part of his 25th book to an account, remarking that one of the worst instances of savagery was the murder of the greatest scientist of the century, Archimedes.

CHAPTER 21

[*Inst. i.* 20]

commentitios. So Cicero speaks of 'commentitios et fictos deos' in *de nat. deor.* II. 28, 70 (cf. next chapter). For Fides, Spes, etc., personified as deities, see abundant references in Lewis-Short's Latin dict. For Robigo, Ovid, *Fast.* iv. 907; for Febris, Cic. *de natur. deor.* iii. 25, 63; and for the temples of most of these deities consult J. H. Middleton, *The Remains of Ancient Rome* (1892).

Stercutum. The name is variously spelt. Tertullian gives it as Sterculus. **Lares,** the spirits of the dead: Frazer, Ovid, *Fast.* ii. 615. **Cuninam,** August. *de civ. Dei,* iv. 8. **Fornacem,** Ovid, *Fast.* ii. 525–7. **Cacam.** For the story of Cacus and the oxen, cf. Virg. *Aen.* viii. 190f.

Terminum, Ovid, *Fast.* ii. 667–70. August. *de civ. Dei,* iv. 23, associates Juventas with T. in resistance to Jupiter, as Livy does, v. 54.

Capitoli im. sax. Words quoted from Virg. *Aen.* ix. 448.

CHAPTER 22

[*Inst. i.* 22]

Faunus. Originally a rustic deity, afterwards identified with the Greek Pan (hence our word 'panic' because he was supposed to excite sudden terror in wanderers in forest places). For the Good Goddess, cf. Ovid, *Fast.* v. 148f.

Numa (Pompilius). A semi-legendary king of Rome, and successor of Romulus. All sorts of traditions attach to that peaceful monarch, e.g. his secret assignations with his mistress, the nymph Egeria: 'nocturnae Numa constituebat amicae', Juv. iii. 12; Livy, i. 21; Ovid, *Amores*, ii. 17, 18. Ancient authorities speak of his religious ardour; Livy, for instance, i. 19; so Tacit., *Ann.* iii. 26, 'Numa religionibus et divino jure populum devinxit'.

Lucilius. An early Roman satirist; unluckily only fragments of his works remain. For an excellent account of his life, writings, and literary influence, consult Sellar, *Roman Poets of the Republic*, chap. viii, and Archbishop J. F. D'Alton's *Roman Literary Theory and Criticism*.

Tullius (Cicero). See note on chap. 21. **Superstitiones aniles.** Cf. Cic. *de divin.* ii. 125, 'superstitio imbecilli animi atque anilis'. 1 Tim. 4. 7, βεβήλους καὶ γραώδεις μύθους παραιτοῦ (ineptas et aniles fabulas devita : so the Vulgate).

computari. Davies' conj. for 'comparari.' **Sacerdos.** He was elected to the college of Augurs in 53 B.C.

CHAPTER 23
[*Inst. i.* 21]

Teucrus, or Teucer. Two heroes in antiquity were so named.

Tauri, a Thracian people. Their savage rites are mentioned by Herodotus (iv. 103); Pausanias (i. 43). It is on this custom of sacrificing visitors to their land that Euripides founded his play, the *Iphigenia in Tauris*. Mayor on Juv. xv. 116.

Latiaris, Min. Fel. xxi, xxx, 'Latiaris Jupiter homicidio colitur'. Cf. Tertull. *Apol.* ix (Mayor). Whether the sacrifice of the **sexagenarii** ever actually took place is not certain; Ovid (*Fast.* v. 621f.) denies it. What he does tell us is that rushes made into effigies were thrown into the river. **ex responso,** so rightly, by conjecture, for 'ex persona'.

Carthaginienses. Their abominable sacrifices were made to Baal-Moloch the fire-god, here identified with Saturn: see art. MOLOCH in *Encycl. Bibl.*

a Siculis, after their victory under Agathocles, 309 B.C. See Grote, *Hist. of Greece*, chap. xcvii.

Bellonae. For this war-goddess, cf. Tibull. i. 6, 45–50; Lucan, i. 565.

Isidis, Osiris. See note on chap. 11. For the curious legend of the murder (by his brother) of Osiris, his dismemberment, and the world-wide hunt by Isis and her final discovery of the limbs, see Diodorus quoted by Euseb. *Prep. Evang.* ii. 1.

COMMENTARY

On the worship of Isis (who has been likened to the Madonna), see Frazer, G.B., *Adonis, Attis, Osiris*, vol. 2, chap. 4. The cult of Isis was popular at Rome in later times; Lucan, viii. 831, 'nos in templa tuam Romana accepimus Isim'; Juv. viii. 29 with Mayor's n.; in Min. Fel. xxi. 7, we find a close parallel to the words of Lactantius. See too Apuleius, *Met.* xi; August., *de civ. Dei*, vi. 10, along with Wiedemann's *Realms of the Egyptian Dead*, and Sayce's Gifford Lectures, chap. vii.

Cynocephalus, Anubis, the dog-headed deity—'latrator Anubis' in Virgil—identified with Hermes as the great psychopomp.

Priapo. The gross indecency of the Priapus cult is frequently stigmatized by Augustine. Lampsacus, a town on the Hellespont.

Herculis. There is a much fuller account of this incident in the *Institutions*. Cf. Erasmus, *Adagia*, p. 623 (ed. 1643); Apollodorus, ii. 5, 10. On the (supposed) beneficent effect of curses, which were sometimes considered effectual in promoting the fertility of crops, cf. Frazer, G.B., *Magic Art*, i. 278.

Amalthea. Ovid, *Fast.* v. 114, does not mention this story of these Corybantes trying to drown the cries of the infant Jupiter with wild music, as he had written about it fully in iv. 203; and Lucr. refers to it (ii. 633): 'Dictaeos referunt Curetes qui Jovis illum vagitum in Creta quondam occultasse feruntur.'

CHAPTER 24
[*Inst. i.* 22, 23]

Didymus, the famous Alexandrian commentator (65 B.C.—A.D. 10), whose labours on Homer have proved of such value. See Sandys, *Hist. of Scholarship*, vol. i; Pearson, *Fragments of Sophocles*, vol. i. p. xl.

Poeta. Virg. *Aen.* vii. 136. The **Deum Matri** is Cybele. The cult of this Phrygian nature-goddess was introduced into Rome during the perilous times of the second Punic war, but it never took much root, as did the worship of Isis. Cf. Min. Fel. xxi. 11; Cumont, *Oriental Religions* (E.T.), pp. 47f.

Belus, 'primus rex Assyriorum ... unde et lingua Punica apud deos *Bel* dicitur', says Servius. Bel is a simple appellative as well as meaning Lord. Identified with Marduk (Merodach in Old Testament): Hebr. בל. The dates given below have no historical importance.

CHAPTER 25
[*Inst. ii.* 1–4]

aureum saeculum. See what Hesiod says in his *Works and Days*, 108f. As the pagan world put the 'golden age' in the past, so the Christian world puts it in the future. Read Browning's splendid poem 'Gerard de Lairesse' in *Parleyings with Certain People* (1887).

solum Deum. The belief in a primitive monotheism, though now scouted by anthropologists, may have something to say for itself. At least the germ of monotheism may be detected in the earliest times, though the actual cult of one God is not manifested. See the words of Ennius in Cic. *de nat. deor.* ii. 2, 4 (Mayor).

lapides. Cf. Acts **19**. 35, where the image of Artemis (Diana) at Ephesus was said to have fallen from heaven (διοπετής). It was probably a meteorite.

Lucretius, i.e. in vi. 52, where some read 'efficiunt'—not 'et faciunt.' For the next section certainly cf. (inter alia) Psalm **115**. 4–8.

qua reddunt, an unintelligible reading. Possibly we should read with Brandt '*quare* [simulacris se de]dunt', cf. *Inst.* II. iii. 9. For this section consult art. IMAGES in *Dict. of Christian Antiq.*, § iii, and Bevan, *Holy Images* (passim).

Dionysius, the first. The reference is to his expedition against the Greek cities of S. Italy (391 B.C.), pillaging the temples as he went. For this 'contemptor divum', see *Inst.* ii. 4, 16, and Grote's *Hist. of Greece*, chap. lxxxiii.

ἄνθρωπος, *quia sursum spectat*: ἄνω ἀθρέω, according to Etym. Magn. This derivation is obviously wrong, though countenanced by Plato in the *Cratylus*, 399. The fact that man, alone of the animal creation, looks *up*, was a favourite theme in antiquity: see my note on *Ep. to Diognetus*, chap. x, and Bünemann on *Inst.* II. i, §§ 13, 14; Mayor on Cic. *de nat. deor.* II. 56, § 140; Min. Felix, 17; Agrippa in Dio *Hist.* liii, τὸ ἀνθρώπινον πᾶν, ἅτε ἔκ τε θεῶν γεγονὸς καὶ ἐς θεοὺς ἀφῆξον, ἄνω βλέπει, to say nothing of the words in *Hermetica* (Stobaei), οἱ ἄνθρωποι πάντες ἄνω βλέπουσιν. More references in Mayor on Juv. xv. 147.

Prometheus. See Hor. *Odes*, i. 16, 13, 'fertur Prometheus addere principi limo coactus particulam undique desectam'. P. is represented in the myth of Plato's *Protagoras* as the creator of man. Cf. Apollodorus i. 7, 1, and Pausanias, x. 4, 4.

spirare dicimus. Virg. *Geor.* iii. 34, 'Stabunt et Parii lapides, spirantia signa'; *Aen.* vi. 847, 'excudent alii spirantia mollius aera'. It is worth noting that the great statue, by Pheidias, of Olympian Zeus was of such beauty and majesty that it was said that the god must have come down from heaven to show the sculpture his 'image', or that the sculptor must have gone to heaven to behold the god himself. See Frazer on *Pausanias* v. 11.

CHAPTER 26

[*Inst. ii.* 5]

elementa mundi here = bodies celestial; *mundi* being used, not of the earth but of the Universe itself. The Greek equivalent is στοιχεῖα; see the learned dissertation by Burton, *Galatians* (I.C.C.), pp. 510f.

Zeno, the father of Stoicism, taught that the gods of the vulgar were all 'elementa': Min. Fel. xix. The τέλος, the 'end', of his philosophy is defined in the well-known formula 'Life in accord with the Law of Nature'. In his system were incorporated some elements taken from Cynicism; see chap. 4 in Dudley's *History of Cynicism*. The famous Hymn of Cleanthes, Zeno's successor, is the high-water mark of Stoic theology. The Mosaic Law strictly prohibited any adoration of the 'host of heaven'.

aeternum. Cf. here, 2 Cor. 4. 18, 'the things which are seen are temporal, but the things which are not seen are eternal'.

CHAPTER 27
[*Inst. ii.* 7, 8–14]

Lactantius here follows primitive traditions on the subject of earliest man, as set forth in Genesis. The short section on the Fall of the Angels ('sons of God' in Gen. 6, as in Job 38. 7) is a piece of unassimilated mythology embedded in the folk-lore surrounding it. The 'fall' of those 'Sons of God' is told us in the book of Enoch 6, 7, and there are many writers who refer to it, e.g. Justin Martyr, Josephus, Tertullian. Augustine combats the notion, and justly disallows inspiration to Enoch, despite the testimony of Jude in his epistle.

With this chapter (27) the relevant sections in Driver's edition of Genesis should be read; for the Eden story consult Frazer, *Folk Lore in the O.T.*, vol. i. chap. 1; and Milton's *Paradise Lost*.

de nihilo. This theory was denied by most ancient philosophers (as it is by modern science for the most part, its principle being known as that of the indestructibility of matter). See Diog. Laert. ix. 44, recounting the opinions of Democritus, which were repeated by Aristotle. And see the note on 67.

centum viginti. Gen. 6. 3.

cataclysmi, viz. diluvii. The word is Greek, κατακλυσμός, and is used by Plato of Deucalion's flood (*Laws*, 677) as well as in the LXX version of the Noachic deluge (Gen. 7).

criminator. A somewhat rare term, but occurring in Plautus and Tacitus, and in Patristic authors.

caedem fratris, Abel. **Delator.** See Mayor on Juv. i. 33. Satan is spoken of as a malicious informer in Job 1, and Rev. 12. 10, ὁ κατήγορος τῶν ἀδελφῶν ἡμῶν.

The idea that the fallen angels (i.e. daemons) will console themselves by corrupting mankind is found in Min. Fel. xxvi. 8, 'ad solatium calamitatis'. In the fourth century the tradition of the 'Fall' was still unsettled. Lactantius gives a different version from that in the Epitome (in the second book of the *Institutes*). There was a curious suggestion made in early Patristic that the place left vacant in Heaven by the dispossessed angels would finally be occupied by the Elect. Milton refers to this in *P.L.* vii. 150–9. There are some interesting remarks on this subject in Saurat's work, *Milton, Man and Thinker*, part iv.

CHAPTER 28

[*Inst. ii.* 14–16]

There are interesting parallels to the statements made in this chapter: I would instance Minucius Felix, in particular chaps. xxvi–xxviii; Tertullian, *Apologeticus*, xxii, xxiii. A belief in daemons was basic with most of the Church Fathers. Paganism used the word daemon (δαίμων) to signify an invisible being, intermediate between the high gods and man; these might be good or evil, but the Christians regarded them as all bad. Cf. E. R. Bevan, *Holy Images*, pp. 90f. In some cases they were looked upon as 'guardian angels', in something like our sense of this rather ambiguous term. See, too, some remarks in Dr. Langton's *Satan, a portrait* (1946).

Socrates. He would speak of his 'sign', that supernatural something which took the form of a warning, a sudden inhibition. For his own account of it, see Plato's *Apology*, 31. Cf. Tertull. *Apol.* xxii, and some interesting remarks in Cic. *de div.* I. 54.

Geniorum. In Roman religion the indwelling spirit (numen) of a man. Cf. Hor. *Epp.* ii. 2, 187, 'Genius, natale comes qui temperat astrum, naturae deus humanae' (Orelli). Cf. our 'guardian angel'. In one of the fragments of Menander occur these words: ἅπαντι δαίμων ἀνδρὶ συμπαρίσταται εὐθὺς γενομένῳ, μυσταγωγὸς τοῦ βίου ἀγαθός, a passage to which Ammianus Marcellinus refers in one of his chapters on Julian, the Emperor. The **Penates**, the spirits of the store-room, and protectors of the family (together with the Lares), akin to the *teraphim* of the Old Testament; cf. Genesis 31. 19.

necyomantias (or necromantias). For this word, see Pease's note on Cic. *de divinatione*, lviii. 132. Lactantius seems to have forgotten that the use of **sortes**, the casting of lots, not only was practised by the Jews, but was employed in the New Testament; see Acts 1. 26.

ambiguos exitus. The pagan oracles were renowned for the ambiguity of their responses; see Cic. *de div.* ii. 56, 115 with Pease's note. There were four main divisions of these μαντεῖα, viz. oral oracles, oracles by signs, oracles by dreams, oracles of the dead. The Delphic oracle was the most famous. The article on Greek oracles by F. W. H. Myers in *Hellenica* should be read.

inesse numen. See Min. Fel. xxvii, 'impuri spiritus, daemones, sub statuis et imaginibus delitescunt'; Cyprian, *de idol. vanit.* iv; August. *de civ. Dei*, ii. 24 f.; id. *de catech. rud.* xix. 32; 1 Cor. **10**. 20. Instead of **plane terroris**, I follow Davies, who conjectures acutely 'plena terroris'.

CHAPTER 29
[*Inst. ii.* 17]

daemoniarchen. Davies' ingenious conj. for 'daemoni archon'. The word occurs once in the *Hermetica*.

Chrysippus (282–206 B.C.), the successor of Cleanthes as head of the Stoic school at Athens. A gossipy account of him is given in the *Lives* of Diogenes Laertius, with a list of his voluminous writings. There was a ceaseless controversy among ancient philosophers whether evil may not be necessary for the better evolution of the good. Cleanthes, in his great Hymn, regards the Supreme Being as having fitted all, evil with good, in one great whole, so that in all things reigns one Reason everlastingly. But the old problem remains unsolved.

Providentia ($\Pi\rho o\nu o\iota a$), a half-divinized word. It is often used to-day as = God; and so it was by Milton, *P.L.* xii. end.

Aulus Gellius. His *Noctes Atticae* consists of notes and comments on books he had read, conversations he had heard, with much miscellaneous matter. His date is sometime in the second century A.D. He is a sort of Burton.

Plato ait, in the *Phaedo* 60 (Socrates is speaking): 'how strange a thing is pleasure, so called! how remarkable its relation to pain, which appears to be its opposite! These will not come together; if a man pursues one and secures it, he is pretty certain to be compelled to accept the other also, as though they were two things united at one end, cf. Diog. Laert. ii. 89. **importunitas** is a difficult word to render adequately: I take it as = 'infortunium'.

CHAPTER 30
[*Inst.* ii. 18, 19; iii. 1, 2]

studium sapientiae, Cic. *de Off* ii. 2, 5, 'Nec quidquam aliud est philosophia praeter studium sapientiae'. A Stoic definition. Contrast the words of Paul (1 Cor. **1**. 21), 'the world by its wisdom knew not God', where by $\sigma o\phi\iota a$ (*sapientia*, that false wisdom of which Lactantius speaks above,) is meant 'speculative wisdom' which the Stoics regarded as the basis of virtue.

grammaticus = scholar, humanist, man of letters; not 'grammarian' in the narrow sense of the word.

CHAPTER 31
[*Inst. iii.* 3]

opinatio, in Greek οἴησις and δόξα. In the *Republic* of Plato Socrates is represented as establishing the true distinction between 'knowledge' and 'opinion'. For the Platonic doctrine concerning the relation between δόξα and ἐπιστήμη (knowledge), see the *Meno*, and the discussion in excursus 7 of E. S. Thompson's edition of that dialogue.

Zeno, the Stoic; not Zeno of Elea.

Cicero, in *de Off*. ii. 2, 5; *Tusc. D*. iv. 26, 57.

Academicis. The disciples of the New Academy, which, like the Old Academy, derives from the School of Plato. Their sceptical views are mentioned by Cicero in *de Orat*. i. 10, 43; *Acad*. ii, 3, 7. The Academics asserted that nothing could be known for certain ('percipi nihil posse'): see next chapter. Cf. Bacon, *Novum Organum*, i, § 37. It should be noted here that if the Socratic method began in scepticism, its object was to re-establish the foundations of knowledge on a firmer basis.

CHAPTER 32
[*Inst. iii.* 4, 5, 6]

nihil sciri. Tennyson, *In Mem*. § 54, 'Behold, we know not anything', and *The Ancient Sage*.

non modo = 'non modo non'. A frequent idem, the *non* being omitted when the two negative clauses have a verb in common.

Eusebius (in the 15th book of his *Praeparatio Evangelica*) cites from Plutarch a large number of examples to exhibit the varying and discordant character of the views held by philosophers in and before his time. Socrates, as we know well, related his own distaste for all physical speculations (see Plato, *Phaedo*, xlv; Xen. *Memor*. i. 1, 11–15). St. Paul's words 'let no man make you his prey through his philosophy' should not be understood as a disparagement of all philosophy, but an attack on those vain speculations which were characteristic of the competing systems of his own day. He would certainly have warmly agreed with the dictum of Pythagoras who, while calling himself a lover of wisdom (i.e. φιλόσοφος), was modest enough to admit that no man could be called 'wise', but only God. The attitude of most Church Fathers was to a large degree hostile to philosophy—Tertullian in particular—and Augustine devotes a whole chapter to the dissensions of its exponents (*de civ. Dei*, xviii. 41); but the Alexandrian fathers (and Clement especially) regarded it as a propaedeutic, training men for the Gospel. Bacon's great aphorism is justly famous (*Essay* xvi): 'a little philosophy inclineth men's mind to atheism, but depth in philosophy bringeth men's minds about to religion'. But read the whole essay, and see Draper, *Intellectual Development of Europe*, vol. i. chaps. v, vi. Cicero's words (*de nat. deor.* II. xxi, § 56) are to the point here: (if any man can view the wonderful order of nature and suppose that no supervising Intelligence is behind all phenomena) 'is ipse mentis expers habendus est'.

CHAPTER 33
[*Inst. iii.* 7, 8.]

summum bonum. In Cic. (*de Leg.*) we read: 'ipsum bonum non est opinionibus sed natura' (viz. 'naturale bonum' = φυσικὸν ἀγαθόν). Horace in the *Satires* (ii. 6, 76) has 'boni summum'; Persius, iv. 17, 'summa boni'. Cf. Cic. *Acad.* i. 5, 21; Lucr. vi. 26. Boëthius, iii, prosa 9, 'Deum summum bonum esse colligimus'. Browning finds the 'highest good' in love. What can be finer than the definition of man's chief end in the words of the document known in Scotland as the 'Shorter Catechism'—'to glorify God and enjoy Him forever'? Cf. the relevant chapter in Boëthius, *de consol. philos.* iii, prosa 10, 'Summum bonum est ipse Deus'. The conception of a Chief Good was a leading one among ancient philosophers (as may be seen in the *Ethics of Aristotle* and elsewhere); but the answers to the question 'What *is* that Good?' were wavering and inconsistent. It is not so in the Hebrew economy, when at its highest, or in the Christian ethic. Modern philosophers are, like the ancient, divided on this question. Kant, for example, by the necessity of his thought, held that the *summum bonum* must be understood as involving not moral virtue alone but also happiness, and that this happiness will be distributed in exact proportion to goodness. On the other hand Bentham laid it down that the *summum bonum* consisted in 'the greatest happiness of the greatest number'. Cf. Locke, *Concerning Human Understanding*, II. xxi, § 56; H. Sidgwick, *Methods of Ethics*, p. 3; and cf. what Cicero says in *Acad.* I. x. 35. For Augustine the 'summum bonum' is found in the knowledge of God (*de beata vita*).

Aristippus, once a disciple of Socrates: he was reputed one of the most refined of the Hedonists. Consult Gomperz, *Greek thinkers*, vol. ii. chap. 9 [E.T.], and cf. the well-known lines of Horace (*Epp.* i. 1, 17): Conington's version:—

'Anon to Aristippus' camp I flit
And say the world's for me, not I for it.'

Several of the minor philosophers named here are mentioned by Cicero, *Acad.* ii. 42, 129–31. **Pyrrho,** the arch-sceptic and universal doubter: Byron, *Don Juan*, ix, § 18. There is a brief notice of him in Euseb. *Prep. Evang.* 763-5. **Peripatetics,** viz. the Aristotelians. Of this company Theophrastus was one of the most eminent.

The place of Zeno in philosophy is of considerable importance; for a good, though brief account of the Stoic school, founded by him, see Schwegler, *Hist. of Phil.*, and a much more elaborate discussion in Caird, *Evolution of Theology in the Greek Philosophers*, vol. ii. Not to be confused with Zeno of Elea.

cum natura congruenter. Cf. Cic. *de Fin.* iii. 7, 26. This celebrated formula of the Stoics has caused difficulty, for 'natura' is an ambiguous word. It seems to imply that we must conform to the law and order as exhibited in the universe about us, and the general course of things, as guided by reason. But *natura* may signify human nature, implying that man, having a fixed place in the economy of the world, and being endowed with reason, finds his true end to live in accord with that reason. The Greek equivalent is ὁμολογουμένως τῇ φύσει ζῆν: Marc. Aur. iii. 4; Diog. Laert. vii. 87; compare Ritter and Preller, *Hist. phil. Graec.* § 413. The Stoics then put all moral perfection into this 'nature' of theirs; yet it was but an abstraction. In practice, however, men like the Emperor Marcus Aurelius felt that to live 'according to nature' (κατὰ φύσιν) was to live according to man's whole nature, and not a part of it. Bishop Butler's second sermon *Upon human nature* should certainly be read in the present context.

CHAPTER 34

[*Inst.* iii. 10, 11]

Cicero ait, *de Legibus*, i. 10, § 28.

commune : so 'communitas'; κοινωνία, is 'society'; 'communis vita' = social union. Below 'communione sensus'.

ab eodem Deo. Cf. Acts **17**, 28, 'for we are also His offspring'.

scilicet here = namely (like δηλονότι in late Greek).

sustinentia. Not found in most lexicons: it is found in the Vulgate.

persequetur, in (I suppose) a legal sense = *prosecute*. Christian believers were not encouraged to bring their disputes into court against 'brethren': 1 Cor. **6**, 1–7. Naturally, as these courts were in heathen hands.

CHAPTER 35

[*Inst. iii.* 12–16]

patientissime. I have adopted this in the text instead of 'sapientissime'.

COMMENTARY 147

non mortalitate = immortalitate, which perhaps should be read. Yet we have in Lucr. i. 1075, 'per non medium'; and in Cic. *Acad.* i. 11, 39, 'non corpus' for 'incorporeum' or 'incorporale'. For the discussion on immortality, see chap. 70.

λογική, **philosophia**, viz. the philosophy of logic, or as we should say 'dialectic', as opposed to ethics.

CHAPTER 36
[*Inst. iii.* 17, 18]

EPICURUS (340–271 B.C.), whose school at Athens was called 'The Garden'. He taught that 'pleasure' was the 'summum bonum'; but this has been often misrepresented; it was not sensual pleasure he inculcated, but happiness, to be brought about by a prudent conduct of life. He did not deny the existence of gods, but thought of them as having no interest in or care for this world. Only fragments of his innumerable works have survived, though some of his letters are extant, together with one treatise discovered in modern times. His system, including the Atomic theory inherited from others, is expounded by Lucretius (with some of its harsher features softened) in his great poem, *de rerum natura.* For full information on Epicurus the reader is referred to the relevant sections in Diogenes Laertius; Cicero's *de natura deorum* and his *Academica* (and cf. note on chap. 1, above).—
PYTHAGORAS was one of the most interesting figures in ancient times; to-day he is mainly known for the proposition given in Euclid, I. 47. His date was 6th century B.C. After leaving his birthplace in Samos, he is said to have travelled in the near and, it may be, the farther East: certainly the conditioning elements in his teaching were largely Oriental —for example, the theory of transmigration of souls (metempsychosis), inherent in Buddhism, the entrance of which into the Vedic tradition is considered to have been late. Pythagoras finally settled in Italy, where he founded a religious brotherhood, somewhat on the lines of monasticism. The rule for initiates was strict. His devotees were instructed to believe (*a*) in an immortality of the soul, (*b*) in transmigration, (*c*) in the duty of abstaining from all flesh diet. He thought he had found the key of the cosmos in his doctrine of Number, with which he identified the One, the Monad, the Absolute Good; his theory involved a partial belief in 'evolution'.

He seems to have left no writings, but he and his followers were frequently referred to in antiquity, e.g. by Plato, Aristotle, Cicero; in later times by Eusebius, Augustine, John of Salisbury, and others. See Schwegler, *Hist. of Phil.*, pp. 11, 352; Burnet, *Early Greek Phil.*, chap. vii; and for a crowd of references, Mayor's note on Tertullian, *Apol.* pp. 457, 8. Traces of Pythagoreanism will be seen in Virgil's *Sixth Aeneid.*

Providentia, personified, as in chap. 29: a post-Augustan use.
nihil curat. Cf. Tennyson's *Lucretius* where he speaks of the Epicurean heaven in which 'no sound of human sorrow mounts to mar their sacred everlasting calm'.
semina minuta, i.e. atoms. Lucr. i. 617f. ii. 522f. (with Munro's notes).
coitu fortuito. Cic. *de nat. deor.* I. xxiv (Mayor).
mente conveniunt. Lucr. ii. 549, 50, 'unde ubi qua vi et quo pacto congressa coibunt materiae tanto in pelago turbaque aliena' (i.e. of atoms differing in kind). **hamata et angulata.** Cic. *Acad.* ii. 38, 121.
suem ... vivere. Hor. *Epp.* I. ii. 26 (with the note of Obbarius).
Euphorbum, one of the Trojan heroes. The whole story as told by Ovid, *Met.* xv, should be read, as well as the long account of Pythagoras in Diog. Laert. viii, where Euphorbus is duly mentioned. It may be added here that there are some noteworthy points of comparison between Epicureanism and Indian systems of philosophy in connection with the Atomic theory.

CHAPTER 37
[*Inst. iii.* 18, 20]

Lactantius, in this chapter, is distinctly unfair to Socrates, whose faults were more than outbalanced by his noble qualities. The late Prof. A. E. Taylor's little book on that great teacher puts his character in a very different light.
oraculo. From the oracular shrine of Apollo at Delphi. See Plato's *Apology*, §§ 21, 22; Diog. Laert. ii, § 37. See Grote's *Plato*, chap. vii.
quod supra nos, etc. Lactantius puts a wrong interpretation on this saying of Socrates (which, by the way, Tertullian assigns to Epicurus). For a just interpretation, see Cic. *Acad.* i, § 15; and cf. *Tusc.* v, § 10 (an oft quoted passage).
per anserem canemque. A matter often referred to in the Platonic dialogues. But Socrates meant no more by it than do we when we say 'By Jove!'
prosecrare. Late Latin. **post se** = 'post mortem suam'. But the conj. 'pro se' may be right. The reference in this section is to the closing scene in Socrates' life, told so movingly in the *Phaedo* of Plato.

CHAPTER 38

[Inst. iii. 21-3]

In this chapter we may see Lactantius at his best. It is marked by plain common sense.

deum philosophorum. Cic. *de nat. deor.* ii. 12, 32. His opinion of Plato is given in a passage that is familiar (*Tusc. Disp.* i. 17, 39): 'errare mehercule malo cum Platone quam cum istis [those who deny immortality] vera sentire'.

Plato's views on community in marriage, in the ideal State, are formulated in the fifth book of the *Republic*. Tertullian, *Apol.* xxxix, says of the Christians, 'omnia indiscreta *praeter uxores*'. Cf. *Ep. ad Diogn.* v, § 6. This revolting piece of doctrine was naturally repudiated by Christians.

quin etiam feminis, etc. Plato, in the *Laws* (804) writes: 'our principle is that there must be the completest association of the female sex with the male in education and *in everything else*'. Plato's original scheme for a community in women and children and also in property was rejected by Aristotle: see Newman, *Politics of Aristotle*, vol. i. pp. 158f.

tanquam morbum. Contrast this horrible doctrine with Bacon's grand aphorism: 'the nobler a soul is, the more objects of compassion it hath'. Coleridge, in his *Aids to Reflection*, can exclaim: 'where Virtue is, compassion is the ornament and becoming attire of Virtue'. Cf. Virg. *Aen.* i. 630, 'non ignara mali miseris succurrere disco'. A hundred years later we find a connate notion in Hebr. 4. 15. Contrast Nietzsche, chapter on the Compassionate in *Thus Spake Zarathustra*.

qui ... excitantur. See the chapter in Seneca, *de clem.* ii. 5.

dissoluti. Cf. Cicero in the Verrine orations (*de suppliciis*, ii. 5, 3): (he preferred to be) 'crudelis in animadvertendo quam in praetermittendo dissolutus'.

paria peccata. For this paradox, cf. Cic. *de Fin.* iii. 14, 48; id. *Parad.* iii.

CHAPTER 39

[Inst. iii. 23, 24; 15, 18]

There is much in this chapter that demands a 'caveat'. Lactantius is unfair in pointing out errors and absurdities in the philosophers he names, neglecting their good things. For example: Xenophanes of Colophon (6th century B.C.) surely deserves credit for his attack on the theogonies of Homer and Hesiod (in that respect a forerunner of Plato), his approximation to some sort of monotheistic doctrine, his ridicule of the Pythagorean teaching about transmigration, the discredit thrown on an anthropomorphic conception of deity: see Burnet (*Early Greek Phil.* chap. ii), who has a valuable chapter on Empedocles, the Sicilian poet-philosopher: see also Matthew Arnold's fine poem *Empedocles on Etna.* He is referred to in Milton, *P.L.* iii. 469. For most of the other philosophers named by L., see Bevan, *Later Greek Religion.* Cato, the younger, seeing that the Republican cause was lost during the Civil War, took his own life. He is one of the heroes of Lucan, who wrote of him this memorable line: 'victrix causa deis placuit sed victa Catoni' (*Phars.* i. 128). Addison wrote a tragedy on Cato's life and suicide.

alia. An emendation by Routh for *illa.*

Antipodes. Cf. Cic. *Acad.* ii. 39, 123; August. *de civ. Dei,* xvi. 9 (with Welldon's note). The existence of the Antipodes was rejected by Augustine and by most of the Church Fathers. One of the Popes actually condemned a bishop for asserting that there were antipodes; see some remarks on the incapacity for conceiving their existence in Mill's *Logic,* v. 3, § 3. Cf. Lightfoot on Clem. Rom. xx; Lecky's *Hist. of Rationalism,* vol. i.

choro canum, viz. the Cynics. Lucian has an amusing (and satirical) dialogue on these people, whose 'school' was founded, according to the orthodox account, by Antisthenes. They might be dubbed the 'mendicant order' or ascetics of antiquity. Cynicism has been dubbed a debased version of the ethics of Socrates, as it exaggerated his austerity to the point, at times, of absurdity, hardening his 'irony' to sardonic laughter at the follies of mankind, but affording no real parallel to his genuine love for, and search after, knowledge. See Dudley's elaborate monograph, *A history of Cynicism* (1937). The most notorious of the Cynics was Diogenes of Sinope, the truest representative of the Cynical 'way of life', and a somewhat disagreeable one at that. Augustine criticizes them with great severity in *de civ. Dei,* xiv. 20. Cf. Davidson, *The Stoic Creed,* pp. 130f.; Gomperz, *Greek Thinkers,* vol. ii. 144 [E.T.]. There is a long chatty account of Diogenes in Diog. Laert. vi.

homicidii crimine. Though suicide was disallowed by Plato (in the *Phaedo*), who is followed by Cicero, it was commended (in certain circumstances) in the Stoic creed, as an act of self-liberation when life had become unendurable. Even Cicero approved of Cato's death. See Mayor's notes on Pliny, *Epp.* iii. 7. Cf. Shakespeare, *Hamlet,* i. 2, 132 [God's] 'canon 'gainst self-slaughter'; and *Cymbeline,* iii. 4, 77. Here is a problem for Casuists. There is a brief but interesting discussion on the moral implications of that problem in Dean Rashdall's *Theory of Good and Evil,* vol. i. pp. 207–13.

It is worth while looking up the following references: Plato in the *Laws* (854, 873); Cic., *Tusc. D.,* i. 30, 74; Seneca, who devotes a whole

COMMENTARY

letter to the question (*Ep.* 77); August., *Epp.* 173, and *de civ. Dei*, i. 19, 20. Dante reserved the second circle of the *Inferno* to self-slaughterers. See too an essay by Montaigne, ii. 23. Suicide is not actually forbidden in O.T. Compare the words of Epictetus, ix, xxix.

CHAPTER 40
[*Inst.* iii. 28, 30]

tenebris. Cic. *Acad.* ii. 39, 102, 'omnia crassis occultata et circumfusa tenebris'.

puteo. Diog. Laert. ix. 72, ἐν βυθῷ ἡ ἀλήθεια = truth lies in an abyss.

Socrates dicit. But what does he say in the *Theaetetus*? that true wisdom consists in 'becoming like God' (ὁμοίωσις Θεῷ). Cf. the *Apol.* 23–24.

CHAPTER 41
[*Inst.* iv. 2, 3]

Deum ... sapientia. Cf. Ecclesiastes 12. 13.
simulacrum suum. Cf. Wisdom 2. 23.
illis, i.e. the philosophers previously named.
neque in sacris. Clement of Alexandria thought otherwise, holding that secular philosophy was a schoolmaster (παιδαγωγός) to lead men to Christ. For the best of early Christian writers the Gospel *is* the philosophy, par excellence: Justin Martyr, for instance. Note what Bacon says at the conclusion of his *Advancement of learning*.

CHAPTER 42
[*Inst.* iv. 6, 7]

fideliter. So I would read for 'fidelem'.

opifice, consiliatore. Here we have two words which in Greek would be δημιουργός and σύμβολος. But in the Hermetic document the former of these words is applied not to the Son, but to the Supreme Deity.

suis spiritibus. Why the plural? Was Rev. 3. 1 in the mind of Lactantius?

Of what passage in Plato was Lactantius thinking, when he said that Plato spoke of a first and a second God? In Scott's *Hermetica* (vol. iv. p. 20) there is a note which says the probable place is *Timaeus* 28ᶜ and especially the end of that baffling dialogue, 92; Lactantius, imagining that the Hermetic document was the earlier, thought Plato was perhaps following Trismegistus. Browning seemed to have had the notion of a *second* God in mind when he wrote *Ixion*:

'Out of the wreck I rise, past Zeus to the Potency o'er him,' where Zeus is no longer supreme (as was supposed) but inferior to the One Absolute. For **sine ipso nihil**, cf. John 1. 3.

in libris, i.e. in the seven books of the Institutes.

Salomon. The old belief that Solomon wrote the book is quite untenable.

in Revelatione, viz. 19. 12.

CHAPTER 43

[*Inst. iv.* 7–11]

In this chapter, as in the last, Lactantius writes as a Subordinationist, and his standpoint does not appear to differ materially from Tertullian's. In a sense Subordinationism has never wholly vanished from the Church, as Bigg remarks in his *Origins of Christianity*, chap. xv. Did the Apologists share in the notion? Origen certainly did not deny it (Harnack, *Hist. of Dogma*, iii. pp. 134f. (E.T.)). Possibly the Subordinationists relied on Paul's words in 1 Cor. **15.** 28. For a criticism of this belief, see Liddon's Bampton Lectures. Calvin treated the Nicene formula 'God, Light of Light' as a dream of Platonizing Greeks. See some observations by Hooker, *Eccl. Pol.* viii, §§ 4, 6.

Lactantius is thinking of the parable of the wicked husbandmen: Matt. **21.** 33–46 = Mark **12.** 1–12 = Luke **20.** 9–19.

sanctus spiritus, '*a* sacred spirit'; not of course *the* Holy Spirit. Cf. here Romans **1.** 3, 4.

CHAPTER 44

[*Inst. iv.* 12]

infirmatus (for which Rendel Harris conj. *insinuatus*). Lactantius is here quoting from the *Odes of Solomon*, xix. See J. B. Bernard's edition of that work (1912), pp. 4–6 and 87. Outside the writings of Lactantius these Odes do not appear to be referred to by any Latin writers. The word *infirmatus* is from the dep. verb, 'infirmor' (see Benoist and Goelzer's Latin Dict.). No sense can be made of either verb here. 'Quaere an legendum *informatus*' (i.e. shaped, moulded for a special purpose)?

The various passages quoted are from the following: (*a*) Is. vii. 14. *Virgo*, in LXX παρθένος, in other Greek versions νεᾶνις (Hebrew 'almah'). Who is this? Probably no ref. is made to the Incarnation, though many commentators think so. See Skinner's exhaustive note in his commentary. (*b*) Is. xlv. 14–16. (*c*) Jeremiah = Baruch iii. 35–7. (*d*) Jer. xvii. 9. (*e*) Is. xix. 20. (*f*) Numbers xxiv. 17; part of the Balaam prophecy.

COMMENTARY 153

medius, as in Virg. *Aen.* vii. 536. In Greek μεσίτης, Hebr. 8. 6.

CHAPTER 45
[*Inst. iv.* 13, 15, 18]

magica, i.e. through daemonic agency. Cf. Luke 11. 14f., and the parallel passages in Matthew and Mark.
Sibyllinis. It is not to be forgotten that these 'carmina' were forgeries, as I have already noted. **excaecavit.** Shakespeare, *Ant. and Cleop.* iii. 13, 111: 'But when we in our viciousness grow hard (O misery on't!) the wise gods seal our eyes.'
Salomon in Sapientia, i.e. Wisdom 2. 12–22. See on chap. 42.
acetum. Mark says 'wine drugged with myrrh'. It was usual to give this to crucified criminals, as a narcotic. Lactantius speaks as if the executioners were Jews; they were Roman soldiers.

CHAPTER 46
[*Inst. iv.* 18, 19, 21]

The scripture references in this chapter are as follows (they differ in wording from the A.V. and R.V. versions in several points; cf. with Vulg.): (*a*) Is. 50. 6; (*b*) Is. 53. 7; (*c*) Ps. 35. 15, 16; (*d*) Ps. 69. 21; (*e*) Ps. 22. 16–18; (*f*) Deut. 28. 66; (*g*) Num. 23. 19; (*h*) Zech. 12. 10; (*i*) Amos 8. 9, 10; (*j*) Jer. 15. 9; (*k*) 1 Kings 9. 7–9 (These words not in our Bibles).
Vespasianus. The revolt in Judaea had long been prepared; it broke out in A.D. 66. Vespasian was in command of the Roman armies, but the actual capture of Jerusalem took place under his son Titus, who succeeded his father as emperor. The date of that destruction, of city and temple, is A.D. 70. For a brief account of the war and its termination, see Bury, *Roman Empire,* pp. 366–73.
Salomon. The words 'et persecuti sunt ... magna' have no place in the original; they are clearly a Christian adscript. Earlier in this quotation the word 'improperium' is peculiar to ecclesiastical writers (= Greek ὀνείδισις, 'opprobrium'). 'Transiet' for the more regular 'transibit' (and similar forms) will be found in various other writers.

CHAPTER 47
[*Inst. iv.* 19–21]

patibulo. A yoke shaped somewhat like a T, fixed on a criminal's back; to its arms he was tied, before being led to the place of execution. Cf. Plaut. *Mil.* 360, 'est pereundum extra portam | Dispessis manibus patibulum quom habebis'. Here used for the cross itself.

exuviae = garments, as in chap. 68 and Virg. *Aen.* iv. 496. Of the shed skin of a snake, Lucan, ix. 718. Often of the spoils of an enemy.

corruptionem. Ps. 16. (=15.) 10. So Vulg.; LXX, διαφθοράν (cf. Acts 2. 27). Brandt would read *interitum*. The Hebrew word here = *pit*.

Osee (13. 13, 14). This rendering, which deviates widely from the Hebrew, is fairly close to LXX. **Aculeus.** May mean either 'goad' or 'sting'. Cf. *Te Deum*, devicto mortis aculeo, translated in P.B. 'sharpness'. Cf. 1 Cor. **15.** 55, where κέντρον is used. This is rendered 'sting' both in A.V. and R.V. **Idem rursus. 6.** 2.

Filius hominis (Daniel **7,** 13, 14). *A* son of man, not as in A.V. *the*. See Driver.

David. These words of the Psalmist were made use of by Jesus in an altercation with the Pharisees: Matt. **22.** 43–5. Here we have an oracle of Jehovah, sent to a king, appointing him as His vice-gerent and priest. Mystically, we may suppose, this psalm predicts the progress of the Messiah, the advance of Christianity throughout the world, and the conquest of the Powers of Evil.

CHAPTER 48
[*Inst. iv.* 18–20]

The scripture references are as follows: (*a*) Jer. **12.** 7, 8; (*b*) Mal. **1.** 10, 11; (*c*) Is. **66.** 18; (*d*) Is. **42.** 6, 7.

The quotation from Esdras is not found in the Bible, but is referred to by Justin Martyr. Cf. 1 Cor. **5.** 7, τὸ πάσχα ἡμῶν Χριστός.

habemus humiliare (for which some would prefer 'debemus'). This use of 'habeo' with infin. is not common in classical Latin outside of Cicero: cf. for example, the *de nat deor*. xxxix. 93.

CHAPTER 49
[*Inst. iv.* 28, 29]

The doctrine here adumbrated corresponds with the teaching set forth in the fourth Gospel. Cf. too 1 John **2.** 23; **5.** 12.

nec . . . habendum. See the *Quicunque vult*.

omnia ei tribuat. John **3.** 35.

unum. John **10.** 30, 'I and my Father are one'. In both cases we have the neuter, ἕν, '*unum*'. What seems implied is not so much a unity of essence as intimacy of communion.

substantia, οὐσία. The natural equivalent of οὐσία would be *essentia*. See Hatch, *Hibbert Lectures* (1888), pp. 277f.

COMMENTARY.

CHAPTER 50
[*Inst. iv.* 22–4]

substringam. Cf. n. in Preface on this word (= lightly touch upon).
derogabit, i.e. detract from. In law = repeal.
verbis ... factis. An early example of this sentiment will be found in Plato, *Laws,* 729ᶜ; Seneca, *Ep.* vi. 5, 'longum iter est per praecepta, breve et efficax per exempla'. Dr. Johnson (in *Rasselas*), 'example is always more efficacious than precept'.
adimpletur. Nowadays we should, in the jargon of latter-day politics, say 'implemented'. The word is frequent in Cyprian.
virtutes. Another reading, adopted by Brandt, is *virtutis.*

CHAPTER 51
[*Inst. iv.* 26, 27]

sacramentum. This was the regular translation (in Vulg. and elsewhere) of μυστήριον = religious mystery (see a note in Gibb and Montgomery's edition of the *Confessions* of Augustine, iv. 3). It cannot always bear its familiar modern sense. It originally meant the military oath by which soldiers promised loyalty to their commander-in-chief. In the Fathers the word has several meanings—symbol, creed, pledge, a sacred ordinance, as Welldon has shown in a note in his edition of August. *de civ. Dei,* iv. 33.
sublimem. John 3. 14. In the previous sentence Lactantius gives a very inadequate and indeed fanciful meaning to 'integris ossibus'.
fugatur. Note present tenses here; they seem to imply that exorcism was still common in the fourth century. **hoc signo.** One naturally calls to mind that these words were inscribed on the cross which was supposed to have been seen in the sky by Constantine, just before his battle with, and victory over, Maxentius. The words—in Greek τούτῳ νίκα—are usually quoted as 'in hoc signo vinces'. See note in Euseb. *Hist.,* p. 298 of Lawlor and Oulten's trans., vol. 2, and the article in Smith and Cheetham's *Dict. of Christian Antiq.,* s.v. LABARUM. Cf. Prudentius, *Cathemer.* vi, where he bids the Devil depart with his co-daemons: '*signum,* quod ipse nosti, damnat tuam catervam'. Compare Gwatkin in *Cambr. Medieval Hist.,* vol. i. p. 4.

For the sign of the Cross in order to *put* the 'cohors daemonum' to flight, see the twenty-seventh chapter of the *Inst.* book iv. The use of the Cross as an instrument of miraculous efficacy was constantly alluded to in the Fathers: Walpole, note in *Early Latin Hymns,* p. 131.

ejus iidem. A good conj. adopted here for ejusdem (cf. *Inst.* iv. 27, 2). **verberanti Deo.** Cf. the oracle (Greek) quoted in *Inst.* i. 7, 10.

CHAPTER 52
[*Inst. iv.* 28; *v.* 1, 9, 12]

With this and the following sections we may compare the chapters in Tertullian's *Apologeticus*, vii. f., *Ep. ad Diog.* v. vi. The pagans accused the Christians of every sort of offence: they showed no signs of guilt when accused; they despised heathen temples; they indulged in nightly orgies; they held aloof from their heathen neighbours; they had neither images nor altars; they refused to attend the public shows; they were guilty of atheism (we may call to mind the yells of the mob when Polycarp was brought to martyrdom—αἶρε τοὺς ἀθέους). These and many other charges are indicated in the *Octavius* of Minucius Felix, or alluded to in Justin Martyr's *Apologies*. As regards the words in the preceding section ('philosophiam . . . pro nihilo'), see Lightfoot on Coloss. 2. 8.

pietas = clementia. Contrast with this the words of Cleon (in Thucyd. iii. 40, § 2), 'Do not be misled by pity, or eloquent pleading, or by a forgiving temper' (ἐπιεικείᾳ).

inter mucrones. Cf. *Inst.* v. 9, 3, 'est locus inter arma clementiae'.

nec victorum = ' ne v. quidem'. So in Juv. 2. 152 (that ghosts exist), 'nec pueri credunt'. A post-Aug. use of 'nec'.

odium . . . veritas parit. From Terence, *Andr.* i. 1, 41. Cicero quotes the words in *de amic.* § 89.

CHAPTER 53
[*Inst. v.* 11, 12, 19]

se ipsos defendunt. 'deorum injuriae dis curae' (a famous saying of the Emperor Tiberius), Tac. *Ann.* i. 73.

verbis . . . verberibus, 'paronomasia'. We have examples of this play on words in the New Testament, e.g. Rom. 1. 29, 31. Such assonances were, in English, affected by the Euphuists.

For the sentiment expressed below one may compare some lines in Seneca's play (*Phoen.* i. 98): 'who forces another to die unwillingly is on a level with one who would hinder him when bent on death. To prevent a man from dying, when he wishes for death, is equivalent to murder.'

utere sorte tua. From Virg. *Aen.* xii. 932.

CHAPTER 54
[*Inst. v.* 13, 19, 20; 11, 9]

impotentes, without self-control. So in Horace, Cicero, and often. Greek ἀκρατής. The meaning 'powerless' is comparatively rare. In Livy ix. 14, 5 we have 'suarum impotens rerum' = unable to manage his own affairs.

In the persecution period the very admission 'Christianus sum' was regarded as sufficient condemnation; torture followed to force a denial from the victim. For a good general account see Gwatkin, *Early Church Hist.*, especially vol. ii. chap. 26; and Bigg, *Origins of Christianity* (passim).

carnificinam. The word has three meanings: (1) office of executioner, (2) the rack, (3) place of torture.

desperatos. Cf. Tertull. *Apol.* 50, 'merito victis non placemus; propterea enim desperati et perditi existimamur' (with Mayor's note); Bingham, *Antiquities,* I. ii. 8.—One needs remember that if Roman emperors persecuted Christians, the Roman Pontiffs, in the heyday of their power, sanctioned the persecution of 'heretics', with torture and death. The pitiless Torquemada, first Inquisitor-General in Spain, followed faithfully in the footsteps of Nero, Domitian, Decius, Diocletian; yet he was counted 'justus piusque' by his Church. 'Tantum religio potuit suadere malorum.'

sacris dii eorum. So I read for 'sacris deorum'.

CHAPTER 55
[*Inst. v.* 19, 20, 14]

addicti = enslaved, as in Seneca *ad Helv.* xi. 6, 'ingenia corporibus suis addicta'. Technically the word indicates the status of a debtor who became a bondman to his creditor.

Aegyptii. See Juvenal *Sat.* xv for some caustic comments on Egyptian worship.

mimi. The ridicule of gods on the stage is alluded to in Arnobius iv. 35, and by Augustine, *de civ. Dei,* iv. 26; Tertullian, *Apol.* xv.

philosophi. Epicurus in particular.

vocabulum boni. A reminiscence of Is. 5. 20.

conciliata. Cf. Lact. *de ira,* vii. 13 (man alone bears rule) 'cetera sibi conciliata sunt'. Note that the following passages are reproduced from Cic. *de rep.* iii. 7. Justice was a favourite theme with most ancient writers on ethics; it is thus defined in the *Institutes* of Justinian: 'justicia est constans et perpetua voluntas jus suum cuique tribuendi'.

Carneades (213-128 B.C.), founder of the New Academy. In one respect his philosophy—which is of a negative kind—somewhat resembles that of bishop Butler; for both of them probability was the guide of life. C. denied the reality of justice apart from what springs from positive law (see next chapter). The result of much of his teaching was a sort of pragmatism. His visit to Rome as an ambassador became famous (155 B.C.), and is briefly described by Mommsen (*Hist. of Rome*). He is frequently alluded to in Cicero. Compare what is said of him in Euseb. *Prep. Evang.* 736, 737. He was a doughty opponent of Zeno, the Stoic, and has been described by Gomperz as the David Hume of antiquity; in one department of philosophy he is in accord with Kant.

CHAPTER 56
[*Inst. v.* 16, 17]

For **Carneades,** see chap. 55, note. His reputation for acuteness ('acumen') and skill in argument is shown by a line in Lucilius, where some problem is spoken of as insoluble even to him: 'nec si Carneades ipsum ad nos Orcu' remittat'. See Cicero, *Academica* (passim), and a passage in *Inst.* v. 14.

casas, lit. 'huts'. Cf. Ovid, *Am.* II. ix. 17, 18.

aurichalco. A Greek word, ὀρείχαλκον, 'mountain copper', as the word originally meant. See Conington on Virg. *Aen.* xii. 87.

CHAPTER 57
[*Inst. v.* 17, to the end of the book]

imaginem, etc. Ovid has a similar thought when he says: 'under a delusion, Virtue has often been arraigned instead of Vice'.

malitia. This word is defined by Cicero, *de nat. deor.* iii. 39, 75. It can often be rendered by 'roguery', 'rascality', as well as 'malice'.

sine noxa. The whole of this passage has a good parallel in Tertullian, *Apol.* xxvii., 'quidam dementiam existimant quod, cum possimus et sacrificare in praesenti et illaesi abire, manente apud animum proposito, obstinationem saluti praeferamus'. Christians were commonly charged with obstinacy (their ψιλὴν παράταξιν, as the Emperor Marcus Aurelius called it): see Pliny's famous letter to Trajan, 96.

judicemus. St. Paul makes a surprising statement that Christians will some day judge angels! See 1 Cor. **6.** 3.

CHAPTER 58
[*Inst. vi.* 1, 2]

In this section and in the chapter as a whole one calls to mind the noble words of Cicero (*pro Cluentio*, lxviii. 194): 'pietate et religione et justis precibus deorum mentes, non contaminata superstitione, neque ad scelus perficiendum caesis hostiis posse placari'.

ipse non indiget. That God needs nothing was commonly held by Greek thinkers from the days of Euripides onward. For many references, see my note in *Ep. ad Diogn.* iii, § 3; and for **in usum hominis** (just below), op. cit. x, note.

non indiget templo. Cf. Rev. 21. 22. The presence of God *is* the 'temple'.

domicilium mundus. Is. 57. 15, 'the High and Lofty One that inhabiteth Eternity',

non luminibus. This was recognized by Seneca—'non lumine dii egent'. Cf. Rev. 21. 23, 24.

cultus mentis. Milton, *P. L.* i. 17, 'Thou, O Spirit that dost prefer | Before all temples the upright heart and pure'. We may call to mind some words of Buddha: 'Greater than the immolation of animals is the sacrifice of self. Better than worshipping gods is obedience to the law of righteousness.'

CHAPTER 59

[*Inst. vi.* 3, and in other chapters]

duas vias. I have dealt with this matter fairly fully in my edition of Plato's *Apology*; but to the references there given add the following: the Didache (init); Persius, iii. 56; Deut. 30. 19 and Jer. 21. 8; note in vol. v of Gifford's edition of Eusebius *Prep. Evang.* p. 196; the Elizabethan play of *Old Fortunatus*, IV. ii. 100–5; Holden's note on Cic. *Off.* i, § 118; Grant, *Ethics of Aristotle* (ed. 4), vol. i. pp. 145, 6. Dante may have had in mind the story of the Two Paths— as told in Xen. *Mem.* ii. 1, 11—in the 19th canto of the *Purgatorio*; cf. Boëthius, chap. i; Loyola, *Spiritual Exercises*.

Elysium. The pagan home of the blessed (a Greek word).— See Heyne, Exc. 8 on Virg. *Aen.* vi.

addicuntur. 'A legal word; see Lewis and Short.

ut praeséntem. So I read for 'ut parentem'. **amor cum timore.** Cf. 2 Cor. 7. 1. Holy fears an incentive to righteous conduct before God.

necessitudine = friendship. Ciceronian word.

jus in viribus. Cf. Lucan, i. 175, 'mensuraque juris vis erat', and the assertion of Thrasymachus in Plato, *Rep.* i. 12, viz. Might is Right. —This chapter in the *Epitome* is noteworthy; much of it has its bearing on events during the troubled days of the present century—in fact, a brief commentary on the dictum of Lord Acton = 'all power tends to corrupt, and absolute power corrupts absolutely'.

CHAPTER 60
[*Inst. vi.* 10–15]

nosmet ipsos nosceremus. The celebrated old saw is in point, written over the extrance to the Delphic shrine, γνῶθι σεαυτόν, 'nosce te ipsum'.

radix. Here Lactantius expands the Golden Rule laid down by Christ.

primum ... proximum. Better, perhaps, as Davies suggested, would be 'primus proximus'.

immortalitatis. Brandt reads 'virtutis'.

CHAPTER 61
[*Inst. vi.* 19, 14–16]

cogunt = urge, press. Actual compulsion is not suggested, any more than it is in Luke **14**. 23, though unhappily Augustine appealed to that text in order to justify forcing people in religion—with dire results later on.

Stoici (as opposed to the Epicureans). They regarded emotions as quite subordinate, an indifferent by-product: cf. Hartmann, *Ethics* [*E.T.*], vol. i. pp. 133f. If peace is to be looked for, complete repression of human desires was to be aimed at. Boëthius (*de consol. philos.*, i. metrum 7) has summed up some of the harsher teaching of Stoicism in these words: 'gaudia pelle, pelle timorem, spemque fugato, nec dolor adsit'. Cf. Sidgwick, *Hist. of Ethics*, chap. ii, § 16. One of the best accounts of the Stoic doctrine (with its central advice, ζῆν ὁμολογουμένως τῇ φύσει) will be found in the introduction to Rendall's translation of Marcus Aurelius; he sums up the main synthesis that took possession of the Stoic mind, i.e. a world a complete and living whole, informed and controlled by one all-pervasive Energy, which 'knew itself' in the consciousness of man. The world is regarded as the *substance* of God: οὐσίαν Θεοῦ Ζήνων φησι τὸν ὅλον κόσμον (Diog. Laert. vii. 148). In Stoicism at its best, perhaps for the first time in Greek thought, emerges the idea of duty.

Peripatetici, the Aristotelians.

abutendum = 'utendum' (and so often).

coercitionem. Cf. Lact. *de ira*, xviii. 21, 'ira ad correctionem vitiorum pertinet'.

CHAPTER 62
[*Inst. vi.* 18, 12, 23, 28]

ad alios. So in the Psalms—'he heapeth up riches and cannot tell who shall gather them'.

COMMENTARY 161

quis putet, for 'aliquis'.
suavioribus. Heumann ingeniously conj. 'canoris et suavisonis'. Needless.
numerosis carminibus traducitur. 'Soft music', said Knox-Little, 'in Church is often like a disinfectant doing away with the sternness of dogmatic facts.'
compositis certe. Here the latter word = 'tamen'. Cf. Cic. *de Fin.* i. 12, 'ut sint illa vendibiliora (more fashionable), haec uberiora certe sunt'.
superius. Cf. 56.

CHAPTER 63
[*Inst.* vi. 20, 18]

spectacula. For full information on these 'shows', and on the 'mimes', consult Friedländer, *Roman Life and Manners*, vol. ii. pp. 19–130 [E.T.]; and for briefer notices Bury, *Roman Empire*, pp. 612, 623; and for the Circus, ibid. 617; along with Middleton, *Remains of Ancient Rome*, vol. ii. chap. 2. The mimes represented low characters speaking in vulgar language: the plots are generally concerned with loose love affairs; cf. Augustine, *de civ. Dei*, ii. 8; iv. 26. Tertullian thus stigmatizes Roman theatres: 'theatrum proprie sacrarium Veneris est'; and the 'spectacula' in these words: 'hinc vel maxime intellegunt factum Christianum, de repudio spectaculorum'. The gladiatorial combats did not cease for a century after Lactantius: see Tennyson's *St. Telemachus*.
editiones, i.e. 'muneris gladiatorii'.
invenit ... vindicavit. One MS. gives 'vindicabit'. For **ac sine legibus,** Davies conj. 'nec sine legibus', but there seems no need for any change. A slight textual difficulty also crops up later, 'nec minus' etc., where Brandt reads **nam.**
disciplina. Cf. Cic. *Acad.* ii. 36, 114, 'd. sapientiae' = a system of philosophy. The word is often used not only for 'school' but for the teaching given there.
lubrica aetas. Pliny, *Epp.* iii. 3, 4, with Mayor's note.

CHAPTER 64
[*Inst. vi.* 18]

The first sentence in this chapter may be held parallel with the words in Cicero, *de Fin.* ii. 35, 117: 'maximas virtutes iacere omnes necesse est voluptate dominante'.
abnegabit q. sp. Cf. Psalm 15 for this and for the rest of the section. **In usura.** This seems strange to modern ears, but moderate rates of interest were almost unknown in antiquity, and the practice

11

was, in the main, condemned by the Greek and Roman moralists of Paganism; for example, Cato, in his *de re rustica*, speaks of the usurer as worse than a thief. It was forbidden in the Old Testament, though this prohibition did not apply to non-Hebrews; it was universally condemned by the Church, at any rate till the Reformation. In the New Testament no rule is laid down; in fact, the legitimacy of usury seems implied. For full information, see Bingham, *Antiquities*, vol. vi. 16, 13; and the article in Smith's *Dict. of Christ. Antiq.* vol. 2; Lecky, *Rationalism in Europe*, vol. 2.

non asper. One naturally thinks of Paul's beautiful letter to Philemon. See Lightfoot's valuable introduction on slavery and the evils of it. Cf. Eph. **6.** 9.

exponere. The horrible practice of exposing newly born children, so common in heathendom, was utterly alien from Christian ethics, and naturally stigmatized as a great sin by all Christian teachers and preachers. [See my note in *Ep. ad Diog.*, pp. 50, 51.]

ut ait poeta. Terence, in the *Andria*, I. i. 41. Τὸ ἀληθὲς πικρόν.

CHAPTER 65

[*Inst. vi.* 10]

spera (not 'hope' but) expect, anticipate (in the sense almost of 'fear'). So in Virg. *Aen.* i. 543; iv. 419.

jubet. The gospel precepts throughout this and the following sections are noticeable

litabilior. Cf. Min. Fel. xxxii. 2, 'litabilis hostia [est] bonus animus et pura mens et sincera sententia'. For the sentiment, see Ps. **51.** 17.

ubi nec fur, etc. Matt. **6.** 19, 20.

Deo custode. Cf. Cyprian, *de op. et eleem.* 19, 'in tuto hereditas ponitur quae Deo custode servatur'.

CHAPTER 66

[*Inst. vi.* 23]

nomen fidei = 'fideles', i.e. Christian believers. Greek πιστοί.

desciscere, viz. apostasy. Cf. 1 Tim. **4.** 1.

interno. Cf. 2 Cor. **4.** 16.

ut qui. The causal sense of 'qui' is heightened by the added 'ut'.

apud Deum quali gloria. See the noble words of Paul in 2 Cor. **4.** 17, 18, 'Our light affliction, which is for the moment, worketh for us a far more exceeding weight of glory', etc.

COMMENTARY   163

Qui habet, etc.   The cautions given in chap. 64 are here amplified.
nisi crimine ad.   Cf. Matt. **19.** 9.   But this saving clause is not in Mark or Luke, and may be a gloss.   Consult n. in McNeile's ed. of Matthew.
itaque justum ... velle.   Depending on 'manifestum est'.
emaculetur.   A post-Augustan verb.
templum Dei.   1 Cor. 3. 16, 17.   Something similar in Philo (*de somn.* i. 23), σπούδασον, ᾧ ψυχή, Θεοῦ οἶκος γένεσθαι ἱερὸν ἅγιον.

CHAPTER 67
[*Inst. vi.* 24, 25; *vii.* 2, 3]

sed enim.   'enim' was originally a particle of asseveration, adding emphasis.
perseverantibus.   Cic. *Phil.* xii. 2, 5, 'cujusvis hominis est errare, nullius nisi insipientis in errore perseverare'.
poenitentiae auxilium.   In a fragment of Democritus occur these words: μεταμελίη ἐπ' αἰσχροῖσιν ἔργμασι βίου σωτηρίη = 'Repentance for ill deeds is the saviour of life'. It is indeed one of the key-notes of the Gospel.
portus salutis.   Cic. *Phil.* xii. 3, 7, 'optimus est portus paenitenti mutatio consilii'.
humilitas, etc.   The story of the Pharisee and the publican is pertinent here.
sequentia ... summam.   I suppose *Summa* is equivalent to our expression 'The Supreme' (= God), and *sequentia* to mean the reasoning powers of man, and his life here on earth.
sua sponte nihil.   See Bacon, *Nov. Org.* ii. 40.   The doctrine 'ex nihilo nihil fit' implies the scientific principle of the indestructibility of matter, with its parallel the conservation of energy.   For statements of this doctrine in antiquity, cf. Diog. Laert. ix. 44, 57; x. 38, οὐδὲν γίνεται ἐκ τοῦ μὴ ὄντος; Lucr. i. 149f.; Persius iii. 84; Marc. Anton. iv. 4 (with Farquharson's note).
sine generante, i.e. a Creator (see chap. 4).   Lactantius may here have in mind Plato's arguments in the *Timaeus*, where that philosopher, in an attempt to solve the problem of the existence of evil, declares that the Supreme Maker first created the universe, and then delegated the creation of men and animals to a lower order of deities, of whom He alone is 'Father and Artificer'.   By the word **conglobatione** is signified the old theory of the 'fortuitous concourse of atoms' alluded to earlier in the book.
alii, the Stoics.

CHAPTER 68
[*Inst. vii.* 4]

quia bonus, etc. The words are derived from Plat. *Tim.* 29, (God) ἀγαθὸς ἦν, ἀγαθῷ δὲ οὐδεὶς περὶ οὐδενὸς οὐδέποτε ἐγγίγνεται φθόνος. The notion that God could be φθονερός was as distasteful to Aristotle as it was to Plato, as is shown in the *Metaphysics*, ii. 983, οὔτε τὸ θεῖον φθονερὸν ἐνδέχεται εἶναι.
Theodorus, like Diagoras before him, rejected all belief in the gods, according to Diog. Laert. ii. 97–8, and became known as the 'Atheist'. Cf. Cic. *de nat. deor.* i. 1, 2; Min. Fel. viii. 2. He is mentioned in Plato's *Theaetetus*.

in materia. The notion that matter (ὕλη) was the cause of evil was widely held in antiquity, and was adopted by the Gnostics. There is no Scriptural authority for such a theory (cf. Gen. 1. 31). There is a discussion on the subject by an ecclesiastical writer, Maximus, in a treatise περὶ τῆς ὕλης, part of which is quoted by Eusebius, *Prep. Evang.* vii. 22. Following the lemma are these words, ὅτι μὴ ἀγέννητος ἡ ὕλη, μηδὲ κακῶν αἰτία. Routh, *Rel. Sacr.* vol. ii. p. 77 [ed. 2].

From section 2 to the end of the chapter, Lactantius is not giving his own opinion (that comes in the next chapter) but is summarizing the arguments of Theodorus. Plato both in the *Timaeus* and in the *Republic* absolves God from any responsibility for evil.

ludum mihi = 'ut mihi videtur'. **nescio quem,** with a touch of contempt. **transmeandi.** The doctrine of 'metempsychosis' was familiar to the Greeks in the time of Plato (see his *Phaedo*, 81–2, besides other references to this theory in the *Republic* 618–20, *Phaedrus* 249, *Timaeus* 42 and 91). In the *Politicus* 'myth' Plato seeks to supply a cause for the evil in the world; cf. J. A. Stewart, *Myths of Plato*, pp. 198 f. Consult Burnet, *Early Greek Philosophy*, chap. 2.

The doctrine of transmigration was attacked or ridiculed by the Church Fathers: see, for example, Tertullian's *Apologeticus*, chap. xlviii; and cf. Min. Fel. xxxiv. Though it became in course of time an accepted part of Hindu religion, it never seems to have impressed itself deeply on the popular mind of Greece and Rome; the Jews may have had some inkling of it, if the passage in John 9. 2, is any clue.

CHAPTER 69
[*Inst. vii.* 5, 6, 8]

summa, sc. 'sententia'; and perhaps this word has dropped out. In this chapter Lactantius harps on his favourite theme—the world made for man's sake. 'Since Copernicus, it has been evident that Man has not the cosmic importance which he formerly arrogated to himself. No

COMMENTARY 165

one who has failed to assimilate this fact has a right to call his philosophy scientific' (Bertrand Russell, *A History of Western Philosophy*, p. 816). It may be worth remark that whereas Celsus wisely hesitated about the old assumption, Origen is quite certain that God had no other object: all things were by God subordinated to man. Compare and contrast what Plato says in the *Laws* 903c., 'the act of creation not in *your* interest; it is you who are created in the interest of the universe'.

dominetur mundo. Gen. 1. 26, 28.

conditorem, parentem. Cf. the words of Plato (in the *Timaeus* 28), 'the maker and father of this All it is hard to find, and having found Him it is impossible to declare Him to all men'. The 'Deus absconditus' of Is. 45. 15.

unde religio nominatur. Cf. *Inst.* iv. 28, 'hoc vinculo pietatis obstricti Deo et religati sumus; unde ipsa religio nomen accepit, non ut Cicero interpretatus est a *relegendo*' (Cic. *de nat. deor.* ii. 28, 72). Lactantius, like Augustine, derived the word from *religare*. See Munro on Lucr. i. 109. But the etymology of the word is uncertain, though Cicero's view is probably right. In any case there is implied in the word a sense of 'awe', reverence—the *numinous*, as Otto calls it.

immortalitatem accipiat. 'Immortality', in other words, is a *gift* from God, conditional on man's earning the right to receive it. It can be had now; presumably it could be lost hereafter. See by all means the late Prof. A. E. Taylor's invaluable book, *The Christian Hope of Immortality* (1938), pp. 63f. Immortality is not a natural quality of the soul, in Christianity; this too is taught in the Book of Wisdom, as distinct from the Greek doctrine of natural immortality. It may not be out of place to quote Calvin here: 'there is no inconsistency in saying that God *rewards* good works, as long as we remember that, nevertheless, we obtain *life* gratuitously.'

CHAPTER 70
[*Inst. vii.* 8, 14]

Plato ait, in the *Phaedrus* 245. Cic. *Tusc.* i. 23, 53, translates a long passage from that dialogue, to which Lactantius is referring.

This passage is important, and begins thus: ψυχὴ πᾶσα ἀθάνατος, τὸ γὰρ ἀεικίνητον ἀθάνατον to be compared with Aristotle's words in *Metaph.* xii. 7, where he speaks of the πρῶτον κινοῦν, the Eternal Being—God, who is the efficient principle, 'first mover', pure τὸ ἦν εἶναι, the Absolute, Soul of the Universe. For the *many arguments* the reader is referred to the *Phaedo* of Plato.

terreni ... concretum (= admixtum). Cf. Shelley, *Adonais*, 'from the contagion of the world's slow stain he is secure'.

quae. I.e. fearlessness in the presence of poverty or death.

solubilis, liable to be dissolved (or destroyed). Cf. 2 Cor. 5. 1. For the word, see Min. Fel. xxxiv. 3.

innovetur = renovetur. Rev. 21. 1, 'I saw a new Heaven, and a new Earth'.

Lactantius girds at the Babylonians for actually estimating that 470,000 years have elapsed since our world began, just as Augustine (*de civ. Dei*, xviii. 40) girds at the Egyptians for putting the period at 100,000. The chronology of Lactantius is based on Jewish speculations, and he gives his reasons in *Inst.* vii. 4. The belief that the course of this present world would be concluded in 6,000 years was once widely held, each 1,000 years being equivalent to one Divine Day, each day of Creation implying a thousand years of the earth's duration (see 2 Peter 3. 8). It is perhaps worth noting that the 'end' was confidently expected in the year A.D. 1000: see Milman, *Latin Christianity* (bk. v. chap. 13). Consult the full note in Christopher's edition of August. *de cat. rud.* 17, and Benson's *Cyprian*, p. 266 (note).

CHAPTER 71

[*Inst. vii.* 15-19]

In this chapter Lactantius, in setting forth a century of coming disasters, has made a patchwork of many Biblical statements regarding the end of the Dispensation. Reference may be made to Thessalonians, 2 Tim. 3, and our Lord's words in Matt. 24. Some of these predictions may well have formed the nucleus for some Jewish-Christian writer, who out of them combined a series of sayings, couched in the conventional language of Jewish eschatology.

manu, by violence. Many of the vaticinations in this chapter have been adumbrated in the New Testament.

decem viri. Is Lactantius thinking of the ten kings mentioned in Revelation? Cf. too Daniel 7. 24, 25 for close parallels. **nomen** (imperii) = formam. This actually took place when Constantine shifted the seat of empire from Rome to his new city Constantinople (now Istanbul).

lucis damna. Cf. Hor. *Odes*, iv. 7, 13 (with Orelli's note).

stellae decident, meteorites, probably. Consult Lane's *The Elements Rage* (1945), chap. 7.

Trismegistus. The reference is to Asclepius, iii. 25. See Scott's *Hermetica*, vol. iv. p. 24f. The Hermetic description of the various cosmic and terrestrial disorders, consequent on man's sin, is comparable with predictions found both in Jewish and Christian Apocalypses: for example, 1 Enoch 80. 2-8, and the Sibyllines, book iii (passim). Compare too the relevant passages in Revelation (and in the 'Little Apocalypse' in our Gospels already referred to).

COMMENTARY

rex impius, Antichrist. See Bousset, *Antichrist Legend,* chap. vi.
coli ut Deum. 2 Thess. 2. 1–10.
resistat for 'subsistat'.
signum in manu. Cf. Rev. 13. 15, 16 (with Swete's notes), and for a parallel case, 3 Macc. 2. 29.

CHAPTER 72
[*Inst. vii.* 20, 24, 26]

intempesta nocte. So in Virg. *Geor.* i. 247, with Conington's note.

anteibit claritas. Milton, *P. L.* vi. 768, 'He onward came; far off his coming shone', and for **descendit,** 1 Thess. 4. 16.

daemonum princeps, Satan. With this passage, cf. the 20th chapter of Revelation, and consult also a recent work by Dr. E. Langton, *Satan, a portrait,* where the subject is treated exhaustively.

diminutionem = 'defectionem', eclipse.

lupus, etc. Is. **11.** 6, and for 'stillabunt' etc., Joel 3. 18.

mille annis. The belief in the Millennium, or personal reign of Christ on earth for a thousand years, is distasteful to modern theologians as it was to the Alexandrian theologians (e.g. Dionysius, and Origen, who was offended by its literalism), as well as to the Roman Church because (as Martineau remarked, *Seat of Authority in Religion*) its fault lay in its interference with the Church's orderly march to the conquest of the world, which was the Roman conception of the kingdom of God. The sensuous aspect of the Millennarian kingdom was apparently taken over from Judaism, like the rococo aspect of the New Jerusalem in the Apocalypse. Apart from the statement in the Apocalypse, the doctrine finds little or no support elsewhere in the New Testament, but it was held by some of the earlier Church writers; the credulous Papias, Barnabas, Commodian, Justin Martyr, bishop Victorinus, and Irenaeus among them. Augustine's opinion was different: *de civ. Dei,* xx. 7–9; but some form of it held its ground till Origen.

For further information the student is advised to consult the following works: Hastings, *D.B.,* iii. 370; *Encycl. Bibl.;* Harnack, *Hist. of Dogma,* s.v. 'Chiliasm', who points out that this belief held its ground all through the third and fourth centuries with those Latin theologians who managed to escape the influence of Greek speculation; Swete's edition of the *Apoc.* p. 260; article 'Eschatology' in Hastings' *Encycl. of Rel. and Ethics;* Cadoux, *The Early Church,* p. 477f., who points out that Lactantius presents the scheme in all its (rather bewildering and fantastic) details. The fact seems to be that the book of Revelation is incorporating an idea which was current at the time and belonged to the ordinary panorama of eschatological and apocalyptical belief, as is remarked in Peake's Commentary. Note that reference should be made to such

168   EPITOME OF LACTANTIUS

passages as Rev. xx. 7, xxi. 1; Is. lxvi. 24. Readers may perhaps like to be reminded that Milton—'that old incorrigible dreamer, kept for the end his most fantastic, his most logical, dream.' He wanted a solid material triumph; so this will be on earth, and will last for 1,000 years. I may perhaps add here that Lactantius gives a long passage in the *Institutes* which, for its main features, is indebted to 1 Enoch; the relevant quotations are set out in Charles' edition of Enoch (ed. 2, 1912); pp. lxxxix. f.   Add Bousset, *Anti-Christ Legend*, chap. xvi [E.T.].

πολυάνδριον, a cemetery, because πολλοὶ ἄνδρες are buried there. This word occurs six times in LXX.

perpetua tormenta ... aeternis ignibus. On this grim note the *Epitome*, more or less, concludes—viz. the eternal punishment of the wicked, a theory which appears to involve the ultimate failure of God Himself to eradicate a plague-spot from His universe. There is a careful answer to all this in Stephen's Epilogue to his *Ecclesiastical Biography* (1849), and another in Farrar's *Mercy and Judgement* (a reply to Pusey's *What is of Faith?*).

EPILOGUE

Hystaspes (= Vistâspa), not the father of Darius but a royal disciple of Zoroaster (= Zarathustra), who became a convert to the new religion, as is shown by the Gâthas, the oldest part of the Avesta. Hystaspes, along with the Sibyl, is mentioned by Justin (*Apol*. xx. 1) as foretelling the destruction of the world by fire; and his books, though he was a Persian 'magus', were—as we should say—'placed on the Index'.

Lactantius constructs his eschatology by combining predictions found mainly in (1) Jewish writings, (2) Christian writings, (3) Sibylline oracles, (4) an apocalypse ascribed to Hystaspes, (5) the prophecy of Hermes in the Λόγος τέλειος (*Ascl. Lat*. ii. 24-6). So Scott notes in *Hermetica*, vol. 4. Result—a strange jumble.

summum Deum. But in the editions 'summum Deum Christum', which Lactantius can hardly have written. Hence conjectures are made (*a*) 'Deum per eum,' (*b*) 'Deum per Christum.' I have simply omitted the word 'Christum' as a pious adscript.

agonem. The word is Greek, ἀγών, lit., 'contest for victory in the public games', and then used by ecclesiastical writers as meaning the spiritual contest against the enemies of man's salvation. 'Agon' in this sense frequent in Cyprian.

coronam fidei, a reference to the crown of martyrdom. Cf. Cyprian, *Ep*. 58, 'quando persecutiones fiunt, tunc dantur coronae fidei'.

COMMENTARY

DETACHED NOTE ON
Pietas (pius); religio; mundus; justitia (justus)

Pietas implies any kind of dutiful conduct towards (1) gods, (2) parents, (3) one's country, and (4) mercy or compassion. The word *pius* means more than our 'pious', a word which at times has a slightly contemptuous flavour. Perhaps 'faithful' (occasionally 'devout') is a good rendering: 'pius Aeneas' being the stock example. The idea seems to be conformity with the divine will, or, as the State-religion of Rome conceived it, conformity with the 'jus divinum' (as in Horace's 'farre pio' = reverential). *Pietas*, says Mackail (Introduction to his edition of the *Aeneid*, p. lxvi) implies 'conscientious', the steady fulfilment of duty to God and man, and is the central quality of Virgil's hero. See Bailey, *Religion of Virgil*. *Pius* can apply to poets, as being those that follow some divine inspiration; in Catullus 73, 2 it may even imply gratitude. **Religio** * has a wider signification than our stereotyped idea of 'religion'. It may signify a conscientious scruple (e.g. regarding oaths), obligation, plighted faith, reverence (in plural = religious rites) and awe—the 'numinous', to borrow Otto's coinage. For the last, cf. Quintilian, *Inst.* x. § 88, who uses it of Ennius. It may be applied to language, as in Longus: 'mihi placet ut in Latino sermone antiquitatis religio servetur' (= respect for antiquity). In Virg. *Aen.* iii. 632, it seems to be used of oracles, prospering signs sent by the gods. For another example of religio = admiration, see Pliny, *Epp.* iii. 15, 'poeticen religiosissime veneror'; for its use as implying superstition, Lucretius, i. 101—a much quoted line. **mundus**, like κόσμος in Greek, means both (*a*) the world, (*b*) the Universe. Which meaning is applicable (in our author or elsewhere) can usually be decided by the context. In classical Latin the word generally means the Universe, as in Lucretius, i. 73, 'flammantia moenia mundi'; but not always. As a rule 'mundus' in ecclesiastical Latin is the world of sin and death, as opposed to the kingdom of Heaven (for examples, see John's Gospel in the Vulgate rendering); in 1 John 2. 15 the old order, pagan society, is called 'the world'. **Justitia** implies in Lactantius our notion of 'justice', but far more often 'righteousness' (δικαιοσύνη): see the valuable note on δίκαιος and its cognates in Sanday and Headlam's *Romans*, pp. 28–31.† There is an elaborate treatise by Lactantius, *de justicia*.

It might be noticed here, incidentally, that the expression 'the righteousness of God' has a double signification in the New Testament.

---

* For a useful note on 'religio' see Max Müller's Lectures on the Origin of Religion (ed. 1882, pp. 11, 12); and Welldon on August. *de civ. Dei*, X 3.

† It is perhaps worth noting that in the A.V. of N.T. δίκαιος is translated by 'just' 33 times, by 'righteous' 41 times.

First, it means the righteousness inherent in the very idea of God, as loving righteousness and doing righteousness; secondly, the righteousness *provided by God* whereby we are accounted righteous before Him: in other words, the righteousness by Him provided is the salvation of the believer.

The meaning of the word often wavers between the forensic and the religious; sometimes it combines both notions: we have no one word quite corresponding. Cicero, in an interesting passage (*Part. Orat.* xxii. 78), wrote thus: 'Justitia erga deos religio, erga parentes pietas, creditis in rebus fides'.

ADDENDA

Chapter

8 **A cock to Aesculapius.** These last words of Socrates have been often sadly misinterpreted, as they were by Lactantius. It was the usual custom to offer a cock to the god of healing, Aesculapius, on a recovery from illness. In the old philosopher's view life was a sickness of which death is the final healing. Compare the following passages: Soph. *Ajax*, 692; the prayer to 'Jovi Liberatori', on Seneca's lips at death; Shakespeare, *Timon*, v. 1, 'my long sickness of health and living now begins to mend'. See too the note in Grote's *Plato*, vol. 2, p. 194.

28 **Daemons.** Cf. Bevan's *Later Greek Religion*, pp. xxviii. 122, and the appendix to Stewart's *Myths of Plato*. There is a good note on this word, by W. H. Thompson, on pp. 238–9 of Butler's *History of Ancient Philosophy* (ed. 2, 1874).

33 **Summum bonum.** See J. H. Stirling's Gifford Lectures (*Philosophy and Theology*), p. 145.

64 **Veritas odium parit.** Mayor on Tertullian, *Apol.* p. 437.

68 It may be pertinent to point out here that the view of many ancient writers and thinkers that good needs some evil as its correlate was held by Lactantius (in the *de ira.* 15): see Reid's n. on Cic. *Acad.* ii. 120, for references to several authors. Modern writers on this problem have felt its difficulty; thus Froude (*Short Studies*): 'where there is no evil, there can be no preference of good'; Schiller, in his *Riddles of the Sphinx* has some interesting comments; Tennyson seems to hint at the doctrine involved, in § 53 of *In Memoriam*; and Browning perhaps does likewise in *Reverie* (at the end of his last volume, 'Asolando'). Cf. the words of Shakespeare in *Measure for Measure*:

> 'They say best men are moulded out of faults,
> And for the most become much more the better
> For being a little bad.'

69 **Religio.** Consult Warde Fowler's valuable chapter (xi) in his *Social Life in Rome*.

72 **six thousand years.** See a note in Benson's *Cyprian*, p. 266/ For the Millennium consult Cruttwell, *Lit. Hist. of Early Christianity*, p. 523 (foll.).

73 **Hell fire eternal.** Not all the Fathers subscribed to this appalling doctrine, but some did, e.g. Tertullian, Cyprian, and Augustine. See the long catena of Patristic authorities quoted by

Dean Farrar in his *Mercy and Judgement*. For Origen's views consult Bigg, *Christian Platonists of Alexandria*, Lect. vi.

This book may perhaps fitly close with the noble words of John Scotus Erigena:—

'Unusquisque in suo sensu abundet, donec veniat illa Lux quae de luce falsò philosophantium facit tenebras, et tenebras recte cognoscentium in lucem convertit.'

SELECT INDEX

(References are to chapters)

Abailard, quoted, 4
Academy (the New), 31
Aculeus, 47
Aesculapius, 8, 37, and *Addenda*
Agon. (Epilogue.)
Alcmēna, 7
Amalthēa, 23
Anaxagoras, 39
Anaximenes, 4
Angels, fallen, 27
ἄνθρωπος, 25
Antipodes, 39
Antisthenes, 4
Anūbis, 23
Apes, 2
Apollo of Miletus, where, according to Strabo, he had a shrine, 70
Apollodorus, quoted, 19
Apollonius Rhodius, quoted, 8
Argonauts, 7
Ariadne, 8
Aristippus, 33, 39
Aristotle, 4, 55, 70
Arnold (Matthew), quoted, 64, 65, 66
Auctoritas, 4
Augustine, 10 (and *passim*)

Bacon, quoted, 32, 38, 41, 67
Bellona, 23
Belus, 24
Boëthius, 64
Browning, 42
Buddha, 58
Butler, bishop, 33

Caelus, 14. [Cf. August., *de civ. Dei*, vii. 19.]
Capitolium, 21
Carneades, 55, 56
Carthaginian sacrifices, 23
Castor and Pollux, 8
Cataclysmus, 27
Ceres, 9
Chiron, 8
Christians, why persecuted, 52, 54, 57
Chronology, 70
Chrysippus, quoted, 29
Cicero (Tullius), 1, 7, 8, 22, 30, 32, 34, 38, 56, 58, 63, 64, 67, 69
Circus, games, 63
Cloacina, 20
Coleridge, 38

Commentitii (dei), 21
Conglobatio, 67
Cross, sign of, 51
'Cum natura congruenter,' 33
Cybele, 24
Cyprian, quoted, 65
Cynics, 39. [The origin of this name is not certain; but see Welldon's note on August., *de civ. Dei*, xiv. 20.]

Daemons, 28 and *Addenda*
Danaē, 11
Deianīra, 7
Delātor, 27
Democritus, 67
Design (argument from), 1
Desperati, 54
Didymus, 24
Diodōrus, 33
Dionysius (of Sicily), 25
Diogĕnes (the Cynic), 39
Diogĕnes Laertius, quoted, 67
Diminutio, 72
Disciplina, 63
Dumtaxat, 12

Elements, 26
Elysium, 59
Enoch, book of, 72
Epicurus, 1, 33, 36, 70
Epidaurus, 8
Erigena, *Addenda*
Eternal punishment, 72
Euhemĕrus, 13, 14, 24
Euphorbus, 36
Europa, 11
Eusebius, quoted, 68
Evil, as necessary, 68, and *Addenda*
Exposure of children, 64
Exuviae, 47, 68

Ganymede, 11
Gellius (Aulus), quoted, 29
Generans = Creator, 67
Genius, 28
γνῶθι σεαυτόν, 60
God made world for man, 58, 69
— needs nothing, 58
Golden Age, 25
Grammaticus, 30

Hell fire, *Addenda*
Hercules, 7, 23

INDEX

Herillus, 33
Hermes Trismegistus, 4, 14, 42, 71
Hermetica, quoted, 4, 71
Hippolytus, 9
Homer, 8
Horace, 25, 28, 33
Hystaspes (Epilogue)

Immortality, 69
Impassibilis, 3
Impotens, 54
Infirmatus, 44
Isis, 11, 23

Justitia, justus (detached note)

Labărum, 51
Laomedon, 7
Larentalia, 20
Lares and Penātes, 28
Latiaris (Jupiter), 23
Liber (a god), 8
Litabilis, 65
Lucan, quoted, 39
Lucilius, quoted, 22, 56
Lucretius, quoted, 25, 36

Marcellus, 20
Marcus Aurelius, 57
Mars (god), 8
Mater Magna, 8
Matter original of evil, 68
Mercury (god), 8
Metempsychosis, 68
Millennium, 72 (Routh, *Relig. S.* iv [s. ind.]).
Milton, quoted, 9, 58, 72
Minucius Felix, 28, 65
Moses, 43
Mundus (detached note)

'Nihil ex nihilo', 67
Numa, 22

Omphăle, 7
Opinatio, 31
Oracles, 28
Orpheus, 3
Orichalcum, 56
Ovid, quoted, 3, 57

Paganism, its fall, 7
Patibulum, 47
Penates, 28
Peripatetics, 33, 61

Philo, 66
Philosophers at variance, 32 (and see 39, 41)
Pietas, 52 (and see detached note)
Pilate, 45
Pistor Jupiter, 20
Plato, 4, 8, 29, 38, 42, 67, 68, 69, 70
Plautus, 47
Polyandrion, 72
Praefiguro, 12
Promētheus, 25
πρῶτον κινοῦν, 70
Providentia, 29 (and *passim*)
Prudentius, quoted, 51
Pyrrho, 33
Pythagŏras, 36

Quindecemviri, 5

Ratio, 1
Religio, 69 (and detached note)
Repentance, 67
Rome besieged, 20

Sacramentum, 51 (and elsewhere)
Sapientia, 30
Satan, 27, his doom, 72
Saturn, 10, 14
Seneca, 4, 38, 50, 53
Shakespeare, quoted, 39, 45, *Addenda*
Shelley, 70
Shows at Rome, 63
Sibyls, 5
Socrates, 8, 28, 31, 37, 40
Solomon, Odes, 44
Spectacula, 63
Stars falling, 71
Statues of gods, 25
Stoics, 61
Subordinationism, 43
Substantia, 49
Substringo, Preface, and 50
Suetonius,
Suicide, 39
'Summum Bonum', 33
Superstition, 22

Tacitus, quoted, 22
Tauri, 23
Tennyson, 4, 32, 36, 63
Terence, 64
Terminus (a deity), 21
Tertullian, 54, 57, 63
Theodōrus, 68
Thetis, 10
Thucydides, quoted, 52
Trismegistus (vide *Hermes*)
Tutela, 11

INDEX 175

Uranus, 14
Usury, 64

Varro, 5
Vespasian, 46
Virbius, 9
Virgil, quoted, 2, 9, 21, 38, 53

Ways, the two, 59
Wisdom, age of, 70, 71
World destroyed, 71
— made for man, 69 (*passim*)

ZAN KPONOY, 13
Zeno, 4, 26, 31, 33
Zeus (= Roman Jupiter), 13

INDEX TO BIBLICAL REFERENCES IN THE COMMENTARY

Acts of Apostles, 25, 34, 65
Amos, 46
Baruch, 44
Corinthians, 26, 30, 48, 57, 66
Daniel, 47, 71
Deuteronomy, 46
Ephesians, 2, 64
Esdras, 48
Genesis, 27, 69
Isaiah, 44, 48, 72
Jeremiah, 44, 46, 48
Joel, 72

John, 42
Kings, 46
Malachi, 48
Matthew, 65, 71
Numbers, 44
Psalms, 46, 47, 62, 64
Revelation 27, 42, 57, 72
Romans, 4
Thessalonians, 71, 72
Timothy, 22
Wisdom, 45

www.ingramcontent.com/pod-product-compliance
Lightning Source LLC
Chambersburg PA
CBHW071451150426
43191CB00008B/1306